DRAGONS

GUARDIANS OF CREATIVE POWERS

BECOMING A CONSCIOUS CREATOR

by Jaap van Etten, PhD

Other Books by Jaap van Etten

Gifts of Mother Earth: Earth Energies, Vortexes, Lines, and Grids
Crystal Skulls: Interacting with a Phenomenon
Crystal Skulls: Expand Your Consciousness
Birth of a New Consciousness: Dialogues with the Sidhe

For print books, visit our online bookstore at LightTechnology.com.

eBooks are available from Amazon, Apple iTunes, Google Play, Barnes & Noble, and Kobo.

DRAGONS

GUARDIANS OF CREATIVE POWERS

BECOMING A CONSCIOUS CREATOR

by Jaap van Etten, PhD

Light Technology PUBLISHING

For information about special discounts for bulk purchases, please contact Light Technology Publishing Special Sales at 1-800-450-0985 or publishing@LightTechnology.com.

ISBN-13: 978-1-62233-066-9
ebook ISBN: 978-1-62233-799-6

Light Technology Publishing, LLC
Phone: 1-800-450-0985
1-928-526-1345
Fax: 928-714-1132
PO Box 3540
Flagstaff, AZ 86003
LightTechnology.com

"All mankind is facing an epic choice: a world of magic or a world of science. Which will it be?"

— Wizard Carolinus to Dragon Gorbesh
in the 1982 animated movie *The Flight of Dragons*
(based on Peter Dickinson's book of the same name)

Contents

Acknowledgments

TO EXPRESS MY GRATITUDE PROPERLY for those who supported me on my journey with the dragons and the creation of this book, I have to start and end with the same person: my wonderful wife, Jeanne Michaels. Without you, I still would have difficulty believing that dragons exist. Your invitation to me to open to dragons formed the basis of my work with them — the research, the workshops, and this book. Thank you, my beloved, for all your sharing and support on this journey.

I would have lost myself in the subtle worlds of the dragons many times without my dragon guide Drasil-air. I am very grateful that you were "suddenly" there in my awareness. You helped me understand dragons to a degree that I would never have been able to without you. I trust that you will never leave because there still is a lot of work to do.

Another essential induction in the dragon work was the invitation from Marie-Ann Mathot and Mayo Hitz. Without your invitation, I may never have started to teach dragon workshops. Your and the workshop participants' enthusiasm have been a key element in my meeting the different dragon species and understanding the energies of which they are the guardians.

I want to thank all the participants of the dragon workshops in the United States and the Netherlands. Without your enthusiasm, my passion for dragons would never have grown to the level that enabled me to write this book. Thank you all for sharing with me many steps of the journey.

A Dutchman writing English needs extra editing support. Thank you, my brave wife, Jeanne for taking on the job of the first round of editing. I am aware that it is a challenging job, and I am very grateful for your courage and not giving up on me.

Thank you, Deborah Downs and Sandi O'Connor, for being supportive during the workshops and your great contribution to the editing of this book. Your support is very important to me.

Thank you, Kristina Arysta, for always being there for me and for being such a great editor even though I know you had some challenges with this book. Nonetheless, or maybe because of the challenges, your editing has been even more valuable.

Thank you, Light Technology Publishing. Thank you, Melody, for your continued trust in me and for publishing this book. I am grateful for your ongoing support and our connection. Thank you, Light Technology Publishing team. Your efforts always lead to books that I can show and offer with pride.

As mentioned, I will end with the person with whom I started — my wife, Jeanne Michaels. Your support is more than in the area of dragons or editing. Your support is there every day of my life. You trust and support the projects I feel guided to do. Without you, I would not be who and where I am today.

Introduction

ALTHOUGH THIS BOOK IS COMPLETELY INDEPENDENT, it is an inherent part of my studies of a subject that I have named metaphysical ecology. I define metaphysical ecology as the study of the interactions between beings who are visible or invisible (subtle beings) and their environment, both measurable and immeasurable (subtle). I used the term for the first time in my book *Gifts of Mother Earth*.[1] While it initially was used to describe the study of the interactions we as humans have with the subtle energies of Mother Earth, over time it included all beings and all subtle energies and worlds.

This subject is so vast that I have only begun to scratch its surface. However, everything that you will read in this book falls within this study. That will become clearer as you read even though the purpose of this book is not meant to go deeper into the subject of metaphysical ecology.[2]

Important

If you are expecting the usual dragon book or an easy read, you may be disappointed. This book is intended to be a guide to help you connect with beings who are the guardians of the elemental powers that are the basis of all creation. This book invites you to connect with them and gives you ways to do that. It invites you on a journey to connect with powerful allies. Connecting with different species and their powers requires both conscious choice and active effort. If you are willing to do that, there will be many rewards and wonderful moments. Most importantly, it will change your life.

The first six chapters help you to understand the energies of dragons and the powers for which they are the guardians. There is a chapter dedicated to each of the five main groups of dragons. To make it possible to work with your chosen group of dragons, each chapter has been presented independently. You may notice repetition if you simply read the book without taking the time to study the groups. However, repetition will make your work with a specific group easier and more efficient.

We Are Creators

Every thought we have will set an aspect of creation into motion. Most of the time, we create from a subconscious level and are not aware of the creation process itself. Also, our lack of understanding often does not lead us to the desired result. Therefore, many people are not happy with their lives. They blame the environment or bad luck, but that does not change their circumstances. If we want to get the results we desire, we need to take responsibility for our lives and gain a better understanding of the elemental powers that underlie all creation.

Most people have no idea how the creation process works. In this book, we will look at the role the different aspects of the elemental powers have in the creative processes. Each aspect has a guardian. We call these guardians dragons. The most optimal way to create is in collaboration with these powerful beings. They love to collaborate with us.

There are many misconceptions about dragons. They are not the reptilian-like, aggressive beings as they are often described. They are not even visible to our physical eyes and therefore belong to the world of the subtle beings. Most people have no interest in them or do not believe in them. However, an increasing number of people have begun to connect with them again. Whether you believe in them or not, it is important to understand the creative processes. In the process of learning to understand these creative powers, you will consciously or subconsciously connect with dragons. However, connecting with them by choice will speed up the expansion and success of your creative abilities.

This book will help you to connect with the different dragon species and the powers with which they are connected to enable you to become a better creator who functions more optimally. Open yourself to this journey because it promises to be very interesting.

How I Became a Believer

Not very long ago, I believed, as many people do, that dragons do not exist. However, I liked fantasy books with stories about dragons and movies in which dragons played a role. I did not like the aggressive dragons very much. I especially liked stories in which there was a special relationship between dragons and men, as in *Eragon*,[3] and stories that describe dragons as beings of great knowledge and wisdom.

Anything we fantasize may exist somewhere in some dimension. Knowing this did not make me accept dragons as an integrated part of our reality. I also believed that dragon stories were fantasies based on the finds of dinosaur bones. One of the many explanations people have for the stories about dragons is the discovery of dinosaur bones. Some people believe that these bones belong to dragons.[4] Besides enjoying the many fantasy stories about dragons, my interest did not go much further.

One day my wife, Jeanne Michaels, came home with a story that would change my way of understanding mystical beings. She told me that during a session with a friend, she was told that there was a unicorn supporting the healing of her daughter. I was very skeptical. Jeanne asked whether it was possible to validate the existence of unicorns. I remembered that any species existing on Earth, visible or invisible to us, had to have a morphogenetic grid and field. I described these grids extensively in my book *Gifts of Mother Earth*.[5] Therefore, if unicorns were only a figment of people's imaginations, there would be no morphogenetic grids. However, if they did exist, I would be able to find their morphogenetic grids. So Jeanne and I went in search of unicorn grids.

With my experience in searching and working with morphogenetic grids, it was easy to find the confirmation even though I did not want to believe they existed. Still, with some resistance, I had to admit that there were unicorn morphogenetic grids with lines and vortexes. Based on what I knew of these grids, finding them meant that there were unicorns connected with the earth.

While we were out searching for unicorn vortexes, Jeanne guided me to another vortex. It took some time and courage to admit that this was a vortex of a morphogenetic grid of dragons. Not only were unicorns part of the Gaia system but so were dragons! I had to admit that my only choice was to become a believer.

In our house, we do weekly meditations supported by crystal skulls. During these meditations, we choose different subjects. Based on our findings of morphogenetic grids of unicorns and dragons, we decided to further explore the subject during one of the meditations. Jeanne's preference was first to work with unicorns.

That evening, I experienced a very surprising meditation. I had no expectations whatsoever. I intended to do a simple crystal skull meditation to see what unfolded. Crystal skulls are amplifiers,[6] so all intentions are amplified by the field of crystal skulls.

During the guided meditation, the unicorns were invited. The powerful and pleasant field that appeared during this guided meditation surprised me. However, I was more than surprised with what happened next. While I was in a meditative state, I suddenly was aware that there were animals in the room. These were not normal animals. I saw that they had single horns on their heads. However, these unicorns did not look like horses, as people usually depict them. They looked more like deer or elk.

I saw two toes instead of one toe, as horses have. I saw three different types of species. One of the unicorn species was the size of an elk or horse, one was the size of a small deer, and the third was the size of a small goat and had long hair. It was difficult for me to trust that what I saw was valid. I thought that they were figments of my imagination. However, they did not disappear.

They moved through the room where we were seated. The small species came over and laid next to me. I became very emotional and was deeply touched. I realized that this was not a fantasy and that I was having a special experience. This experience took away the last doubts I had about the existence of unicorns and dragons.

Without Jeanne and the support and interest of the group that comes to our meditations, I would never have written this book. This support and stimulation made me look for more vortexes and grids, both to confirm what I was beginning to believe and to gather more information. When I found more morphogenetic grids of dragons, a whole new world opened for me. It was not a world of understanding but rather a world full of many questions.

Dragon Workshops

In Eastern stories, people describe unicorns as highly benevolent beings. However, in the Western world, dragons have a strong negative image. According to stories, people fight and kill dragons. They are described mostly as destructive beings who hoard treasures and hold princesses and other women captive. However, in the Eastern world, there is an image of dragons as benevolent beings who support people.

Once I had felt the energies of the vortexes of the dragon grids, I knew that these were not energies of frightening creatures. There were two possibilities: (1) I had found grids that did not belong to the dragons, or (2) the legends and stories of the Western world were incorrect. I chose to believe the latter. I trusted that I had found dragon grids and that dragons were beings with positive and supportive energies.

Usually, I would have been satisfied with this conclusion about dragons and continued with other research. However, our guidance sometimes stimulates us to go in a meaningful direction even when we may not favor that direction at that moment.

While I was planning a trip to Holland in 2013, I talked with two dear friends, Marie-Ann and Mayo, who organize workshops for me in the Netherlands. We planned two one-day workshops on crystal skulls. The other two were not clear. Because they both love dragons, they asked me to do a one-day workshop on dragons. My initial response was no, but after meditating on the subject, I felt such a strong yes that I was shocked. I decided to do it. The preparation for the workshop, which we called Dragons 101, formed the start of a more expanded study of dragons. The results of these studies form the basis of this book.

My studies and the increasing enthusiasm of the participants at dragon workshops stimulated me to continue to study dragons. The more information I collected, the clearer it became that dragons are important. They are important for working with the earth, learning how to work with elemental powers, learning how to create our reality, and finding balance within ourselves.

The study of dragons contains challenges. As mentioned, many dragon legends, especially those in Western society, are often negative. Because both Western and Eastern dragon legends and stories lead to certain beliefs about how dragons look, people depict them as physical creatures that are reptile-like and lay eggs. The fact that there are no remnants found of dragons leads researchers to the belief that they do not exist and never have. Ernest Ingersoll ended his book *Dragons and Dragon Lore*: "I go out where I came in: There are no dragons — there never was a dragon; but whenever in the West there appeared to be one there was always a St. George."[7]

Everything that is not visible but is believed to be part of our reality belongs to what is called the subtle worlds. As mentioned, these worlds are part of the Gaia system and are studied in the subject of metaphysical ecology. These invisible worlds are the worlds of angels, devas, elementals, nature spirits, unicorns, and other beings.

People have written many books about these subtle beings, especially about angels. A person with a deep connection to the subtle worlds is David Spangler, who spent a large part of his life studying them.[8] Although people describe many subtle beings, people rarely place dragons in subtle worlds. It is one thing to be serious about nature spirits or devas, but dragons and even unicorns are not part of such studies. In my opinion, because we are not able to perceive dragons with any of our five senses, the fact that there are dragon grids leads me to say that dragons are part of the subtle worlds. Because they are part of the subtle worlds, they deserve our attention, as do all subtle beings.

The Challenge Is Perception

Assuming I am correct and dragons are subtle beings, we encounter another challenge. If dragons belong to the subtle world, how do we study them? Suddenly we are faced with the same challenges as other people who study invisible subtle worlds. There is no accepted procedure. It is like learning a new language while there are no books to teach us. The challenge we have when we study dragons is that we cannot see, hear, or touch them. We cannot perceive them with our five physical senses. We can only sense them, connect with them, and learn to feel with increasing subtlety who these beings are, what they offer us, and how they help our journey.

For those who have difficulty believing that there are other worlds apart from the world we can see, I offer this: The universe as we think we know it consists only of 4.9 percent ordinary matter. Most of it is dark matter.[9] One of the aspects of matter of the universe is radiation, which we measure as photons. Photons form the light we can perceive, and they form an even smaller part of the energy matter of the universe.[10] Of this small part of the existing energies, only a small part is visible: the visible spectrum. Our eyes receive an enormous number of bits of information. However, different systems prevent the brain from becoming overwhelmed by too many visual stimuli.[11] Therefore, we do not process all the information we receive into a perception.

When we summarize the presented information, it becomes clear that what we think of as our grand reality is only a tiny fraction of the reality that exists. Realizing this, we may become more open to believing that there are energies we cannot see. It is an invitation to expand beyond the perception of the physical senses and to develop other senses to obtain information that is beyond the physical, sensory world. When we choose to study dragons, that is the path we need to take.

When we enter a world where we do not yet have the same verification systems as our sensory systems, we may choose not to accept all the information emanating from observations of the invisible subtle worlds. I believe that this is a wise decision. The subtle worlds we explore can easily lead to interpretations based on our belief structures. We already do that in the physical world, as Michael Shermer extensively describes in his book *The Believing Brain*.[12] We tend to look for confirmation of what we already believe. Therefore, it is important to share information and collaborate to understand the subtle worlds.

An important key to processing information from the invisible worlds is to learn to work from the heart. According to research from the Noetic Sciences and HeartMath Institute, the heart can receive information that is beyond space and time. It can receive information from the subtle worlds as well as information from the past and the future.[13] Therefore, it is important for each of us to learn to screen information from the subtle worlds through our hearts because the heart *knows*. The heart can help you decide which information about the subtle worlds and other dimensional realities you can resonate with. What this book presents about dragons needs to be looked at from this perspective. When you read this book, feel from your heart whether you can resonate with the information.

Understanding Dragons Is a Journey

In no way do I claim to fully understand dragons. Only through sharing will we expand our understanding of these important and most interesting beings. This book presents information based on my experiences with dragons as well as a number of meditations that can help you to connect with and explore dragons yourself.

One of the key characteristics of dragons is their connection with the elemental powers. Dragons help us to connect with the different aspects of the elemental powers. With the help of dragons, we learn to work with the elemental powers in such a way that we can learn to function and optimally create in the physical reality in which we live. The dragons also help us to understand the powers that govern the world in which we live. They truly are allies that help us to function optimally in this world.

There are many books about dragons. Those who love dragons will notice that this is not the usual book on dragons. It presents dragons from a different perspective. Dragons are not reptiles or related to reptiles. They are subtle beings with the ability to shape-shift and will appear in the image you want to see. The information in this book will help you to see that dragons are not beings to fear and distrust but beings who are allies in creating a world that supports all life within the Gaia system.

Much of the information in this book was received while sitting in meditation on the vortexes of the dragon grids. Also, the experiences during workshops that I facilitated alone or with Jeanne over several years have been very important. The best way to get to know dragons and how they can support us is by working with them.

I did not go through this process alone. Besides the support of many people in the Netherlands and the United States, there is a being who calls himself Drasil-air, who has guided my research almost from the beginning in preparing workshops as well as writing this book. I have given this being several roles and functions during my process of understanding dragons. As you will see, it took quite some time in my research and working with dragons to finally understand what an honor it is to work with this wonderful being.

Although this book contains a lot of information, there is much more to learn about dragons. This book provides a foundation for those who wish to study and work with dragons. It provides enough information to continue as you feel personally guided.

In the first chapter, I will provide background information of the current beliefs before presenting a new perspective about dragons. This book invites us to let go of what other people think about dragons. Most people are familiar with a saying that is believed to come from Einstein: "We can't solve problems by using the same kind of thinking we used when we created them." We cannot change our thinking about dragons if we hold on to the way we learned to think about them. Therefore, I invite you to be open to thinking differently about dragons, which will open a door for an exploration of dragon energies in a completely new way. From this new perspective, it will be possible to connect and explore more fully the gifts dragons offer.

Working with dragons will also contribute to a way of living that creates harmony between the visible and invisible worlds. I consider this to be the most important gift of working with dragons. If we want to understand the world in which we live, we must consider both the visible and invisible aspects that lead us to a different and more realistic understanding of our world. This approach is what I have already described as metaphysical ecology.

The study of dragons is important because by learning to see beyond the physical and learning to trust beyond our current collective beliefs, we recognize greater value as the basis of creating a new world, a world of higher vibrations in which all life, including Earth, is respected and seen as one dynamic, interactive system.

Working with dragons is a choice that determines the importance and intensity of your connection with them. Whatever your conscious connections are, you will work consciously or unconsciously with their powers as the guardians of the elemental powers. Being aware and receptive to their support will only help you to function more optimally and evolve more quickly as a cocreator.

When I started my journey with dragons, I had the naïve idea that I had embarked on a simple and interesting journey. I now know that this worthwhile expedition will continue for the rest of my life. As my connection intensified, so has my excitement. It is as if we had been friends for many lifetimes. I no longer understood all the negative feelings toward them, and it upsets me that there are so many stories creating negative images of such wonderful beings.

Experience the Extremes to Achieve Harmony

One day during meditation, my dragon guide, Drasil-air, confronted me. He confirmed that I had worked with dragons over many lifetimes. He made me aware that in certain lifetimes, I adored dragons and did everything to become a dragon master. However, in other lifetimes, I hated them and became a dragon slayer. It was a shock to be confronted with both my light and dark sides. Drasil-air wanted me to experience this context not to make me feel bad but to show me that people in different lifetimes have to experience various aspects of polarity.

Polarity is an inherent part of all creation. We tend to get stuck in the problems of polarity because we believe that one pole is better than the other. However, without understanding both poles, we will never be able to see that they are just different degrees of a single phenomenon. For example, success and failure are the polarities of a result and therefore are different degrees of the result. Cold and warm are but different degrees of temperature. Only when people have had these contrasting experiences do they not need to experience extremes.

Drasil-air has said to me: "You have experienced extremes in the past. Now it is time to harmonize and collaborate based on the guidance of your heart. Then the collaboration will be optimal for the fulfillment of your soul purpose. It is not about defining the form of the relationship you want to have. That will lead to a situation in which the form of the relationship is more important than the collaboration. Now that you have experienced extremes, we can finally work together in a balanced way."

Most likely everyone has experienced polarity in different lifetimes. Nevertheless, no matter what has been experienced, now is the time to choose your journey from your heart, continuing onward as a cocreator. Allow the dragons to help you become a creator who optimally supports the world in which you live.

CHAPTER 1

About Dragons

IT IS AMAZING HOW MANY IMAGES THERE ARE OF DRAGONS. The fact these beings are so heavily portrayed as connected with human cultures implies that dragons have existed or may still exist. They also may symbolize something significant in the human psyche. Whatever the case, there is no doubt that dragons are important, or they would not be so abundantly present in human consciousness.

If dragon symbolism was not noteworthy, it would be difficult to renew interest in them. However, the opposite is true. The interest in dragons is rapidly increasing, and it is surprising to hear how many people claim they have connections with them. Although it is often not easy to understand what that connection means or stands for, the fact that these connections exist is important, and it becomes increasingly difficult to dismiss them as childish fantasy.

When people mention they have a connection with dragons, they usually see this connection as important and beneficial. These positive connections that people describe seem to be in contrast with most depictions of dragons in our modern Western society. Usually,

IMAGE 1.1. On Chinese New Year, the dragon dance is performed
to ensure a prosperous year.

books and movies depict dragons as vile, dangerous creatures that
need to be killed. Killing dragons is evident in many stories; for example, you see it in Christian lore with St. George or Archangel Michael
slaying dragons.

There also are many stories in which heroes kill dragons to save
the maiden or princess or to reclaim the treasures that dragons have
stolen. Many stories show dragons as hoarders of riches — money,
gold, and precious materials like gemstones. An example of a dragon
hoarding a treasure is Smaug, the dragon that plays an important role
in Tolkien's *Hobbit*.[1]

While dragons in the West serve a dubious role, in Eastern countries such as China, Japan, and Vietnam, people revere dragons
because they bring luck and wealth. The Chinese New Year starts with
people carrying around a snake-like dragon to ensure that the new
year will be prosperous (see image 1.1). It seems that there are big differences in beliefs in the East and the West about dragons. However,
in some Western traditions, we find positive qualities attributed to
dragons, such as wisdom, knowledge, and service to people. We also

see dragons with positive attributes in some movies and TV series. A pleasant example is the movie *How to Train Your Dragon* and its sequels.[2]

I first began investigating dragons while I was writing *Gifts of Mother Earth*. I searched for information from channelings and books in which dragons were associated generally with Earth energy grids and particularly with crystalline grids. These stories offered a different perspective and reflected diverse beliefs about dragons and the roles they play. These stories specifically refer to dragons as the creators of distinct energy lines. The Chinese even name certain energy lines as dragon lines.[3]

As we formulate a new view of dragons, we need to consider the historical view that people held. There are many different thoughts about dragons. I will summarize some of these points of view. The dragons asked me to include this information for the following reason: We are collectively affected by beliefs about dragons from the past as well as from the present. When we know what the collective beliefs are, we can clearly identify which are inaccurate and then choose to release them, opening ourselves to new ideas and perspectives about dragons.

The First Dragons

It is difficult to find information that identifies when dragons first appeared in human history. Some people believe that this challenge is the consequence of a lack of consistency in the understanding of what dragons are. Initially, people may not have used the term "dragon"; however, we cannot be certain. More importantly, we do not know much about history before the Sumerians. We have limited written information about the beginning of history, and often the historical tablets are incomplete.

Moreover, we interpret the information we have from the viewpoint of current reality without enough knowledge about the conceptual thinking of the people who provided the original information. The shared history comes mostly from those who were the conquerors or leaders. The ruling group does not always provide information directly, because accurate information may have resulted in a loss of power over those they ruled. Thus, the rulers often wrote symbolically, hiding the real message in a metaphoric or symbolic description. Therefore, written history does not necessarily represent the true story of the people.

Since most of the stories about dragons are myth, it is important to consider information about dragons throughout time from such perspective as to determine whether there are common and essential aspects that help us to understand them. Ernest Ingersoll does not believe dragons exist. He believes that dragons are the embodiment of the underlying principle of morality — the eternal contrast and contest between good and evil typified by the incessant struggle of humankind with the forces of nature and their twofold selves.[4]

According to Ingersoll, in the East, the dragons, like primitive gods, were either deity or demon. He believed that although the idea of dragons originated in the East, only the negative, demon aspect migrated West. He also believed that the dragon is as old as the human imagination and may have been part of the original artistic expression.[5] In summary, his vision is that dragons do not exist but that they are a figment of human imagination trying to express fluctuating and primitive belief of god-like powers.

A weak spot in Ingersoll's story is no cave paintings depicting dragons have been found anywhere. He attempted to argue that the famous half-human figure painted on the wall in the Cave of Trois-Freres (Montesquieu-Avantès, France) by people from the Magdalenian period (about 13,000 years ago) was an attempt to paint a dragon.[6] Few agree with him.

Peter Dickinson explains why there are no rock paintings of dragons. According to him, dragons are animals to fear. People in ancient times painted animals that they needed for food and saw painting as a magical way to attract them. Thus, as you do not want to attract a dragon, you would never paint one.[7]

The Book of the Dragon by Judy Allen and Jeanne Griffiths[8] provides a more extensive overview of dragons throughout history. According to these authors, dragons and snakes are the basis of creation stories. One challenge a researcher has is that the word "dragon" is Greek and there is no known word for dragon in pre-Hellenistic times. Therefore, there are no textual references.[9]

In early stories, dragons are identified by their appearance and attributes. The most basic attributes being serpentine, reptilian, associated with water, and possessing immense power. Secondary attributes such as legs, wings, the ability to change shape and size, fire breathing, and treasure hoarding are mentioned. Although stories frequently mention these attributes, they are not universally included in author descriptions.

A shared connection in many stories is that snakes and dragons possess a strong relationship with water. In these stories, water is both the power of creation as well as the power of destruction. Once again, the polarity between good and evil — constructiveness and destructiveness — are ever present. Therefore, snakes and dragons had to be pleased to ensure that the water was creative and not destructive. Often the dragon was portrayed to oppose creation and needed to be defeated by a god, just as humanity had to vanquish the chaotic and destructive aspects of nature to build a livelihood.[9]

Tiamat

Several authors trace the first stories about dragons back to the ancient civilization Sumer. They refer to the story of Tiamat. The principle of the story is the same in all texts. Because it is important to understand the symbols, a summary follows. This story is largely based on the one found at Wikipedia[10]; however, there are many variations.

In the religion of Mesopotamia (which includes Sumer, Assyria, Akkad, and Babylonia), Tiamat was known as a primordial goddess of the ocean, and she mated with Abzû (known as the god of freshwater) to produce younger gods. Tiamat is regarded as the symbol of the chaos of primordial creation, which is depicted as a woman. She represented the beauty of the feminine and was referred to as the glistening one.

There seem to be two parts to the Tiamat mythos. In the first part, Tiamat was a creator goddess, who, through a sacred marriage between salt and fresh water, peacefully created the cosmos through successive generations. In the second part, called Chaoskampf, Tiamat was considered the monstrous embodiment of primordial chaos. Some sources identify her with images of a sea serpent or dragon.

In the Enûma Elish, the Babylonian epic of creation, Tiamat gave birth to the first generation of deities. Her husband, Apsu (or

Abzû), assumed correctly that there was a plan to kill him and usurp his throne, so he commanded war and was killed. Enraged, she too started a war with her husband's murderers. She took on the form of a massive sea dragon. Enki's son, the storm god Marduk, slayed her but not before she had brought forth the monsters of the Mesopotamian pantheon, including the first dragons, whose bodies she filled with poison instead of blood. Marduk then formed the heavens and Earth from her divided body.

Tiamat was later known as Thaláttē (a variant of *thalassa*, the Greek word for "sea") in the Hellenistic Babylonian writer Berossus's first volume of universal history. It seems that the name Tiamat was dropped in secondary translations of the original religious texts (written in the East Semitic Akkadian language). Some Akkadian copyists of Enûma Elish substituted the ordinary word for "sea" with "Tiamat" since the two names had become essentially the same by association.

Allen and Griffiths also traced the history of the dragon lore back to the Sumerians. While the tablets that form the basis of the story were incomplete due to damage, the essence of the story seemed clear. These stories are myths. The earliest myth is that of Ninurta, a god-hero, and Asag, a monstrous dragon-like demon. There is also the story of the giant sea dragon Labbu, who appeared so horrifying that the very gods trembled before him and had to appoint a champion to slay him.[11]

Like Allen and Griffiths, Boulay[12] also believed that the dragon stories originated in Mesopotamia, in particular from the Sumerian culture. These stories spread to the West and the East. Each culture added or changed information in the stories, leading to different depictions of dragons and their qualities.

What History Tells Us

The creation stories of snakes and dragons, especially the story of Tiamat, offer important clues. Tiamat is a female who connects with water, the primordial ocean. Water is a creative element. As we will see later, this creative element also holds wisdom. However, creation cannot happen without proper induction: her husband. Tiamat became destructive when the creation — the children — tried to take control. From my perspective, the story of Tiamat encompasses the creation story and informs about our (the children's) downfall because of our attempts to control the creative process.

Equating the feminine (Tiamat) with a dragon, who can both create and destruct, relates to how we choose to use creative powers: either for the greater good of all or for personal benefit. The choice to use creative power for personal power increasingly leads to the destruction of the natural world, as we currently see all around us.

Construction and destruction are the polarities of creation. Polarity is an inherent aspect of our universe. There is no benefit in judgment because polarity is simply a fact. It invites us to look at the essence of the two poles to offer us the possibility to learn to use creation for the greater good of all. Thereby we move away from our tendency of destruction. Dragons are simply dragons. They are neither good nor bad. They are guardians of creative powers. We choose how to connect with them: either to collaborate or to be afraid and fight.

Another belief about dragons is that they hoard treasure people usually define as gold and precious stones. As was discussed, the real treasure is understanding the creative process. Dragons are the guardians of these treasures, the power of creation. As guardians, the dragons stand in the way of those who search for power and control; therefore they must be slain.

While there are many opinions about dragons, an increasing number of people consider them as positive creatures, and they depict them in a generally acceptable manner. As previously discussed, once we are aware of the common ideas, we can choose to let go of them and to see them in a new light. Therefore, before we consider the results of new research and describe dragons in a new way, we should review the collective beliefs about dragons, the different types of dragons, and the various ways people see them. These general ideas about dragons affect our beliefs and may hamper our ability to look at them in an open, unbiased, new way.

Beliefs About Dragons and Their Forms

Although we have looked at dragons historically, we still have not defined them. What does the word "dragon" mean? It comes from the Latin word *draco* and the Greek word *drakon*. The root of these two words is *drak*, or *derk*, and is believed to derive from the word *derkomai*, which means "to see." Its deeper meaning is "sharp-sighted." The Greek word *drakon* was originally used to describe any large serpent and the dragons of mythology.

As mentioned, the general belief about dragons is that they are reptilian-like creatures. Most images of dragons depict a type of reptile, sometimes more snake-like and sometimes more lizard- or crocodile-like. In Western culture, most dragons have wings and can fly as well as spew fire. They all seem to possess some mystical power, which suggests that they have qualities beyond those of normal physical animals. That does not mean that people have not considered them to be animals.

An ecologist named Rob Colautti from the University of British Columbia developed a relationship overview of dragons using biological techniques. Based on internet sketches, drawings, and sculptures, which are dated from the dark ages to the twentieth century, he defined seventy-six dragon species[13] based on biological techniques. He concluded that there was a considerable difference between dragons from Asia, which he calls Orientalia, or Lung, and Eurasian dragons. Colautti suggested that this might indicate different evolutionary lines. This idea is fascinating, as it is based on drawings and descriptions and not on biological material.

Another extensive description of dragons as biological animals is found in *Dr. Ernest Drake's Dragonology: The Complete Book of Dragons*.[14] Beautifully illustrated, it describes different species and the general biology of dragons. The descriptions (true for most descriptions) are based on the idea that dragons are reptilian creatures. Therefore, these types of books describe dragons as reptiles who lay eggs. These eggs hatch to create cute baby dragons.

The Orientalia — Chinese Dragons

The Orientalia (as named by Rob Colautti[13]) are the Chinese dragons; however, the forms of the dragons from Japan and other Eastern countries are similar (see images 1.2, 1.3, and 1.4). Dragons influence a very important aspect of Chinese culture. They traditionally symbolize potent and auspicious powers, particularly control over water, such as rainfall, typhoons, and floods. The dragon is also a symbol of power, strength, and good luck for people who are worthy of it. Hence, during the time of Imperial China, the emperor used the dragon

IMAGE 1.2. This is a picture of a statue of Quan Yin standing on a dragon in water.

IMAGE 1.3. This is a golden Chinese dragon named Fucanglong.

IMAGE 1.4. This is a Japanese dragon.

symbol to represent his imperial power and strength.[15] This dragon had five claws and two horns (image 1.2). The dragon with five claws was reserved strictly for the emperor. The dragon with four claws was reserved for princes and nobles. Nowadays, the dragon with the four claws is used commonly (image 1.3).

Initially, the dragon was benevolent, wise, and just, but the Buddhists introduced the concept of malevolent influence. Just as water destroys, they said, so can some dragons destroy via floods, tidal waves, and storms. They suggested that some of the worst floods were the result of a mortal antagonizing a dragon.[15]

From this perspective, it is illuminating to consider one of the many statues of Quan Yin. In China, Quan Yin is a Buddhist deity known as the goddess of mercy and compassion. One sculpture depicts her standing on a dragon riding water waves (image 1.2), presenting her as a being mastering these powers. Primordial water represents creation, and dragons are the guardians of the elemental powers of creation. Quan Yin represents the feminine wisdom and often holds the pearl of wisdom (in some stories called the pearl of light[16]) in her hand. The dragon is also seen as wise and in the statue holds the pearl of wisdom or the orb of knowledge. Much symbolism is evident in this statue, demonstrating the many conscious and unconscious aspects of the role of dragons as the guardians of creative powers.

Dragons or dragon-like depictions have been found on archaeological sites from the Neolithic period throughout China.[17] Chinese literature and myths refer to many dragons in addition to the famous Long (or Lung). The linguist Michael Carr analyzed over 100 ancient dragon names found in Chinese classic texts. Many such Chinese names derive from the suffix "-long."[15]

The Chinese separate the dragons into nine types of which the horned dragon, or lung, is the most powerful. It is associated with water and rain. This dragon is considered deaf.[17] To the Chinese, the imperial dragon, or lung, is considered the primary of four benevolent spiritual animals, the other three being the phoenix, the unicorn, and the tortoise. There are four types of lung: the Tien-Lung, the celestial dragon; the Shen-Lung, the spiritual dragon; the Ti-Lung, the earth dragon; and the Fut's-Lung, the underworld dragon. The celestial dragon protects the places of the gods. The spiritual dragon controls the wind and the rain. The earth dragon controls rivers and water on Earth. The underworld dragon guards precious metals and gems.[18] In general, the Chinese believe that dragons are made up of nine different animals. While different sources use different animals, the number does not vary. One of the more common descriptions mentions the following parts of animals[18]:

Head: camel (also mentioned crocodile)

Scales: carp (fish) 117 scales total — 81 infused with yang (the good) and 36 infused with yin (the bad), balancing the dragon's temper and personality

Horns: giant stag (deer)

Eyes: hare or rabbit (also mentioned having the eyes of a demon)

Ears: bull or cow

Neck: snake

Belly: clam or tortoise

Paws (soles): tiger

Claws: eagle or hawk

Eurasian Dragons

Rob Colautti defines the Eurasian dragons as a completely different group of beings of Orientalia, or Chinese dragons. He believes that
the Orientalia and mammals have a common ancestor because they
have four legs. They may lose a pair or even both pairs of legs, but fundamentally, they have four legs. The situation is different for the Eurasian dragons. They must have a different ancestor because instead
of four appendages they have six: four legs and two wings (image
1.5). According to him, two groups of dragons have four legs and two
wings: the *Dracopteronidae* and the *Dracoverisidae*. This description
of six appendages assumes that complex appendages such as wings
and legs evolve from something.

The next group of dragon species, called the *Wyvernidae*, gradually lost two legs. The ancestors of the *Serpentidae* lost two more legs
before losing wings in the more recently derived *Serpentidae* species.
It is intriguing how a specialist in systematics can use images from
fantasies to develop an evolutionary view of various dragon species.

The wyvern species is more generally known, defined as a cousin
to real dragons because they have only two legs (image 1.6). They are
described as smaller than dragons, and they do not breathe fire, but
their breath is poisonous, and they are malignant.[19]

Western dragons look mostly like reptiles; both are depicted with
scales. Dragons also have tails like lizards. Their heads look similar
to a crocodile's. If we look at the shape of the crystal dragon skulls
(dragon skulls carved from crystalline materials), which have become
very popular over the past five years, it becomes clear that the shape
of these skulls looks very similar to a crocodile's skull. They have
added some spikes and horns to make it look more dragon-like, but
from a biologist's view, the similarity to a crocodile is striking. Some
people believe that crocodiles (alligators) may have been the inspiration for many dragon drawings.[20] Also, the legs have a certain similarity with those of crocodiles and lizards.

Although most books depict dragons with four legs and two wings,
some people created their own categories of dragons. For example, the
wizard's apprentice Sindri Suncatcher in *A Practical Guide to Dragon
Magic*[21] separates the dragons into two groups. The first group —
the chromatic dragons — is destructive, selfish, ambitious, greedy,

IMAGE 1.5. This is a depiction of a typical Western dragon
(called a steampunk dragon).

IMAGE 1.6. This is known as a wyvern dragon (image by Fafnirx).

proud, cruel, and fickle. The chromatic dragons are further separated
by color: red, blue, black, green, and white. The second group — the
metallic dragons — embraces all that is good and useful about the elements. Spontaneous and with a bright nature, majestic as mountains,
and warm as fire, the metallic dragons are nature's blessings in the
world. Listening to the people's stories, most people talk about this
type of dragon. Also, the metallic dragons come in different colors:
gold, silver, copper, bronze, and brass. In Suncatcher's delineation,
there is polarity: the evil and the good dragons.[21]

 In chapters I and II of *Dragonology,*[22] Dr. Ernest Drake describes
different dragon species with familiar names, such as the wyvern: the
dragons with two legs. Drake states that the wyvern are from Africa.
He continues to create new species based on geography, such as frost
dragons from the Arctic and Antarctica; Knuckers, with very small
wings and snake-like bodies, who live in Europe; and from Australia,
the *Draco marsupialis*, the marsupial dragon.

Dragons Exist

Some authors suggest that dragons still exist while there truly is no evidence for any of what they describe, confirming Ernest Inger-soll's conclusion: "There are no dragons — there never was a dragon; but whenever in the West there appeared to be one there was always a St. George."[23] From a physical perspective, his conclusion seems cor-rect. However, our perception of the physical world is highly limited. Except for those who have developed their intuition, hardly anybody looks beyond their physical senses. Moreover, our brains are highly selective when processing information, and we prefer familiar and accepted beliefs. Ernest Ingersoll strongly represents this approach.

In my previous book, *Gifts of Mother Earth*, and also in this book's introduction, I mentioned data that indicate how extremely limited we can see reality.[24] We only see a small part of the electromagnetic energies, which are only 0.005 percent of the energy and matter that is estimated to exist in the universe. Also, only a small part of what our eyes see translates into awareness. In other words, we live completely in the illusion that we think we know the world in which we live while our concept of reality is so limited that we should be ashamed to have such arrogant thoughts.

Nikola Tesla, who some consider the greatest inventor and most knowledgeable person of modern times, made some interesting com-ments. "If you want to understand the secrets of the universe, think in terms of energy, frequency, and vibration." That is, understand-ing the universe is not through that which is only perceived with the senses, which are too limited to observe all energies, frequencies, and vibrations. Tesla proceeds further: "The day science begins to study non-physical phenomena, it will make more progress in one decade than in all the previous centuries of its existence." This statement is bold. It confirms that perception is highly limited, leading to illusions and thereby accessing only a fraction of reality. We must free our-selves from such limitations.

Scientists may have started the research of nonphysical phenom-ena, but this research is still very limited. Therefore, it is important that we not wait for their results and instead start to study nonphysi-cal phenomena in whatever way possible and to the best of our abil-ity. It may be easy to decide that we want to do so, but the challenge is in how we proceed.

We have brains that are capable of more than we think, especially since we now realize that the location of our brains is not limited to our heads but in three different places: the gut, the heart, and the head. The whole body is a sensory system capable of receiving information. Because receiving information through our whole bodies is not logical, people tend to call it intuition.

The HearthMath Institute defines intuition as follows. "Intuition is the process of perceiving and knowing something without conscious reasoning: knowledge of events such as an act of nature that has yet to happen; or knowledge of a distant material object such as an unseen obstruction blocking the highway ahead."[25] I believe that intuition is far more than this definition. It includes knowing about other worlds and the beings who live there and are invisible.

The development of our intuition will lead to a true change in our perception of the world. Bob Samples interpreted Einstein's works as thus: "Albert Einstein called the intuitive or metaphoric mind a sacred gift. He added that the rational mind was a faithful servant. It is paradoxical that in the context of modern life we have begun to worship the servant and defile the divine."[26]

Even though many authors suggest otherwise, it may be clear by now that dragons do not exist in the physical realm. Therefore, we need to use our intuition and other extrasensory gifts to explore the world in which dragons do exist. This world is not of fantasy. This world is of nonphysical phenomena. Some people call it the world of subtle energies, beings, and phenomena. Let us begin the exploration of what dragons really are.

CHAPTER 2

Connect and Work with Dragons

DRAGONS ARE BEINGS FROM THE SUBTLE REALMS. Therefore, we need to look at them from a subtle energy perspective instead of a physical perspective. Dragons are not visible to our physical eyes. We use our eyes to explore the world, our reality. This approach does not work for investigating dragons. The fact that they are not visible makes it understandable why those who believe in dragons only see them with their third eye while in a meditative or a dream state.

Their invisibility makes it difficult for most people to work with them. If they are not visible, how do we know they exist? It could all be in our imagination. If they exist, how do we connect with them? How do we know whether we have connected with them?

A Species Potential through the Morphogenetic Field

We first have to answer, "Do dragons exist?" In the previous chapter, books about dragons were separated into two groups: books that conclude there is no proof of their existence and books that accept their existence even though there is no strong physical evidence to confirm these beliefs. However, the deep-rooted belief in dragons throughout the ages necessitates a bit more of an answer than belief or no belief.

I mentioned that when I want to know whether a species (visible or invisible) exists, I use a particular system. Every species on Earth has a system that holds the information needed to make its existence possible. I call this system a morphogenetic field, which is a coherent field of information that exists as a layer around Earth. No species can exist without such a field. It holds the information of the full potential of a species.

All species, including humans, rarely use the full potential of information in their morphogenetic fields. They actively use only a certain part of it, which is located in the morphogenetic grids. The grids are located on Earth's surface in the form of lines.

There is a connection between the grids and the field through what is called a vortex. A vortex is an energetic connection through which information can flow between a field and a grid. The movement of the energy induces a spiral, hence the name vortex. The word "vortex" comes from the Latin *vertere*, which means "to spiral."

Morphogenetic grids can be found all over the world. That means that you can access information about the different dragon species everywhere on Earth. You can find a more extensive description of the morphogenetic system in Gifts *of Mother Earth*.[1]

The morphogenetic field, the grids, and the connecting vortexes are supposed to be dynamic systems; however many are currently rather static. The purpose of evolution is to bring the information in the grids into complete alignment with the field. Then the potential of a species is realized. However, the overall energy of Earth "co-determines" to what degree this is possible.

Human beings have chosen to be the stewards of the Gaia system: Earth with everything that lives on her. We came to Earth for a number of reasons: to experience physicality, be stewards of the Gaia (Earth) system, and help the Gaia system raise its vibration to make ascension possible.[2] As stewards, we have a powerful influence on the Gaia system, which is much larger than people realize. Without knowing it, humans are the reason most species of animals and plants are not able to express their full potential. This limited expression of potential is a consequence of the reality in which we live. This reality is only a fraction of the potential the Gaia system has. It is the consciousness of the human species that creates this limited reality because we as a species realize only a small part of our potential.

You may wonder why our limitations are relevant when we talk about connecting and working with dragons. From my perspective, there is great relevance. Because dragons are not perceptible to our five senses, we need to develop our extrasensory perception. We all have this perception; however, developing extrasensory perception is not supported as part of our general educational program. If we want to connect to all aspects of the world we live in, the visible and the invisible, we need to develop skills other than the ones we primarily use.

The placements of our eyes in the front part of our face suggests that we are beings who primarily experience the world through vision. Being visually oriented, if we cannot see it, we do not believe it exists. This limitation makes it difficult to work with the huge number of beings not visible to us.

In the previous chapter, I discussed the limited way in which we perceive our reality. Given this limitation, how can we rely on such a restricted system in our efforts to study and understand the universe? Our limited use of the potential of the morphogenetic field along with being constrained by a limited expression through the morphogenetic grids make it difficult to go beyond the information our visual impressions provide.

Most people are happy believing that what they see is the total world in which they live. However, people on their spiritual journeys need to be willing to look beyond. That is especially true for those who want to study beings from the invisible worlds such as dragons.

Morphogenetic Grids of Dragons

A species can only exist when there is a morphogenetic system holding the information needed for its existence. In the introduction, I mentioned that my wife, Jeanne, challenged me to look for morphogenetic grids of unicorns and how that led to finding not only the grids of the unicorns but also of dragons. Finding the morphogenetic grids of dragons and studying them after this discovery was the beginning of a journey that has endured for many years and is likely to continue for many more.

Initially, I thought there was only one species of dragons with a lot of variations. It turned out I was wrong. I am grateful that the twenty-six years of training in dowsing made it possible for me to sense differences between grids and to find more than one grid. When there are more grids, there are more species. The discovery of more grids was the beginning of the discovery of different dragon species and the study of their roles and functions.

Finding a morphogenetic grid is not difficult for a dowser. However, understanding the information contained in the grid is a different matter. When I started finding the grids, I also wanted to know and understand the kind of dragon connected to that grid. Does this dragon have a form, and if so, what is that form? What is the role this dragon plays within the Gaia system? What is its relationship to other dragons? Sitting on the different vortexes, I realized that the information on dragons in books and on the internet did not help me in my attempts to understand dragons. I even began to doubt whether the grids I had found belonged to species I labeled as dragons. Maybe I was looking at different beings altogether. These are thoughts that come up when you work with beings you cannot see and can only approach with extrasensory perception that is always in development. The only thing you can do in such a situation is continue with your research and trust that you will find enough information to develop a deeper understanding and insight.

In studying the morphogenetic grids, patterns emerged. These grid patterns had certain characteristics. It soon became clear that the first grids I found were irregular rectangle shapes, sometimes close to being squares (see image 2.1). Some of these grids had roughly the same sizes while the size of others varied. Seeing the similarities and the differences of the shapes and sizes of the grids, the lines, and the vortexes were the first steps in recognizing groups of related species.

The second important aspect of understanding a species is sitting in the center of a vortex and meditating. By sitting in a vortex, you can connect with both the grid and the field. By sitting in a meditative state in a vortex, you can receive information very optimally.

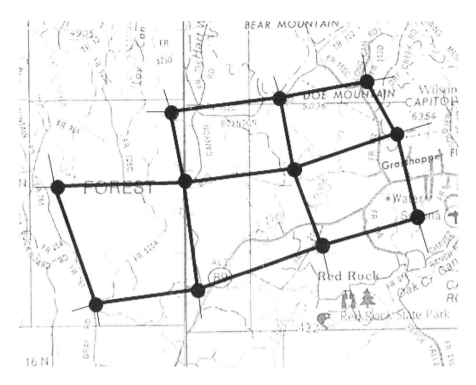

IMAGE 2.1. This image shows the most common form of the morphogenetic grids of dragons. This grid is from a duality dragon: a dragon of the northeast (see chapter 7).

After repeated effort, an image of the species connected to that field and grid may emerge. I compare this process of receiving information and learning to translate it into an understanding similar to learning a new language. It takes some time before sounds become words with a meaning. The process of connecting with subtle energies is similar. Initially, it is energy, and it takes time before it has an image or information with meaning. It is important to give this process time. As with learning languages, you can speed up the process through sharing and training with other people.

The first step is to learn to work with the information already available: the information contained in the grids. Once we can work with the energies and information held in the grids and we are ready to expand, we will automatically begin to tap into the field. This approach is more efficient, more successful, and also more natural than forcing attempts to go to the field directly. After all, we live on

Earth and experience first what is here before we expand to what exists beyond it.

As we will see when we work with the different groups, there is a specific dragon for each group that helps us connect to the grids of all the dragons of that group. We call these the black dragons because that is how they tend to show themselves to me. In chapter 11 we will connect with the master dragons and see that there is a master grid dragon. Every time we connect with a dragon through its grid, we also connect with the black dragon of that group as well as the master black dragon. That indicates that when we open ourselves, there is a lot of support for us to connect with dragons and the powers of which they are the guardians.

Vortex Essences

Another very helpful approach for studying dragon energies is to make an essence of the vortex. We define an essence as a substance that holds the key energies of a system. An essence should contain enough of the energies of the original place or system to allow a person to connect to the fullness of that system. Jeanne and I create vortex essences in water because we believe that water holds the vortex essence fully and optimally. Water has unique qualities. One of these qualities is its ability to receive and hold energy and information.

You can create an essence with water as the carrier in the following way: First, you connect with the essence of water. At the same time, you connect with the essence of the energies of the vortex with the intent that the water will fully take on the essence of the energies of this vortex. While holding your connection with both the energies of the water and the vortex, you allow the fullness of the energies of the vortex to be transferred into the water, thus creating the essence.

To be able to induce the full potential of the vortex into the water requires training. You will always get some aspects of the vortex into the water. However, if you cannot make a strong enough connection to activate that vortex, you will only get a part of it. It also takes training to activate a vortex. This ability takes time and practice. Over time, you will be able to activate a vortex to greater degrees.

People believe that simply placing a bottle of water or another fluid on a vortex for a while is enough to create a vortex essence. However, that is not my experience. Water will then take on a certain part of the energies of the vortex, but it is only a part. Which part depends on many factors, mainly on the unconscious abilities to connect and on the level of activity of a vortex, which depends on the consciousness that connects with that vortex.

Many think that a vortex shows all aspects all the time. However, that is not the case. It is the consciousness of the individual who connects with it that determines what is active. Therefore, you will only create an optimal essence when your consciousness activates that vortex to this optimal state. Just placing a bottle in a vortex will not create an optimal essence.

I am aware that not everyone will agree with what I share about making vortex essences. However, I invite you to play with this principle to see whether you achieve different results. You will always create some results. However, my personal experience has taught me that the ability to connect with both water and the vortex at the same time, as fully as possible, will add to the process in such a way that it creates an essence that holds the energies more completely.

The gift of a vortex essence is that it can be utilized with groups to create temporary vortexes. It is also possible to amplify your experiences with these essences and the temporary vortexes they can create by working with crystals and crystal skulls. We use the vortex essences in our circle of crystal skulls to create an optimal temporary vortex. The presence of this temporary vortex allows people to experience the energies of the vortex without the need to go to places that often are not easy to access.

Working in a group with an essence makes it possible to share experiences that help our understanding of the dragon species. Using vibrational essences makes it possible to work with a whole group of dragons in one day, which would be impossible if you have to go to the vortexes of the grids outdoors. You can also use these essences for personal experiences simply by sitting with them and holding them.

Unfortunately, it is not possible to put an essence in a book. The alternative we use in this book is a photo of a vortex of the morphogenetic grid of the dragon species with which we want to connect. A photo also holds the energy of the vortex. It is a way to connect with the energy of the grid and field because focusing on the picture also creates a temporary vortex, similar to working with an essence. That will make the connection with a particular species easier.

I highly recommend that you connect as optimally as possible with the energies of a picture before connecting with the species to which that grid belongs. It is important to trust that by looking at the picture, you create a vortex and make that connection, whether you feel it or not.

Crystalline Beings and Dragons

Chapter 4 dives deeper into the subject of crystalline beings and dragons. This chapter introduces the subject to support the way you will see dragons and the way you will develop your connection with them.

In our research, we discovered that there is a relationship between dragons and crystalline energies. Earth is a crystalline being. We soon discovered that dragons have a deep connection with Mother Earth. They are an inherent part of Earth, Earth's energies, and the way Earth's system functions.

While studying crystal skulls, we encountered beings that we later described as crystalline beings. We discovered that these beings could be called pre-dragons, which will be discussed later. For now, the important aspect is that the pre-dragons can only exist in crystalline material when it contains enough of a certain life force, which will also be described extensively. The key point for now is that crystals with crystalline life force help you to connect with dragons. Crystals with crystalline life force are like beacons telling the dragons that the person who holds the crystal is capable of making a connection with energies that are important in working with them. The subject of crystalline beings and crystalline life force is so important that we dedicate a whole chapter to it.

Our work with crystalline beings led to an important discovery. Each crystalline being works with and has a connection with all four elemental powers, and one of these four elemental powers is dominant. This discovery brought up the question of whether dragons, like the pre-dragons, also are connected with elemental powers. That turns out to be correct: All dragons are connected to all four elemental powers, and for each dragon, one of the elemental powers is more dominant than the other three.

Elemental Powers and Dragon Species

The discovery that dragons have a connection with elemental powers was a great help in defining the different dragon species. It was the last part of the information that was needed to begin to understand the dragon energies, which was the basis used to define them. The morphogenetic grids, the connections with the elemental powers, and the increasing amount of information that became available during meditations and workshops ultimately led to the understanding that there are forty-five species of dragons, excluding the pre-dragons. These forty-five species hold all the energies of the elemental powers needed to be a creator at the full potential that the morphogenetic field of the Gaia system holds. Therefore, the dragons can help you to become a conscious creator.

Within Gaia's morphogenetic field, there is a morphogenetic field that holds the full potential of all dragons within Earth's system. This morphogenetic dragon field expresses itself in forty-five different grids that hold the information of the forty-five species as they express themselves at this moment. The grids do not hold the optimum of what dragons can offer us, but they offer what is directly available in this phase of the evolution of the Gaia system.

Each of the dragon species has a specific function as the guardian of a creative power that we can use to create a reality in harmony with the Gaia system and supports all living beings in an optimal way. We are invited to work with these dragon species. Interestingly, originally there were only five species. As we will see later, these five species held all the powers needed in this reality to create anything we want. At the time when there were five dragon species, there was a collaboration between dragons and humans. However, people misused the powers and wanted to eliminate the guardians. The need to control the powers without the interference of the dragon guardians forms the basis of all the stories of defeating the dragons. The attempt to control the powers led to the destruction of what we call Atlantis.

Working with dragons was no longer an integrated part of the new society. What was left was the idea that dragons were bad and dangerous and that we needed to destroy them. That is the basis of the attitude of those in the West, who are the descendants of Atlantis.

Some people are beginning to reconnect with dragons and

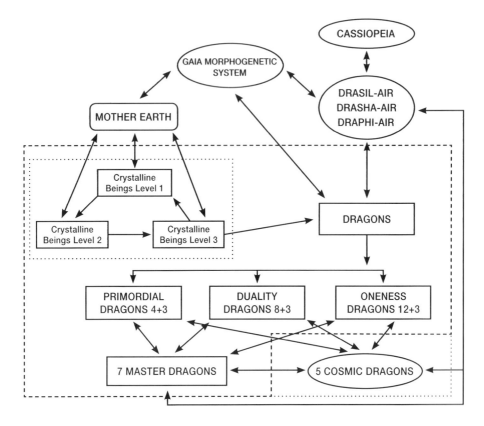

IMAGE 2.2. This diagram provides an overview of the existing dragon species connected with Earth. The overview will be easier to understand after you've read the descriptions of the different groups (chapters 7-11).

understand who they are: our allies. However, dragons are aware that humans need more development to overcome their egos and desire for power. To prevent a repetition of the misuse of the elemental powers while at the same time being able to work again with humans in the current time frame, dragons decided to split their powers into subpowers. Thus, humans require more preparation to use and master the full power of each of the elemental powers. The dragons expect that during the process of working with the different subpowers and energies, people can gather enough wisdom to use the full powers wisely. We will further explore these powers in the chapters ahead.

In image 2.2, a summary is given of the forty-five different species (which will be discussed in detail in chapter 6). As the image shows, there are five main groups of dragons. The first group is the primordial dragons, numbering seven species (indicated as 4 + 3, as will be explained in chapter 9). These are the dragons that help us to work with the powers of the elements. We live in a world with four elements that are physical, tangible, and measurable. These are earth, water, air, and fire.

People talk about soil and stones when they refer to the element of earth. When they talk about water, they refer to the water we drink, swim in, and know as rain. We experience the element of air as wind or, even stronger, as storms as well as the air we breathe. We know the element of fire as that which burns and gives warmth and energy. The power locked in these elements is very strong and far greater than our limited understanding. The primordial dragons help us to work with the powers of the elements, which will allow us a certain mastery over the world in which we live.

The second group is the duality dragons, numbering eleven species (indicated as 8 + 3, as will be explained in chapter 7). We live in a world of duality, a world of polarities and differences. We are supposed to learn from these differences. They help us to understand what we do and do not resonate with, allowing us to find a point of balance between opposites. Unfortunately, many people cannot see that polarity (duality) defines the same thing but from different angles. Consequently, they choose one of the points of view as their truth, turning what is but a perspective into a fact and an absolute truth.

These different opinions lead to opposition, and that leads to fights, racism, fanaticism, and even wars. Learning to see the gift in duality and learning to understand the energies involved in creating from the perspective of duality will help us to overcome duality as a problem. The duality dragons help us with this.

The third group is the oneness dragons, numbering fifteen species (indicated as 12 + 3, as will be explained in chapter 8). We can only move to oneness when we have sufficiently mastered duality. That is why it is important to work with the duality dragons before starting to work with the oneness dragons. These dragons help us to achieve a state of oneness, which is the first step on the path to enlightenment. However, it is important to state that one group is not more important than the other. They all are needed to master creation within physical reality.

The fourth group is the master dragons. Each of the previous three groups has dragons that work with aspects of each of the four elemental powers. As we will explain in chapter 10, there are six aspects of each elemental power in these three groups and, therefore, six dragons for each elemental power. There are four master dragons responsible for the six aspects of each of the four elemental powers. They bring the energy of the six aspects, guarded by six dragons together, into a deeper understanding of how to work optimally with them. When we work with the four master dragons, we learn to become masters of the way this physical reality of the Gaia system works. Then we understand these powers and can apply them in our lives.

There are three more master dragons. They bring the three dragons of the grids of the previous three groups, the fields of the previous three groups, and the three central dragons together in harmony and mastery. The functions of the groups and individual dragons will become clear in chapters 7 through 10.

The fifth group is the cosmic dragons, numbering five species. As will be explained in later chapters, the cosmic dragons have no connection with the crystalline life force. Their energy is completely in alignment with their star system of origin: Cassiopeia. Their responsibility is to make sure that the dragon energy will not move away from its original intent due to the effects of the low vibrations of our current Earth reality.

That completes the delineation of the forty-five dragon species. However, in the overview of the dragon species (image 2.2), three more names are mentioned. They also can be called cosmic dragons, but they are different because they do not have a grid. As discussed later, they are a bridge between the forty-five species and the star system from which the dragons originated, Cassiopeia. They are like the ambassadors of that star system to Earth.

I met one of them at the beginning of my dragon resioearch — Drasil-air. I had no idea who this being was. He presented himself as my guide in the world of dragons. I am deeply grateful for his support and guidance. I only recently discovered what his role in the dragon realm is. I also learned that he is part of a trinity and that his two partners are Drasha-air and Draphi-air. We will connect more deeply with these three magnificent beings later.

Most people do not need to reach a state of mastery (however, it is helpful to have at least a basic understanding of the elemental powers) to be able to function in this world. Those who have certain agreements to fulfill in this lifetime that include connecting with the master and the cosmic dragons will have an opportunity to learn to do so. We all have to find our unique optimal state. In this process, we all can use and, from a certain perspective, need the support of the dragons.

Dragons Respond to a Call from the Heart

Working with dragons is not the same as working with pets. Dragons are beings I prefer to view as allies. They are powerful, independent beings who are here to help us on our journey to regain connection with our essence. They also help us to become more conscious creators.

Dragons need to be approached with respect (as we should approach any being, whether visible or invisible). If we want dragons to help us, it's important to behave with respect and to work at a deep connection. The only way to achieve this deep connection is through our hearts. The following meditation can help you to create an optimal connection with the dragons' energies. In the following chapters, we will learn to connect with all the dragon species. This meditation helps us to open our hearts and minds to dragons in general. It also is an opportunity to connect with those dragons who may want to function as guides in the complex world of dragons and dragon energies.

I am aware that there is a tendency to skip this meditation in the interest of gaining more information. You are free to do so. However, if you are serious about connecting with dragons, I recommend you do this meditation as often as feels helpful in expanding and deepening your connection.

―――〜〜〜―――

MEDITATION TO CONNECT
WITH DRAGONS AND DRAGON GUIDES

It is important that you create a quiet space where you will not be disturbed. It would be nice to have a special designated place to meditate, visualize, and connect. (This chapter is not meant to describe the preparation of such special rooms or altars. You can find enough information on the internet or in other books. In the least, a quiet place is important.)

I do not recommend a special posture. Use a posture that allows you to be comfortable so that you are as relaxed as possible. Take care of yourself. Have respect for yourself and for those beings (in this case, the dragons) with whom you want to connect. That is the most fundamentally important aspect.

- Take a few deep inhalations and exhalations, and relax.
- Allow your whole body and mind to relax as optimally as possible. Feel yourself sink into this relaxation.
- Bring your awareness to your heart. Feel your heart and become aware that your heart is also the seat of your essence.
- You can imagine your essence as white light in your heart — for example, as a sphere. Allow that white light to expand throughout your whole physical body and your aura.
- Be aware that this white light of your essence holds the energy of unconditional love. Feel unconditional love for yourself, exactly as you are right now. It is great to want to make changes, but they are not needed to love yourself unconditionally, here and now.
- Set the intent that you will do all your work with dragons as optimally as possible from this place of unconditional love.
- Feel unconditional love for the Gaia system — Earth and all life connected with her — realizing that you are an intricate part of her. Feel gratitude for all she unconditionally provides you.
- Set the intention to connect now with the energy field of dragons in a way that is most optimal for you. Feel yourself enveloped in the dragon energy.
- Set the intention to use all dragon energy only for the greater good of all and for the evolution of the whole Gaia system and yourself.

- Ask the dragons to help you to become a cocreator to the degree that is in alignment with your soul purpose and to the most optimal level possible for you at each moment.
- Ask the dragons to connect you with a dragon who wants to step forward to help you as a guide on your journey of becoming a cocreator.
- Sit in these energies for as long as it feels right. Allow the energies to unfold, and be an observer of all that happens.
- When you feel ready, take a deep breath, bring your awareness back to the room or place you are in, and open your eyes.

After the meditation, take the time to feel what you experienced. To the best of your ability, bring what happened to your awareness. Making a connection with the field of dragons is an essential step of your journey with them. Make a connection with the dragon(s) you invited to become your guide(s).

If you did not feel a dragon step forward, trust that, nonetheless, a connection was made. Dragons always respond to a call that comes from the heart. If it helps you, give your dragon a name that you will use to call it as your guide. Maybe you will hear a name. If that is the case, trust that it is the name of your dragon guide. If you do not hear a name, use the name you chose as the vibration that will help you to connect with your dragon guide.

Whether you feel it or not, the connection exists once you set a clear intention. After that, the key is to trust and work from and with that trust.

CHAPTER 3

Crystalline Beings and Their Cosmic Relatives

ALTHOUGH I HAVE MENTIONED SEVERAL ASPECTS ABOUT DRAGONS, the best way to introduce them is by describing my journey with them in more detail. The start of my journey with dragons began at a time when I did not believe in them. It started at the beginning of my journey with crystal skulls.

In *Crystal Skulls: Interacting with a Phenomenon*, I described my emotional encounter with my first crystal skull.[1] This emotional reaction ignited my desire to understand the strong reaction I experienced with what I called "an ugly thing." (I got over that judgment.) Afterward, I purchased a clear quartz crystal skull, and it took a long time before I became a caretaker of one. Before Sam, the clear crystal skull, I obtained a white marble skull (Egaddon), both pictured in image 3.1.

One day, while I was still living in the Netherlands, I was sitting with a friend in the same room with my two crystal skulls. My friend was also my teacher in intuitive development. Together, we regularly explored the subtle energies and worlds. Suddenly, she asked me whether I was aware of some small lights jumping in and out of the

IMAGE 3.1. This is a picture of the crystal skulls named Egaddon (left) and Sam (right).

white marble skull. Initially, I had no idea what she was talking about. After some attempts, I saw what she meant.

To me, it looked as if little lights were moving in and out of the skull. They had slightly different colors, but it is possible that they changed colors every time they moved in and out of the skull. We decided to call them crystalline beings because they were tiny, a little bit like small fairies. Interestingly, the quartz crystal skull, Sam, did not seem to have these little beings.

As exciting as this discovery was, after a while, I forgot about it. I did not know what these beings were doing or what their role was, and I lost interest. I might have completely forgotten about them except for another experience almost fifteen years later in the Sedona, Arizona, area.

I was very active in working with crystal skulls at that time. One day, somebody called me and left a message saying he wanted to show me an ancient skull. During that period, such a call was not unusual,

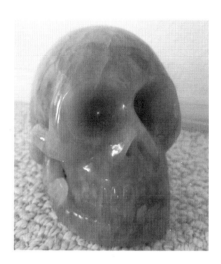

IMAGE 3.2. This is the crystal skull named Aires, in which went the crystalline being of the same name.

and it almost always turned out to be a false claim. So I did not call back and forgot about it. When he called again, it felt that this time I needed to meet him.

When he came into our house and unpacked the skull, Jeanne immediately kicked the skull and us out of the house. The energy of the skull was very dark and negative, and Jeanne is very attuned to these energies. Being a good caretaker and protector of our crystal skulls, she demanded that we remove the skull. Outside, I felt into this skull. She was right; it was a skull that had been used as a tool for black magic. However, I also could feel that it was indeed an ancient skull. The only thing I knew at the time was that I needed to clear its energy.

I had no idea what I was getting myself into with that decision. I worked with the skull for months, removing layer after layer of negative energy, often being very frustrated with a very difficult and challenging process. One day, I had the feeling I had made a lot of progress. The skull felt much clearer, so I believed that I could work with it in the house.

I will never forget the next event. I was working with the skull at my desk while Jeanne was with me in the room. I removed a layer of energy that I thought was the final step. Suddenly a being was freed that had been locked by black magic spells. The being went straight to Jeanne and entered her, which was a shocking experience for Jeanne. For whatever reason, it was clear to me what needed to happen. Jeanne needed to get a crystal skull, hold it, and the being would move into the crystal skull. Indeed, that is what happened: The being moved out of Jeanne and went into the crystal skull she held (image 3.2).

Now Jeanne and this being are great friends. We call her Aires and gave the skull the same name. We thought that after the final clearing of the ancient skull, Aires would go back into it, but that did not happen. Aires never was part of that skull. She was part of the black magic system, and we had no idea from where she originally came. She prefers to stay with the skull she inhabits, which holds energies that she resonates with. She can move around wherever she wants to go, but she stays connected with the same crystal skull, which has amazed us from the beginning. We truly are grateful. She is a wonderful companion, and she has taught us a lot.

Crystalline Being Creation

In trying to understand Aires, I realized that her (we felt that this being was feminine) energy was familiar. It took a while to realize that her energy reminded me of the energy of the little crystalline beings that I saw in the white marble skull many years ago. Aires is also a crystalline being, dependent on crystalline energies. She can move around, but she can never stay long without the support of crystalline energies. There were, however, differences between the crystalline beings in the white marble skull and Aires; namely, their size, the amount of energy, their presence, and their power.

The realization that Aires is also a crystalline being raised many questions. The most important questions we asked were: Who are these beings? What is their role? What does it mean for the crystalline materials in which these beings exist?

Studying the crystalline beings was not easy. They are not physical, so we could not measure anything. I was unable to find any references to them. If I had not met people who were aware of their existence, I would have believed that it was all imagination. However, it felt important to obtain answers, especially because of Aires's presence in our circle.

During the subsequent months, we learned much about these crystalline beings. Through training, it was easier to follow them and observe what happened. We also noticed that since Aires was present, we observed more crystalline beings in our crystal skull circle. This expansion of their numbers was most noticeable after we did a meditation that was specifically dedicated to Aries. It seems that giving her attention made her grow, and this growth resulted in the presence of more small crystalline beings. Over weeks and months of observation, we discovered a third type of crystalline being. We also discovered a pattern that was confirmed by participants during workshops.

Because we could not define names, we delineated the crystalline beings as level 1, level 2, and level 3. We called the tiny beings I met many years back in the white marble skull level 1 crystalline beings. We called Aires a level 3 crystalline being. The level 2 crystalline beings had a size and energy between levels 1 and 3.

While observing the crystalline beings, their energies and movements revealed fascinating phenomena I initially qualified as unbelievable. However, the patterns were consistent. When we focused on Aires during meditation, we observed that Aires was building energy. When she reached a certain level, she began to split off parts of her energy until it decreased. This decrease in energy always returned to a specific level, never decreasing further. This lower level is difficult to describe but is a familiar and characteristic amount of energy we associated with Aries from our first encounter. However, the fascinating aspect of this process is that the parts that split off resulted in level 1 crystalline beings. Aires was like a mother giving birth.

If the creation of level 1 crystalline beings by a level 3 crystalline being was the only process that would take place, we would get an increasing number of level 1 crystalline beings in our circle, or in a circle of crystals and crystal skulls during a workshop. However, this is not what we observed. Interestingly, these small level 1 crystalline beings can blend and form level 2 crystalline beings. Depending on how strong these level 1 beings are, which means how much energy they contain, twelve to twenty of these level 1 crystalline beings are needed to blend into a level 2 crystalline being.

The blending we observed with level 1 crystalline beings also could happen with level 2 crystalline beings. To form a level 3 crystalline being, eight to twelve level 2 crystalline beings need to blend. The level 3 crystalline beings appear to have a choice. They can become the producers of level 1 crystalline beings, or they can also merge. Again, the number required for this merging depends on the power of each level 3 crystalline being but seems to be at least eight.

Initially, it was unclear what determined the choices of a level 3 crystalline being. However, the fusion of level 3 crystalline beings was crucial for understanding dragons. Most of the fusions of level 3 crystalline beings happened during workshops when it was observed that the merging of the level 3 crystalline beings resulted in what we define as a real dragon. We were aware that during this creation of a real dragon, the energy was quite different from the energies when level 1 or level 2 crystalline beings merged. Something else was happening in addition to merging.

The Crystalline Life Force

I mentioned earlier that our clear quartz crystal skull, Sam, had no crystalline beings when we examined it many years ago. In the process of studying crystalline beings, we realized that they did not use every crystal skull or crystal available. We observed that this phenomenon did not depend on the type of crystal. Rather, something else defined which crystals or crystal skulls were suitable to hold the crystalline beings. We discovered that what was lacking in some crystals and crystal skulls was an energy we named the crystalline life force.

The crystalline life force is an energy not commonly known, and few people work with it. You need to learn how to feel this energy. Once you recognize the energy, it is easy to determine whether a crystal, in whatever shape it is, has this energy or not.

All that exists, whether it is organic or inorganic, has life force. Life force is an inherent part of all that exists and has an infinite number of variations and frequencies. Crystalline life force is one of the expressions of life force and is present in the earth. However, it is far less present in stones and crystals. The loss of crystalline life force is a consequence of the way people mine and collect crystals. The crystalline life force may leave a crystal or stone when people do not mine it consciously with love and gratitude. There are other reasons as well. You can compare it with cutting a branch from a tree. When you do that without awareness and communication with the tree, the tree will pull all life force out of the branch. The cut branch no longer holds life force and is dead. Something similar happens when people mine crystals.

Most crystals and stones no longer have a crystalline life force. However, the good news is that we can bring the crystalline life force back into stones, crystals, or crystal skulls when we are in the proper state of being, have the correct connection with Mother Earth, and have the appropriate intention.

Bringing crystalline life force into a stone, crystal, or crystal skull is different from awakening the potential of your crystal or crystal skull, which we see expressed in different energy layers. I described the process of activation and the resulting energy layers in *Crystal Skulls: Expand Your Consciousness.*[2] Re-introducing the crystalline life force into a crystal or stone results in an increase of a certain quality that is as important for crystalline beings as life force (chi/ki/prana) is for us. Crystalline beings cannot exist in a stone or crystal without it.

Although most people do not connect and work with crystalline life force, it is important to reconnect with it. I will provide a meditation that will help you to connect with these energies. It is important to do this meditation a couple of times to train your system to connect again and also to train your system to recognize the energy.

In the process, you will notice that your stone, crystal, or crystal skull will change, becoming more alive. When your crystal or stone becomes more alive, it also becomes easier to work with and to access the unique qualities of the crystalline material. In this way, you prepare your crystal (skull) for the crystalline beings, and it becomes a source of support for your journey.

Connect with Mother Earth

The success you will have in bringing crystalline life force into your crystal or stone depends on your connection with Mother Earth. We all have a connection with her, or we would not be alive. However, that does not mean we can bring crystalline life force into a crystal or crystal skull. Mother Earth will not allow this to happen if the connection is not deep enough. I do not understand all the details, but I know that a certain kind of connection is needed to make it possible to be the intermediary between Mother Earth and the crystal or crystal skull. Therefore, the most important part is your connection with Mother Earth.

As we will see, this is true for all the work we do with dragons. They will work with us to the degree that we have a connection with Mother Earth. After all, dragons are expressions of Mother Earth and work for and with her. Therefore, it is important to meditate to deepen your connection with Mother Earth and, in turn, to work with the crystalline life force and dragons. From my perspective and experience, this meditation is very important. You can do it in whatever variation you choose as part of your journey.

MEDITATION TO CONNECT DEEPER WITH MOTHER EARTH

- Take a few deep inhalations and exhalations, and feel yourself relaxing in the space you are sitting. Feel your brain relaxing and your heart opening.
- Bring your awareness fully to your heart area, and feel your essence in the center of your heart. Feel your essence connect with unconditional love. Focus this love on yourself. Feel love for yourself — for who you are, for what you have achieved. When you feel doubt or even judgment, bring your focus back to your heart.
- Focus your love on your physical body. This body is the temple of your soul. Be fully aware that everything you do affects your physical system.
- Become aware that every atom of your physical system comes from Mother Earth. Feel Mother Earth in every atom of your body.
- Feel gratitude and deep love for the mother who gave and gives you all you need.
- Feel your connection with her deepen. Allow yourself to merge with her because you are not separate but one with her. Feel that oneness with her as optimally as possible.
- See yourself as an extension of her even though you can move around freely.
- From this place of oneness, you can act as one and access and work with her energies.
- Trust that you have established this connection and that you always can return to it.
- Sit in this connection for a couple of minutes to allow it to integrate into your system as deeply as possible.
- Take a deep breath, and slowly bring your awareness back

to where you sit, knowing that your relationship with Mother Earth has deepened.

—〰〰—

Bring Crystalline Life Force into Your Crystal, Independent of Its Form

Creating a deeper connection with Mother Earth allows you to create a deeper connection with crystalline life force because it is an inherent part of her. Your connection with her makes it possible to bring crystalline life force back into your crystal or stone or, in case some crystalline life force is already present, to increase that crystalline life force.

There is an interesting relationship between crystalline life force and carbon-based life force. Although this is not yet very well understood, it seems that the crystalline life force is a kind of foundation, a basis, for the life force in carbon-based life forms. In other words, working with Mother Earth to bring crystalline life force into stones and crystal skulls stimulates your life force as well and thus is an empowering activity that stimulates your health and overall well-being.

Life force in all its aspects is also called the breath of the Creator and represents the love of the Creator. Life force is not one frequency but a range of frequencies that are beyond our current understanding.

The following meditation helps you to train yourselves to connect and work with crystalline life force. Doing this meditation will also create a basis for your work with dragon energy. You can do this meditation with any stone or crystal. However, it is recommended to use a crystal or stone you have in your home. It will improve the quality of your environment. Also, you will have this crystal or stone available to work with to increase the amount of crystalline life force even further every time you do this meditation with it.

—〰〰—

CONNECT WITH CRYSTALLINE LIFE FORCE, AND BRING IT INTO YOUR STONE OR CRYSTAL

- Make yourself comfortable, and hold the crystal or stone of your choice in your hand.
- Begin with some deep inhalations and exhalations, and

with every exhalation, relax a bit deeper. Allow yourself to be in the present. Realize that at this moment, the only thing that matters is this meditation.

- Prepare yourself by connecting with your spiritual essence and unconditional love.
- Feel the love expand through your whole system.
- From this place of unconditional love, connect with Mother Earth in such a way that you feel as fully connected as possible, just as you experienced in the previous meditation. Feel love and gratitude for her. Feel how you are merging with her, becoming one with her.
- From this place of merging with Mother Earth, connect with the crystal or stone in your hand.
- Now invite the crystalline life force to come into the crystal (skull) or stone that will support and sustain crystalline beings. Ask Mother Earth to help you with this process, and trust that it unfolds exactly in alignment with your intention to the most optimal level possible.
- Sit in this energy awhile.
- When you feel ready, take a deep breath and become aware of the room you are seated in, and when you are ready, open your eyes.

Expressions of Earth's Consciousness

While a part of the story of crystalline beings is that they connect with stones and crystals, it is even more important to be aware that they are expressions of the consciousness and energies of Mother Earth. Therefore, we can ask Mother Earth to put the parts of her that we call crystalline beings into crystals or stones. In that sense, we contribute to the return of the dragon energies because the crystalline beings are an essential part of dragons.

You now have prepared your crystal or stone, and you have made a deeper connection with Mother Earth. We are now at the point of determining whether your connection is deep enough to bring crystalline beings into your crystal or stone. This process is not about how good you are; this is about understanding where you are on your journey without judgment and to learn from the experience, expanding who you are.

Once you have crystalline beings in your crystal or stone, your meditations will help them to grow and expand. In this way, you will also deepen your connection with Mother Earth and physical reality. Once you have crystalline beings in your crystal or stone, your meditations will increase their number. If you have more stones and crystals, they will move into those as well once there is enough crystalline life force in them. You now possess the ability to bring all your stones and crystals into a state that will allow crystalline beings to live in them.

For the following meditation, you need to use a crystal or stone that sufficiently holds the crystalline life force. To be sure, use the crystal or stone you used to bring in crystalline life force during the previous meditation, trusting that there is sufficient life force to continue the process. However, you may want to do the previous meditation several times to bring the life force in the crystal or stone of choice to an optimal state.

—⁓—

MEDITATION TO INVITE CRYSTALLINE BEINGS

- Take some deep inhalations and exhalations, and with every exhalation, relax even more.
- When you feel sufficiently relaxed, bring your awareness to your divine essence, connect with unconditional love, and let it spread throughout your whole being.
- From this place of love, connect with Mother Earth. Know that she can support you by bringing crystalline beings into your stones and crystals because they are expressions of her. Therefore, you need her support to do this. You only get this support when you are ready to receive it. You already created a deep connection with her so that you can reconnect with her again.
- Once you are connected, bring your awareness to the crystal or stone you hold. Set the intention to activate the crystalline life force inherent within the crystal or stone to an optimal level. Next, set the intention to expand the crystalline life force to the most optimal level possible.

- Ask Mother Earth to bring crystalline beings into your crystal or stone.
- Sit in this energy as long as feels right. Trust in it, but do not be attached to the outcome. Know that everything that happens will be for the greatest good of all involved, including you.
- Express your gratitude for the gifts, which always will be there, whether or not there are crystalline beings in your crystal or stone.
- Take a deep breath again, and bring your awareness back to the room. When you feel ready, open your eyes.

—〰—

Going through this process provides many benefits. Your connection with Mother Earth deepens, which is important for your process and for your reconnection with Mother Earth and all that lives on her and is part of her. Also, you connect with the crystalline life force that stimulates the life force within you. Consequently, your system will function better and will heal and balance.

We connected with the energies of the crystalline beings because crystalline beings are part of dragon energies. Another important aspect of crystalline beings for our work with dragons is their connection with elemental powers. Chapter 4 focuses on the topic of elemental powers exclusively. However, we need to mention some basic points here that are important for understanding the crystalline beings and dragons.

There are four elemental powers: fire, water, air, and earth. When we studied crystalline beings, we felt that each of them fully connects with all four elemental powers and one is dominant in each crystalline being. Thus, when the elemental power of fire is dominant in a level 1 crystalline being, we call it a fire being.

When crystalline beings merge, the elemental power that becomes dominant depends on the composition of the beings. A level 1 crystalline being who has fire as its dominant elemental power can become part of a level 2 crystalline being that has water as its dominant elemental power. We find the same situation when level 2 crystalline beings merge and also when level 3 crystalline beings merge to become

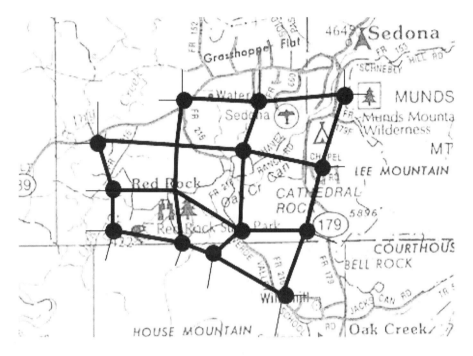

IMAGE 3.3. Depicted here is the morphogenetic grid of the three types of crystalline beings, or pre-dragons. These beings have one grid, indicating they are one species.

a real dragon. Such a dragon has all four elemental powers of which one is dominant. This is true for all dragons, including the ones Mother Earth creates directly without going through the steps of the crystalline beings. The connection of dragons with elemental powers is more complicated, but that does not change this underlying principle.

The Real Dragons

As discussed, crystalline beings are part of the dragon's energy system (image 2.2 in chapter 2). The energies of level 3 crystalline beings can merge and result in a real dragon. As was mentioned, there was additional energy involved that crystalline beings do not possess. Many years of research on morphogenetic grids and connecting with the morphogenetic field were required for comprehension.

While studying the grids of crystalline beings, it was observed that there is only one grid for all three levels of crystalline beings (image 3.3). Finding only one grid implied that crystalline beings constitute one species that can grow, split, and merge. Conversely, there are many grids for real dragons. When comparing the energies of the grid of crystalline beings to those of the grids of real dragons, there is additional energy in the dragon grids.

I might never have been able to understand these additional dragon energies without guidance. My friend Daniel and I have been studying portals[3] for many years. Portals are like vortexes, but instead of connecting the surface of the Earth (grids) with fields within the Earth system, they connect Earth with systems outside the space and time construct of our world. The main group we've studied is portals that connect Earth with star systems. Learning to recognize and define the energies of a star system that expresses through a certain portal is like learning a new language.

One day, we discovered a portal that we finally determined was connected to a star system called Cassiopeia. The energy felt familiar. I thought this familiarity related to the fact that Cassiopeia is one of the star systems connected with crystal skulls.[4] However, I kept feeling that there was another connection. Finally, it became clear: The energies of Cassiopeia and the energies of the dragons resonate with each other and have relationships. The energies that merged with the crystalline beings' energies during the creation of a real dragon were Cassiopeia's energies.

It might seem strange that energies from a star system are part of an Earth species. However, this is far more common than you may think. This book is not the appropriate place to delve deeper into this subject. However, we are not as isolated from other star systems as most people think. A seemingly infinite number of energies from different star systems enter Earth's energy system through many portals. We are just beginning to discover the amount and the variation of energies that enter Earth's system.

We do not know the nature of the effects of all these energies. However, we are sure that Cassiopeia contributes to the morphogenetic field that makes it possible to create the different dragon species in collaboration with Mother Earth. Because Cassiopeia is important in our being able to work with dragons, we will return to this subject in a later chapter.

During workshops, people often ask whether dragons are

abundantly present in our world. People ask this question because they wish to know whether it is easy to find and meet dragons. I would have answered this question differently in the past, as ten years ago, dragons were rare. However, the increasing interest in dragons induces the creation of more dragons, especially for two groups of dragons. The process described in which level 3 crystalline beings merge and create new dragons has led to a noticeable increase in this type of dragon. These are the dragons we will discuss in chapter 7. However, before defining the different groups of dragons and the species within these groups, we need to understand the powers associated with the elements.

CHAPTER 4

The Powers of Elements and the Elemental Powers

A BASIC UNDERSTANDING OF THE ELEMENTAL POWERS and the power of elements is necessary to know how to create and work with that creation. Also, if you desire to understand dragons, their function, and how they help us create our reality, such information is very helpful. However, this chapter also gives a lot of detailed information and a dominant analytical quality to the creation story and its progression.

Not everyone interested in dragons may be interested in what is presented in this chapter. However, without this information, it might not be as easy to understand the powers of which the dragons are the guardians. Nonetheless, if the amount of information is too much or if you do not resonate with it, please proceed to the next chapter or to the chapters that describe the different dragon species and the powers for which they are the guardians (chapters 7–10).

When people talk about the elements, they refer mostly to the physical, measurable elements. When they talk about earth elements, they refer to stones, sand, clay, and crystals. They refer to the material in which plants and trees grow. They often also refer to the planet as a whole: the planet Earth as an expression of the earth element. In the same way, they talk about water as the element we drink, swim in, and ride on in boats, as well as the substance that falls from the sky as rain and that all living beings need to survive. Air is what we breathe and also wind and storms. Fire is what warms us, what destroys, and what creates the basis for new life. Books have been written to help us work with the powers of these elements.[1]

We can use the term "element" for the creative powers of the universe. When we use the term in this way, I prefer to use "elemental powers." They have the same four names, but the description is different. When we talk in a general way about the elemental powers, the earth element represents the manifestation process. Water represents creativity and emotionality. Air represents life force and thoughts. Fire represents energy and consciousness.

As mentioned earlier, dragons are the guardians of different aspects of the four elemental powers. However, they are also guardians of the powers of the elements. Therefore, to understand the roles of the different dragons and the way they can support us in becoming conscious creators, we need to consider in greater detail the elements and elemental powers.

Three and Four Elemental Powers

In our reality, we work with four elemental powers, often referred to as elements. Initially, there were only three elements. I use the term "element" rather than my preferred term "elemental power" because the books and texts I refer to use the term "element" when referring to the power, not the physical element. Understanding the role of the three elements and the shift from three to four elements is important in many ways. I base much of my sharing on *Sefer Yetzirah: The Book of Creation*[2] and on information from working with dragons.

Sefer Yetzirah is an ancient Hebrew kabbalistic text. This chapter is not intended to be about the Kabbalah. Rather, the text is a description of helpful principles for understanding the energies of dragons and the connection dragons have with ancient wisdom.

Every attempt to understand ancient wisdom is exactly that: an attempt. No matter what ancient wisdom we study, we are trying to understand vast ancient knowledge with the limited perspective

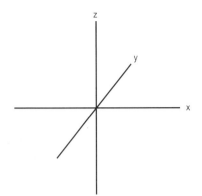

IMAGE 4.1. These three axes
(x, y, and z) are used to define
a point in space.

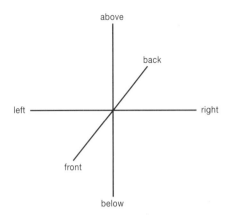

IMAGE 4.2. These three axes
(left-right, above-below, and front-back)
define the six directions.

currently held by most humans. Nonetheless, it is important to at least attempt to describe this ancient knowledge as a support to our understanding of the world in which we live.

The general belief is that initially there was chaos. I prefer to say that there was not yet an ordered expression. Therefore, what is called chaos is better described as infinite possibilities. It also can be described as infinite consciousness, which is unexpressed. Also, it is a state called the void.

Whether we refer to either the Flower of Life or the Tree of Life as the next step of understanding creation does not matter. The Tree of Life, as kabbalists use it, is an inherent part of the Flower of Life. Both are ways to describe the process of creation, which also can be called the process of the infinite consciousness expressing and exploring itself.

The first step in the creation process is the moment that the infinite consciousness became self-aware. It is a different way of saying that the infinite, that which is called chaos, became organized. This first step of the infinite was the need to define itself. Therefore, it created a reference point, being itself. To define this point in space, it needed three axes (image 4.1). These three axes are equally important and, therefore, have the same length. They also represent the three mother elements. The three axes create six directions, or seven if you see the center as a direction (image 4.2). The six directions also define a sphere (image

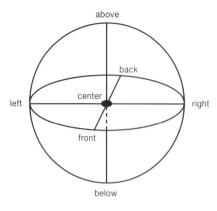

IMAGE 4.3. When assigned a center point, the six directions can define a sphere.

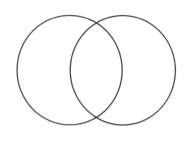

IMAGE 4.4. Two equal, intersecting circles create a vesica piscis.

4.3). The sphere, therefore, is the first step in creation. The sphere is also important for understanding the different dragon groups.

The Creator went to the edge of the sphere and created another based on the same radius. This sphere is a reflection of the first one and creates two opposing forces, the I versus the other (the reflection of the I). Doing so, the Creator created polarity through self-awareness. Therefore, polarity is an inherent part of all creation. This second sphere has an edge that goes through the center of the first sphere. The two circles represent spheres in two dimensions, which create a famous aspect: the vesica piscis (image 4.4).

The number 2, considered by itself, is divisive by nature (polarity). The 2 represents the principle of multiplicity; unchecked, 2 is the call to chaos. The number 2 is what we define as the fall. But 2 is reconciled in unity, included within it is unity, by simultaneously creating 3. The 3 represents the principle of reconciliation or relationship (trinity). The vesica piscis contains the third aspect, the trinity, which inherently exists in everything. By creating the next step, the next circle (the sphere), the trinity becomes manifest.

This trinity contains the three mother elements: fire, water, and air. Everything created will always hold the information of the previous steps as well, meaning that everything contains duality (polarity), and through these three elements (trinity) also contains oneness.

The next step creates the fourth circle, representing the four

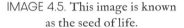

IMAGE 4.5. This image is known as the seed of life.

IMAGE 4.6. Outlined is the Tree of Life within the Flower of Life.

elements, which adds the elemental power of earth. Without going into the details of all the steps, the sixth addition of a sphere (which corresponds to the sixth day of creation) completed the first phase of creation. This first phase resulted in seven spheres (circles) and is called the seed of life (image 4.5). Each new sphere added information; therefore creation expanded. This expansion continued, creating the Flower of Life (image 4.6).

The *Sefer Yetzirah* describes a similar process. As mentioned, the *Sefer Yetzirah* is a kabbalistic book based on the Tree of Life, which is a part of the Flower of Life (image 4.6), as is the seed of life. The Tree of Life has ten aspects called sephiroth (image 4.7). The top sephirah, Kether, is the highest spiritual aspect (also called the cause) while the lowest sephirah, called Malkhuth, represents creation — physical creation, the world in which we live (the effect). The other eight sephiroth and the twenty-two connections between them indicate the steps that need to be taken to bridge Kether and Malkhuth in a functional enlightened system.

The twenty-two letters of the Hebrew alphabet define the qualities and energies of the twenty-two connections between the ten sephiroth. We can divide the twenty-two letters into groups of three (the mothers), seven (the doubles), and twelve (the elementals). The important aspect for our discussion is the three mother elements. In the Hebrew

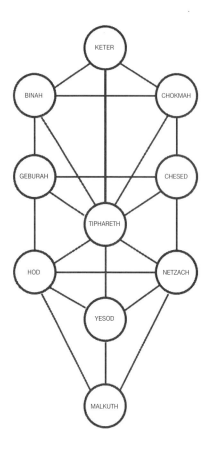

IMAGE 4.7. This image shows the ten sephiroth of the Kabbalah as displayed in the Hebrew Tree of Life.

alphabet, the letters mem, shin, and aleph represent these three mother elements. They are called the mother elements because they connect to the elements of water (mem), fire (shin), and air (aleph). The three mother elements also connect to the divine names yud, heh, and vav. These are called the fathers. There is a relationship between yud and mem (related to water), heh and shin (related to fire), and vav and aleph (related to breath and air).

The three mothers (alef, mem, shin) represent thesis, antithesis, and synthesis, the basic triad of the *Sefer Yetzirah*. Thesis and antithesis represent two opposite directions in a one-dimensional line. Together with synthesis, they yield three elements.

The three father elements can be permuted in six different ways, creating six directions. As we saw earlier, to define itself, the infinite consciousness needed six directions (three axes) (images 4.1 and 4.2). Hence, space is defined. Once space is defined, creation can begin. Here, the *Sefer Yetzirah* arrives at the beginning of the unfolding of the seed of life, as it was described.

The *Sefer Yetzirah* describes many more aspects of the three mother elements. However, within the context of this book, they are less important and therefore are not discussed further.

The Fourth Element: Earth

The story in the *Sefer Yetzirah* mentions only three mother elements. The earth element is not considered a mother element. The book is very clear about this point. Earth is not a basic element but a confluence of the other three.[3] Earth represents a solid state. It is a state in which matter exists with a minimum of space (matter is the most condensed state of energy). However, in my perspective, this is only one aspect.

The three mother elements exist from the beginning of creation. They are a consequence of the infinite consciousness becoming self-aware and are the basis of all creation. They exist in creation whether physical or nonphysical. However, as soon as creation goes to the next step and manifests in physical forms, a fourth element is needed. Because the three mother elements are at the basis of all creation, the manifested creation — represented by the element of earth — has to include the three mother elements. Therefore, all manifested forms always have all four elements. That means that all dragons will always work with all four elemental powers to help us to be cocreators in this physical reality.

Gregg Braden added an interesting perspective about the three mother elements and the creation of the fourth element, earth. His point of view is important to understand the manifestation of form and relates especially to the powers of which the primordial dragons (chapter 9) are the guardians. Braden also follows the *Sefer Yetzirah* and starts with the three mothers, alef, mem, and shin, which are air, water, and fire respectively. These are the building blocks of the universe. For Braden, however, it was important to find a link between these building blocks and the modern elements of our physical world.[4] According to the *Sefer Yetzirah*, the mothers are more than just symbols of nature's elements. The verses in the book show us how knowledge of the power in each of the three mothers is the key to understanding the forces of the universe. That is how I, based on working with dragons, perceive the elemental powers: as the creative forces of the universe.

Braden also believes that the *Sefer Yetzirah*, using the language of that period, describes nothing less than the building of the universe.[5] The *Sefer Yetzirah* states that clearly: "He made the letter Alef king over breath, bound a crown to it…. He made the letter Mem king over water, bound a crown to it…. He made the letter Shin king over fire, bound a crown to it." The crown represents a higher spiritual nature to the letter.[6] Braden's question is: What ties these primal letters of creation to the chemistry of modern science?[7]

In ancient alchemical texts, the element of air is never clearly defined. Later interpretations assume that it refers to the air we breathe. Modern science shows that our atmosphere nourishes us with an element that gives life to every cell: oxygen. According to Braden, if you correlate ancient alchemy with modern chemistry, oxygen seems to be the equivalent of alchemical air. Although this is the element we need to live, what we breathe in as the most dominant part of the air is nitrogen. Therefore, Braden assumes that nitrogen correlates to the alchemical air. He uses the same line of thinking for the other elements.[8]

Water, which covers a large part of Earth, contains more than 85 percent oxygen. In line with his thinking, oxygen, therefore, is the chemical correlated to alchemical water. Alchemical fire links to the Sun. As fire burns, it releases the energy of the Sun. The dominant element of the Sun is hydrogen (about 71 percent); alchemical fire correlates with the chemical element of hydrogen.

In the Hebrew alphabet, every letter has a numerical value. The study of the relationship between letters and numbers is called gematria. Braden uses this aspect to make the next step to help us understand the role the mother elements have in forming the fourth element, earth. In gematria, words with the same numerical number have a similar meaning; they correspond. From a spiritual perspective, words with the same numerical value correspond independent of the meaning we may give them today.

According to Braden, of the many possible characteristics that describe each element, his studies reveal only one that stands out as a bridge between the four elements of life and the Hebrew alphabet: the quality known as atomic mass.[9] In gematria, you simplify numbers to one digit. In simplifying the numbers, hydrogen has a simple mass of 1. Nitrogen (atomic mass 14) has a simple mass of 5 (1 + 4 = 5), and oxygen (atomic mass 15) has as simple mass of 6 (1 + 5 = 6).

Next, Braden studied the corresponding numbers in the Hebrew alphabet. As we have seen, the mother elements are alef, mem, and shin. These letters were created first and are the letters of chaos. They belong to the same world as Tiamat, who was described in the first chapter. The letters yod, hey, and vav are the counterparts of the letters alef, mem, and shin, and they are the letters of God's name and source of all creation. While the letters alef, mem, and shin are the mother letters of the world of chaos, the letters yod, heh, and vav are the mother letters of the world of order.

The results can be summarized as follows: The alchemical element of fire corresponds to the chemical element of hydrogen, which has a reduced atomic mass of 1. The alchemical element of air corresponds to the chemical element of nitrogen, which has a reduced mass of 5. The alchemical element of water corresponds to the chemical element of oxygen, which has a reduced mass of 6. The question is, which letters of the Hebrew alphabet have hidden number codes that match the simple mass of the ancient elements of creation? There are three letters in the Hebrew alphabet that do. It is yod to the number 1, heh to the number 5, and vav to the number 6. As Braden puts it: This concrete and verifiable relationship speaks volumes to us about the knowledge of our ancestors.[10]

According to the *Sefer Yetzirah*, the fourth element, earth, came from the mother elements.[3] Therefore, all of creation comes from these three mother elements. If Braden is right, this will also reflect in the Hebrew letters, chemical correspondence, and simple atom mass. Using the principle of the simple masses of the three chemical components that correspond to the letters yod, heh, and vav results in the number 12 (1 + 5 + 6), which reduces to the simple number 3 (1 + 2).

Braden then considered the human body and the most common elements. There are four that account for over 99 percent of the human body: hydrogen, nitrogen, oxygen, and carbon. Carbon is the only one that does not yet have a letter or element. The mass value of carbon is 12, which means its simple mass is 3. Carbon is the only one of all 118 possible elements that matches the number 3 produced by combining the letters of God's name: yod, heh, and vav. Carbon is the only one of the four that makes us solid; the other three are gasses. When the ancients recorded that we are made of fire, water, air, and earth (in the language of their day), they were saying that we are made of hydrogen, nitrogen, oxygen, and carbon — precisely the findings of modern science.

Braden's final step was to find the corresponding Hebrew letter.

This letter is gimel. From the perspective of numbers, gimel is carbon in the Hebrew scriptures, and in ancient alchemy, it is earth.

The Trinity

Based on the sharing so far, it might become clear that there are two important systems in our reality. Both are important for understanding dragons and the role they play in the Gaia system. One system is the trinity, and the other system is based on the number four. Both systems are a reflection of elemental powers. The trinity is represented by the three mother and father elements, as we have seen earlier. The number four is a reflection of the four elements needed for the manifestation of the world in which we live.

To understand dragons and creation, it is important to consider in greater detail the trinity and the different ways the trinity expresses itself in the world in which we live. While there are many ways, we will restrict our discussion to some major aspects to understand the importance of the trinity.

It has already been mentioned that the three mother elements (fire, air, and water) are the Mothers of Chaos. They existed before creation. They lead to the three mother elements (also called father elements) of the world of order. What we call order is potential expressed in creation. These three mother elements lead to the formation of the fourth. The fact that the three mother elements lead to the formation of manifestation, form, and order means these elements are an inherent part of everything that exists.

The trinity forms the oneness in our world that comes forth from duality. To see the underlying oneness in everything is the purpose of our spiritual journey. Seeing the underlying oneness in everything will shift dramatically the way we see the world from a world of opposites (polarities, duality) to a world of oneness. This way of seeing the world will lead to a new consciousness.

The easiest way to represent the trinity is in the form of a triangle (image 4.8). Each point represents one of the three qualities of the trinity. Although the basis is the three mother elements, we also know the trinity as the masculine (fire), feminine (water), and child (air). In Christianity, these three aspects are known as the Father, the Son, and the Holy Spirit, in which the Father represents fire, the Holy

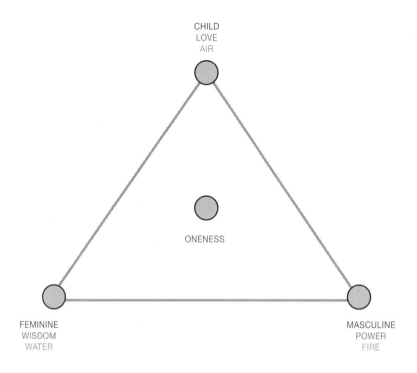

IMAGE 4.8. This image offers several definitions of the trinity.

Spirit represents water, and the Son represents air. The Hebrew tradition replaces the name Holy Spirit with Shekinah.

There is another way to define the three elemental powers I often call the three cosmic principles. In this approach, we describe the element of fire as power, or energy. We describe water as wisdom and air as love (image 4.8). Air, which is the breath of the Creator, is life given in love.

Each description of the three mother elements reflects a different way of understanding these three elemental powers. They are different points of view of a system inherently built into everything in this physical reality. All these points of view correspond to each other.

Almost all people live in duality, which is based on seeing and thinking in polarities. They base the way their consciousness functions on learning from differences. It is the most important way to understand ourselves and to learn how to choose. Unfortunately, when we are confused, fearful, or self-doubting, we do not make clear choices,

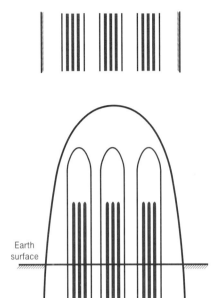

Earth
surface

IMAGE 4.9. This image shows
three triads to illustrate the grid line,
or triad line, of human
consciousness.

vacillating from one pole to the opposite and back. Such wandering creates instability, and sadly, most people live this way.

Even though we function mostly from a duality consciousness, inherent within this consciousness is the essence of the oneness, the trinity. We align with the principle of oneness when we understand that the polarities reflect gradients of a system, for example, the third part of the trinity.

If there is any truth in the statement that two (polarity) tends to move to three for stability, the trinity should be built into the way our consciousnesses function. That can be demonstrated by looking at Earth's energy lines that hold the morphogenetic grids of humans. I originally called these human consciousness grids. *Gifts of Mother Earth* provides an extensive description of these grids.[11]

It is important to look at the construction of the lines that form such grids. Within each of these grid lines, there are sublines. These sublines are constant throughout all grids, and they always have three wires, or sub-sub-lines (see image 4.9), which are named triads. These three wires (triads) represent the trinity, which means that oneness is inherently built in the way our consciousnesses function.

Although we learn through duality by noticing what works for us and what does not, there is always a hidden invitation to move in the direction of oneness. When we function in oneness, we are aware that there are opposing forces, but we are also aware that these two forces are two aspects or gradients, which we can call the essence. This essence brings in the third aspect, and that shifts us in the direction of functioning within the trinity system.

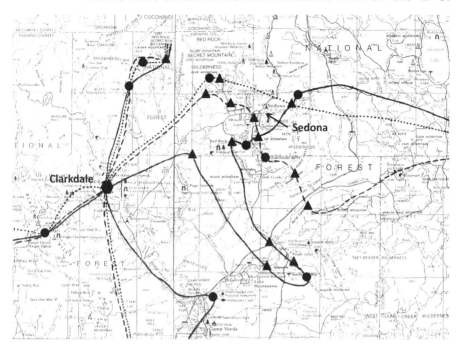

IMAGE 4.10. Depicted is a part of the grid near a cross point of lines in the Sedona, Arizona, area. The Christ consciousness grid shows triad lines (internal trinity) plotted with triangles and three lines plotted with spheres to define the grid system (external trinity).

An example is cold versus hot. They are polarities of each other. At the same time, they are gradients of what connects them: temperature, the third aspect of the phenomenon. Another example is the polarity of success and failure. They both are gradients of the third aspect: result. We define a result as a success or failure.

When we are on our spiritual paths, we will function increasingly from oneness. We call this oneness consciousness Christ consciousness. When we look at the grids of the Christ consciousness, we see triad lines (lines with triads), as in the lines of the grids of our duality consciousness, but we also see that these grids are always defined by three triad lines that flow together, regularly crossing over each other[12] (image 4.10).

Christ consciousness grid lines reflect to us through the appearance of three parallel lines (triads) that the consciousness of that level and frequency has inherent oneness, as do all consciousness grids. The three grid lines also indicate that on that level of consciousness, the oneness is expressed and visible in the way we function. In this state of consciousness, oneness is reflected both internally and externally.

There are many examples available, as all ancient civilizations were aware of the trinity and expressed it in many ways. Richard Cassaro wrote a whole book dedicated to the sacred number 3, delineating how it is present in structures and symbols all over the world.[13] The subtitle of his book is *Decoding the Secret Masonic Religion in Gothic Cathedrals and World Architecture*. He described that many that were built by Masons have a triptych; that is the name that he gives to buildings with three doors or windows. Many American monuments have three entrances, such as the Lincoln Memorial, the Jefferson Memorial, the Federal Reserve, Union Station, the Library of Congress, the Federal Triangle, and the Organization of the American States, for example. The triptych also exists in the New York Public Library and the post office in Glendale, California. Many Masonic temples also have a triptych. Moreover, Cassaro demonstrates that the triptych existed in ancient civilizations, such as in Mexico (the Maya), Egypt, Indonesia, and India. Throughout history, people were aware of the importance of the trinity and expressed it in many ways, including in plain sight in structures all over the world.

The Trinity and Chakras

While a whole book could be dedicated to the trinity (like Cassaro), I offer one final important example, shifting from the outside world to the inside, our energy system. Human beings have a subtle energy system called chakras. Chakras are the most important energy centers of our human energy system. You can define chakras as centers within the physical body that reflect different ways of dealing with the world around us.

The best way to look at chakras is to see them as the colors of fractionated white light. Before the soul embodies (enters a physical body), it radiates white light. The white light reflects the connection of the soul with Source. When the soul enters a physical body, white light is refracted into the colors of the rainbow in the same way white light is refracted by a prism or as sunlight through rain creating rainbows. Each color is a chakra and represents an aspect of the soul that tries to express itself optimally in this physical reality through the physical body.

When we lose our connection with these colors (qualities), or chakras, or when our connection is disturbed due to our personal experiences, we are not able to express the totality of our souls in this physical reality. The colors lose their aliveness, and they become murky (dirty), preventing our light from shining.

Most humans have lost the ability to use the chakras or soul qualities optimally. They even have forgotten, at least partially, what these qualities are. Therefore, it is important to again learn about these centers — the chakras — and their qualities.

These centers are named chakras (which means "wheel" in Sanskrit) because they are places where energy, and thus information, enters and leaves the physical body. They are places where the soul and the surrounding environment exchange information. Energy spirals at these chakra locations, and when you look at them from the outside, it seems as if you are looking at a spinning wheel, hence their name. A chakra is a type of a vortex.

Most books and articles enumerate seven chakras; however, there are an increasing number of people that discuss higher numbers. In addition to the chakras connected to the physical body, there also are chakras above the physical body. In *Gifts of Mother Earth*, I mentioned that there are five chakras above the crown chakra.[14] These five chakras are the connections between the five energy bodies. Therefore, there are twelve main chakras. This number is in alignment with the number and type of chakra vortexes found on Mother Earth.[14]

The study of the chakra vortexes of Mother Earth led to a relevant discovery. We tend to view the twelve chakras as a single system; however, our studies of Mother Earth's chakra vortexes indicate that each chakra vortex has three aspects. Given that our twelve chakras resonate with the chakra vortexes of Mother Earth and that there are three versions of each of these chakras, we have in total thirty-six different chakras.

By now, it should be clear that these three aspects of each of the twelve chakras reflect the trinity principle. Each chakra has a masculine aspect that represents the active aspect that reflects how we use the energies connected with the chakra. The feminine aspects hold the wisdom and feelings connected with the experiences of how this chakra functions within the whole system. The child or neutral aspect of the chakra helps us to lovingly use the qualities of the chakra to allow the life force energy that belongs to each chakra to function as optimally as possible.

While this is an important understanding of the total chakra system, there is yet another trinity within the system of seven chakras connected with the physical body. The three higher chakras (crown, third eye, and throat) represent the masculine, the spiritual aspect of this trinity. The lower three chakras (the root, sacral, and solar plexus) form the feminine, the physical aspect, and the heart chakra forms the neutral, or child, aspect.

There is one more trinity aspect connected with the chakras. There are three flows of energy moving through the chakras. There is a feminine flow (through a channel called a nadi), which is called the ida. The masculine flow goes through the nadi, which is called the pingala, and the child aspect flows through the central nadi, which is called sushumna.[15] Optimal functioning occurs when the flow through these nadis is favorable. When the chakras are functioning optimally — creating white light, the light of the soul — we call that enlightenment.

Some of you may question the existence of thirty-six chakra vortexes, but hopefully you understand that the trinity exists in everything even though it is often hidden. You might be more challenged to accept that the twelve chakra system is similar to the system of the oneness dragons: a system of three times four. The "four" refers to the four elemental powers, and the "three" refers to the trinity. I was challenged to understand chakras in this way.

Chakras are commonly correlated with elements or elemental powers. However, because there are only five elements, the fifth being Aether, five chakras are associated with these five elements in many articles. The root chakra connects to the earth element, the sacral chakra connects to water, the solar plexus connects to fire, the heart chakra connects to air, and the throat chakra connects to Aether.[16]

While there is value to the above approach, that is not relevant to this discussion. I refer to a universal system that links chakras and

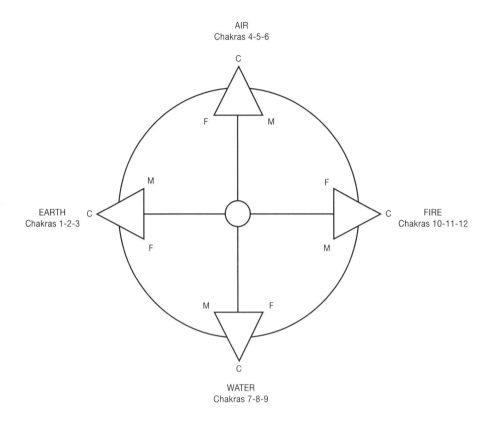

IMAGE 4.11. Pictured are the twelve chakras separated in four groups of three, corresponding to the four elemental powers. The three represent the sacred trinity, indicated as F (feminine), C (child), and M (masculine).

dragons and also links each with angels and devas. This system separates the chakras into four groups of three. The four groups refer to the four elements, and three chakras form the trinity of each element (image 4.11).

The lower three chakras connect with the earth element. They are the chakras that deal with the way we function in physical reality. The tenth to the twelfth chakras connect with the spiritual aspect some people call the soul or higher self, and these connect to the fire element. These two combinations are easy to accept; more challenging might be the remaining groups. The seventh to the ninth chakras connect with the water element. These chakras receive the information from the spiritual world to help us create reality from this spiritual aspect. The fourth to the sixth chakras express this creation, thus, give it life. Therefore, these three chakras connect with the air element.

The latter approach may lead to correspondences beyond the traditional ways of looking at chakras. However, I feel there is a possibility that there may be truth to this approach. Later, we will discuss the deeper meaning of this approach and its correspondences and resonances with dragons and other subtle beings. One correspondence has been revealed, but there are several more. Undoubtedly, we need to understand chakras as a complex system that can function in different ways, depending on our vibrational states and the situations we experience.

In summary, the trinity is an inherent part of our functioning and consciousness as well as every system of creation. Therefore, it may not surprise you that the trinity is also part of the dragon system, which, as the chakras, is based in the four elements. There's more to follow in the chapter about the oneness dragons. We will see that these dragons have a system that resonates with our twelve chakras. Working with the dragons stimulates all systems. This stimulation may be noticeable throughout our systems but mostly affects our chakras.

Chakras, Four Worlds, and Four Elemental Powers

The chakras have a second relationship with the number four. The energies of these four aspects of the chakras also connect them with the four elemental powers and, through these powers, with the dragons. However, in this case, the connection is at a different level.

In *Gifts of Mother Earth*,[17] I mentioned that chakra vortexes have four frequency levels, which increase, and are related to the different energy bodies. I connected the lowest chakra frequency with the physical system, the second level with the emotional body, the third level with the mental body, and the highest frequency with the spiritual body. Since then, more information has become available, which I will explain.

The first group of souls that came to Earth as part of the human consciousness is called the Founders. The Founders have guided me all along, and thanks to them, I found the thirty-six different chakra vortexes mentioned above. The Founders realized that the frequency of their consciousness and that of Earth was too vast to bridge. Therefore, they created twelve levels of consciousness in addition to theirs. Over time, different groups of people created civilizations that anchored the various levels of consciousness into the earth grids. We know some of them as Lemuria and Atlantis.

Starting with the Founders level, these levels of consciousness decrease in frequency. In the system, the Founders created barriers to prevent consciousness increasing instead of decreasing, as the natural tendency for any consciousness is to evolve. To prevent this tendency, barriers were needed. Otherwise, the consciousness would never align with the lower physical vibrations of the Gaia system.

There are a total of three barriers that create four different realities, or worlds. The idea of the existence of four worlds is not new, as is evident in different cultural traditions, such as that of the Maya, the Aztecs, and the Hopi. We also find this idea in the Kabbalah.

There are different opinions about the meaning and role of these four worlds. I believe they are related to the four elemental powers: fire, water, air, and earth. The first world is dominated by the element of fire, spirituality, consciousness, and energy (I am aware; I Am). The second world is dominated by water, creation, wisdom, and feeling (I feel). The third world is dominated by air, thoughts, and mental structures (I think). The last world is the world in which we live. This world is dominated by the earth element, physicality, and materialism (I have).

Returning to the chakras, the 4 levels of chakra energy of the 36 chakra vortexes that create a total of 144 chakra frequencies (4 x 36) resonate with these four worlds. Integrating the four levels of the chakras in one functional system is the same as integrating the four worlds into the fifth world, which is the world of Aether — the world in which we reconnect with the universe based on an integrative use of the elemental powers. This integration results in the promised Golden Age.

The dragons can help us to enter the fifth world. They can support us with every frequency we need within this physical reality. While working with dragons is essential on an individual level to become a cocreator, it is equally, or possibly even more, important for the shift within our collective consciousness that will help us to move from the fourth world of materialism to the fifth world of creating harmony.

The Cross and the Circle: a Symbol for the Four Elements

The circle with a cross is an ancient symbol that exists in many places in the world. It even exists on the walls of mountains in the Sahara, estimated to be more than 3,000 years old. The symbol exists in the Western mystical tradition, and it is an integrated part of indigenous traditions in the Americas, known as the medicine wheel.

The circle with the cross is a very important symbol that connects directly with the four elemental powers; therefore, it can help us to understand the different dragon species and their role in our reality. Similar to the trinity, there are many definitions. Across different indigenous traditions, the details of the medicine wheel symbol differ, but the principles are the same. The definitions I share are aligned with the way the dragons present themselves and their function.

The basic symbol is a circle with a cross (refer to image 4.11). The four points where the cross touches the circle represent four systems. They represent four points with four different qualities. In the basic symbol, these points represent the four directions: east, south, west, and north. Indigenous people from the Americas designate power animals as guardians of the four directions. The animals designated as the guardians depend on the specific tribe. The same is true for the colors given to the directions.

Therefore, the purpose of the symbol is to understand principles and is not meant to be a discussion about what is the right animal or the right color for each of the four directions. The Western mystical tradition designates four archangels as the guardians of the four directions: Archangels Michael, Raphael, Uriel, and Gabriel.

The four points also represent the four elemental powers. I define the east as the place of the fire element, the spiritual direction as the place of intent and the place of all beginning. On the same axis on the opposite side is the west, the place of the earth element, physicality, and manifestation, and it shows the results of the intent we set into motion in the east.

The second axis is the north-south axis. I call it the axis of the

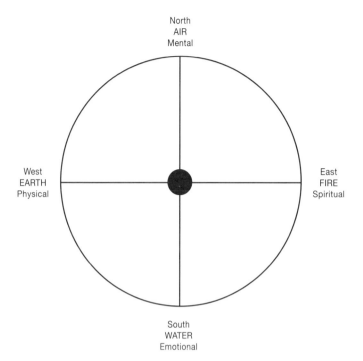

IMAGE 4.12. Displayed here are the circle and the cross with the four directions and their various definitions.

mind. It is the axis of emotions and creativity; it is connected with the water element in the south and with thoughts and beliefs connected with the air element in the north. Our emotions and beliefs determine whether we produce the results (in the west) that we intended (in the east). This description illustrates one example of how we can use this interesting symbol we refer to as the medicine wheel.

Image 4.12 provides an overview of different terms associated with the four directions. The key point for our work with the dragons, however, is the definition of the four directions as the four elements.

The circle with the cross is a basic symbol. There are also circles with two crosses, creating eight directions. The circle with eight directions is also known in indigenous traditions as a medicine wheel with four main and four secondary directions. The wheel with eight spokes is an important tool in certain traditions. This symbol represents the second group of dragons, the duality dragons. We have yet an even

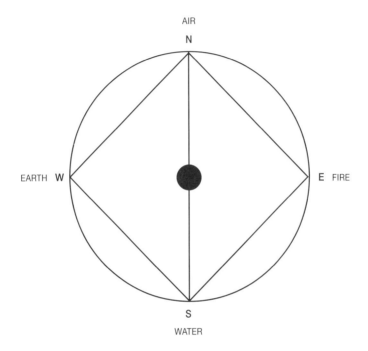

IMAGE 4.13. Shown is the square of the four directions
with the two triangles — spirituality (right) and physicality (left) — separated by the
north-south axis, representing the mind.

more complex system that describes another group of dragons. This
system is the wheel with twelve spokes. As a medicine wheel, it is less
familiar. However, Sun Bear, a medicine man, has popularized this
form of the medicine wheel.[18] The wheel with twelve spokes symbolizes the oneness dragon, as is mentioned above and discussed further
in chapter 8.

The Relationship between the Trinity
and the Symbol of the Circle with the Cross

The essence of the symbol of the circle with the cross is to help
us understand the process of manifestation in physical reality. Also,
the three mother elements refer to creation. When two systems reference creation, they must have similar principles.

The four directions represent the four elements. When we connect the four directions, we create a square. There are several ways to

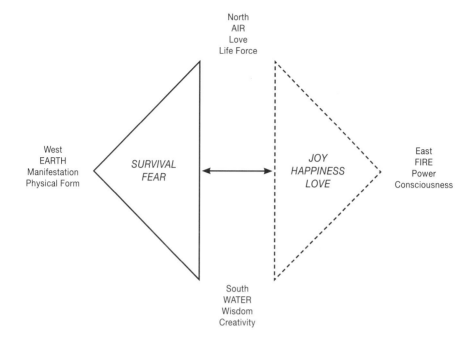

IMAGE 4.14. This image displays the spiritual (higher mind: right) and physical (lower mind: left) triangles separated.

separate the square into triangles. Here, we focus on the two triangles that are created by the north-south axis (image 4.13). Due to the way most people function, the two triangles were separated (image 4.14). The left triangle represents the way most people function in the physical world during their day-to-day activities. They often have an emotional reaction to what they think and believe, and they act based on their thoughts, beliefs, and emotions. That is how they manifest their reality (the west). We call this the physical triangle. In this triangle, people's actions are based on survival instincts, which are directed by their mind, referred to as the lower mind. The function of the lower mind is to ensure functional survival and optimal safety.

When we meditate or are in a more spiritual mode, we connect with aspects of the other triangle. The right triangle is the spiritual triangle, which represents the higher mind (thoughts and feelings) and our spiritual essence. Our evolutionary journey is to align the lower and higher minds so that they function as one system instead

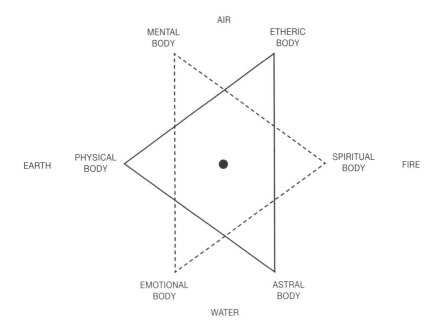

IMAGE 4.15. This image shows that the spiritual and physical triangles
form the Star of David (the six-pointed star).
Also indicated are the energy bodies connected to the six points.

of distinct systems. When the two minds function as one, the two triangles reconnect. We create a situation in which the spiritual essence
becomes the primary driving force in our lives instead of the lower
mind of our personalities.

As a consequence, the two triangles begin to function in such a
way that they form the Star of David (image 4.15). That is the state in
which we have overcome duality as a limitation. Then duality becomes
an asset, leading us to a spiritual view based on a higher level of consciousness. This path brings us to the state called oneness.

To bring the two triangles together, we need to transform, heal,
and balance all that keeps the left triangle in a lower vibration, preventing the two minds from unifying. This path is completely supported by the dragons, as will be demonstrated in the next chapters.

The Powers of the Elements

When we work with the elemental powers, we are working with

the four powers of creation. It is part of our journey to learn how to use these powers to create a reality for the greatest good of all and supports the ascension of the Gaia system.

When we look at the elements, we look at systems that exist as manifested phenomena, as part of the manifested world in which we live. All manifested phenomena in physical reality will always contain all four elemental powers. For example, water contains all four elemental powers. Working with elements is therefore quite different from working with elemental powers. **Working with elements is not about creating but about learning how to work with creation.** It helps us to master the world in which we live for the benefit of all that live in it.

Although each element contains all four elemental powers, one of these powers is dominant. That power is so dominant that people confuse the elements with the elemental powers. That is understandable because we perceive the elements as a manifestation of the elemental power. Therefore, the elements mainly display characteristics that we also see in the corresponding elemental power. Consequently, studying the elements helps us to understand the elemental powers. As we will see in chapter 9, there is a group of dragons, the primordial dragons, that will help us to work with the powers of these four elements.

CHAPTER 5

The Four Elemental Powers and Aether

IN THE PREVIOUS CHAPTER, WE SAW THAT THE MAIN ROLE OF DRAGONS IS TO BE THE GUARDIANS of the elemental powers and the powers of the elements. Each of the elemental powers has six aspects, and each of the six aspects has a dragon as a guardian or caretaker. We will look at these six aspects when we work with the different dragon groups. However, before we do that, I would like to expand the general understanding of the elemental powers and the roles they play in working with dragons in the creation process.

The power of the elements can be described in many ways. The mother elements — fire (alef), water (mem), and air (shin) — exist in a state of chaos before anything is manifest. When things move into a state of order (as in creation), the mother elements are renamed as the letters yod, heh, and vav. These three letters also connect to the three elemental powers of fire, water, and air, and they are called the mother elements of creation. Sometimes they are called the father elements. The fourth element, earth, came out of the three mother/father elements.

Some qualities of the four elements have been discussed. However, to understand dragons, we need to study these elemental powers and the expressed elements in greater detail. There are claims of a fifth elemental power, Aether. In this chapter, we will look at these elemental powers from different perspectives, which will allow us a better understanding of the gifts of the dragons.

The Four Elemental Powers

We use the circle and the cross again as the basis for this discussion (see image 4.12 in chapter 4). The four points where the cross touches the circle, we have called the four directions, and we have connected an elemental power to each of these directions. The decision to place an elemental power in a particular direction is a choice. I based my choice on the preference of the dragons, and we will use that throughout this book. In this chapter, we will look at the many correspondences that the four directions and the four elemental powers have. They are what we call correspondences because they are not identical. They correspond with each other. Therefore, we can use this information to understand the way the dragons support us on our earthly journey.

We discussed the steps that led to the number 4 and the connected four elements in the previous chapter. Based on the information about the mother elements and the four elements, we can describe a process called densification (image 5.1); that is, descending from the spiritual to the material — into the physical reality. Human consciousness decreased in vibration, as is reflected by the increasingly dense realities. Consequently, the human system began to lose its spiritual connection. Image 5.1 shows the main steps of the descent into physicality. These steps are part of a spiral of descent into the lower vibrations and functioning from lower levels of consciousness.

We start with chaos and the three mother elements at the top. The next steps are the process of creation in which the father elements create order. The steps from chaos to order are part of every creation in every dimension. The next step, however, applies to the physical, manifested world. When souls came into this physical world as humans, they were not as dense as the physical world of Earth. In the image, this is indicated by the broken line, which is in contrast to

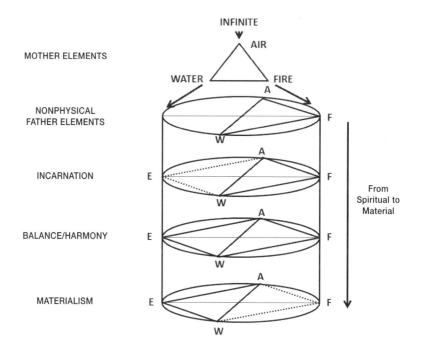

IMAGE 5.1. Densification is the process of descending into lower vibrations.

the solid line connected to the three spiritual elements (the right triangle). At that stage, we were mainly spiritual beings having a physical experience in an etheric/astral form.

The purpose was to find a balance whereby the souls who were on Earth needed to create a situation in which the four elemental powers and all the connected aspects were in harmony. For them, that meant they needed to become more physical, which was the next step.

At a certain moment in human development, people reached a state in which the four elemental powers were in balance; however, humans were not able to maintain this balance. The physical aspects became stronger and began to overtake the spiritual aspects. Based on the fear of lack and also due to power games in which some people controlled others, people began to sink deeper into the material aspects of this world. This deep connection with the physical/material world and the loss of connection with the spiritual aspects resulted in the last step shown in image 5.1, which depicts the current state of our species. We can describe this state as scientific materialism, a

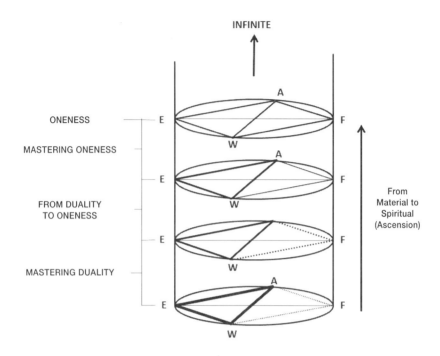

IMAGE 5.2. Ascension is the process of increasing vibrations that lead to a new world.

state in which technology and the need of the mind to be satisfied by what we have dominates the way we live and make choices. This last step also indicates a phase of deeper descent into the physical world.

Although we descended into this physical world, we do not understand or respect it, and we use it without consideration of consequences. We have descended into the manifested world but lost the connection with it. In this phase of our development, we have reached a point in which we cannot sink deeper. We are already destroying our world. The only step we might add would be the complete destruction of our world. However, it seems that people are increasingly realizing what has been created and are choosing to initiate change.

It might seem that we are still proceeding down a path of descent; however, this is no longer true. There is a dramatic increase in awareness that we are spiritual beings having a human experience. People are searching once more to connect with their spiritual essence. We are beginning to move in the direction of the path of ascension (image 5.2). The step at the bottom of the image is the same step at the bottom of image 5.1. The lines of the physical triangle have been made thicker to indicate a stronger contrast with the spiritual triangle at the right.

To move more into a state in which the spiritual and physical triangles are balanced, we need to learn to work with duality. It is a phase in which we need to understand that we learn through differences, which in our society are often considered a curse. We need to reframe differences as a gift. Duality is a gift that facilitates our being able to learn how to function in physical reality. The dragons of duality (chapter 7) can and will help us with this process if we are willing to follow.

Once we have mastered duality, even to a certain degree, we begin the process of learning to live in oneness. In the state of oneness, we understand that the aspects of duality are opposing qualities that describe the same thing but to different degrees. We learn to understand the third aspect that binds the opposites together and moves us into the state of oneness.

The dragons of oneness will help us with this process. In the state of oneness, the physical triangle and the spiritual triangle are in balance and function as one system. The moment of balance represents the beginning of the process of true ascension. Once we have reached the state of balance between the physical and spiritual, we can see the world as one. This one world will be raised in frequency to allow this world to function in higher spiritual dimensions, reconnecting the Gaia system to higher consciousness levels of the universe.

Fire

The east is the location of the elemental power of fire. Corresponding aspects are spirituality, consciousness, and energy. Fire is the elemental power connected to consciousness. It also is the element of energy and power. It corresponds to our spiritual bodies, one of the three bodies part of what some people call the higher self, soul, or soul aspect (fragment).

Fire, as one of the three mother elements, is inherently present in the state of chaos and is also inherently present in the state of order — creation. This presence is obvious when we realize that fire is the consciousness that provides the energy and the information to set things into motion. It is the basis of Divine intent (the beginning of order), and as a consequence, it forms the basis of all intent. Whenever we wish to start a process of creation, we require the element of fire to be able to create consciously. Only when we start the creation process using the element of fire, will we be able to create in alignment with the infinite and therefore in alignment with all of creation.

There are many associative aspects when considering fire as the starting point. For example, the possibility of life on Earth depends on the Sun, which is a key example of the element of fire. The main element connected to the Sun is hydrogen. As we have discussed, hydrogen is connected to the element of fire.

When we accept the Sun as a symbol of the element of fire, it is not surprising that the dragons prefer to place the elemental power of fire in the east. The Sun rises in the east; thus the east symbolizes the beginning of creation using the element of fire.

Fire has been described as an elemental power; however, fire also has a physical aspect: the fire that burns. We can use this fire for many purposes, such as to warm ourselves and to cook food. Although there are alternative ways to cook food, they all require energy.

The physical aspect of fire connects to another quality: transformation. Fire transforms. We often see fire as destructive; for example, a forest fire. However, forest fires have always been a natural aspect of life on Earth, allowing new beginnings of life. Fire transforms the forest, heather, or grass fields into new growth, starting another succession cycle. In the same way, the fire of consciousness enables us to transform ways of thinking and feeling that no longer serve us, as symbolized by the phoenix, a mythological bird that, while it burns spontaneously, allows a new bird to rise out of its ashes. We are invited to use fire to transform what no longer serves us to allow something new to emerge.

All processes that produce energy have a connection with the element of fire. Living beings cannot function without the production of energy. We take in food that needs to be burned to produce the energy that makes it possible to be alive and to be functional.

Many people all over the world use fire in ceremonies. The best-known example of the use of fire in a ceremonial way is the cremation of the dead. While there are different details in the beliefs why cremation honors the dead, the most common belief is that it supports the process of transformation from this life into the afterlife. There are, of course, practical aspects as well. If there are insufficient places to bury the dead, cremation seems to be the best option. However, the practical aspects in most traditions are secondary, as the burning of the dead is a ritual to honor the process of death and transformation.

Fire also functions as a cleanser, both practically and symbolically. People burned the bodies of the dead during epidemics as a way to prevent the spread of disease. On a personal level, people do ceremonies to cleanse negative energy. A popular approach is to write down what you wish to transform, and with this intent, throw the paper in the fire. There are several variations of this ceremony, all holding the intention to transform unwanted behaviors and experiences.

Water

In the systems related to dragons, the location of the elemental power of water is in the south. Water is the element of creativity and emotions, and it belongs to the emotional body. Just as the spiritual body is part of the higher self, soul, or soul fragment, so is the emotional body. It is to remind us that the higher self/soul is made up of the three mother/father elements.

As with fire, water is part of both chaos and order. Mythology abundantly mentions the state of chaos and its relationship with water. The Sumerian story of Tiamat may be the oldest recorded example. Water is the element so widely considered as a basic aspect of creation that it is included as the major element in most creation myths. The fact that on a physical level all creation and development takes place in water is undoubtedly part of the reason water is included in all creation myths.

You also can define the elemental power of water as wisdom. Water can receive the energy and information of fire and consciousness and use it to create. This process is true in both nonphysical and physical situations. All life is born in water. Water is the system that sets into motion to create from the energy that it receives. Energy (e) in motion is emotion.

In a creative process, it is important that energy flows; thus, it is in motion. Without flow, the energy in a system will clog up, and the system will become blocked. The statement that energy needs to be in motion is a very important aspect that we will talk about in working with dragons and the powers of which they are the guardians.

While it is true in general that energy needs to be in motion — that emotions need to flow — it applies equally to us. We also need to allow emotions to flow. Otherwise, energies get stuck, leading to diminishing functions and ultimately diseases and even death. In our society, many people tend to hold their emotions in and suppress them. Saying that this is unhealthy is an understatement. As part of our journey, we need to learn again to allow emotions to flow, which will result in optimal health and functioning.

While water is an elemental power involved in the creation process, water as an element is extremely important for life on Earth. Without water, there would be no life. This statement is accepted as fact. When scientists look for the possibility of life on other planets, they always search for water. Although this is a limited way of looking at whether potential life forms exist, seen from a human perspective, it is understandable. We look for life forms that we can recognize. The life forms that we are familiar with all need water.

While we are aware of the importance of water, we know little about its qualities. Recently, water became a more extensive subject of study. One of the important questions that scientists seek to answer is how water can hold so much information. Work by people like Dr. Masaru Emoto has shown that water reacts to intentions, thoughts, and sounds. Emoto showed that the shapes of crystals formed by frozen water are affected strongly by the frequencies, sounds, and thoughts to which water was exposed.[1] When the thoughts were positive, the crystals were regular and beautiful. When thoughts were negative, the water did not create crystals, or it created only deformed ones. The same was true for music. Harmonious music, for example, classical music, created beautiful crystals, but disharmonious music did not create crystals.

Water crystals have six points, like snowflakes, and their shape is hexagonal. The hexagonal shape seems to be important for understanding water and its functions. Research has shown that water molecules can bind together. When water is dirty, polluted, or affected by negative thoughts and energies, the structure is irregular. When the structure is irregular, the water cannot create the regular six-pointed water crystals.

To be able to create beautiful, crystalline water crystals, the water molecules need to cluster. There are differences of opinion about what optimal clustering is. The most commonly accepted form of optimal clustering is the hexagonal form. Dr. Mu Shik Jhon works with optimal clustering in a hexagonal shape. He wrote a book[2] that provides scientific evidence of the existence of hexagonal water and its positive influence on health.

The Aerospace Institute of the University of Stuttgart in Germany used a different method to prove water has memory. They found that although they used drops of water from the same source, the images of these drops of water were different for the different experimenters, and each experimenter got consistent images. For example, when you put a flower in water, all drops consistently produced a similar image different from any other flower.[3] Water truly can hold information and hold it consistently.

The most optimal water is water that flows in natural systems, like seas, rivers, and creeks. However, most water on our planet no longer has sufficient life force, for which there are many reasons. Water loses its life force when it is stored in tanks and pipes. As Schauberger showed, water needs to move in natural ways to maintain its life force.[4] Schauberger calls water a living substance. It drives everything from our metabolic processes to weather patterns and climate change. Moreover, the real significance of water lies in its role as a medium for metamorphosis, recycling, and exchanging energy and information. Bartholomew describes water as a conscious organism that is self-creating and self-organizing.[5] However, due to human action against Earth, water no longer carries the balanced constituents or the energetic components to sustain life to its full potential. When water lacks balance and life force, so do humans.

Although water always has been seen as critical for life, we are only beginning to understand its importance. More knowledge about this subject is necessary. Fortunately, an increasing amount of books on water are appearing. Working with water and fully understanding its power and its qualities is something with which the dragons can help.

Air

While fire is the elemental power that provides the information that comes from the consciousness received by water for creation, we need air to give that creation life. Air, in its highest vibration, is equated to being the breath of the Creator. On that level, air gives life to creation. Without air, there would be no life.

Air is the third of the mother elements that existed in the state of chaos and continued when order arrived. Air is an essential part of creation. This life force, which is so difficult to define, is an inherent part of the elemental power of air. It is the breath of the Creator that gives life, which by definition includes the life force. Without life force, there is no life.

Life force is taken in by every living being. We take it in through breathing and nourishment from food. When we eat food in its original form, it contains life force because every plant and animal takes in life force. However, due to the way we grow plants and treat animals, they no longer have a sufficient amount of life force. Also, we pollute our air, and consequently, there is less life force. We are creating a world that is less supportive of us. Consequently, the human race as a whole diminishes in power and vitality in mental and physical health and in the ability to think clearly.

To receive air and life force, we need to breathe. Breathing is essential because otherwise, we die. Because breathing is so important to many traditions, techniques for proper breathing have been developed. Whether it is yoga, tai chi, chi gong, or martial arts, these practices rely on life force (chi, ki, prana).

In a modern Western society with its hectic pace and intense demands, many people suffer to various degrees from stress. While it is most important to breathe properly to deal with stress, most people begin to hold their breath, which creates more stress. Therefore, breathing and being aware of your breathing is significant.

In our daily functioning, the elemental power of air connects to the mental body, which represents thoughts connecting to the process of thinking. Our thoughts have a powerful effect on the way our system functions, such that positive thoughts create a healthy system just as we have seen that thoughts affect water. Therefore, thoughts affect the quality of the water throughout our system, and consequently, they have a powerful effect on the health of our system.

Many people do not adhere to the discipline of maintaining positive thoughts, which would support the optimal functioning of their whole system. Often people are not aware of the effect of their thoughts or even most of their thoughts. Negative thoughts eradicate life force and diminish our vitality. Once you are aware of the effect of your thoughts, you may be more willing to take proper care of the way you think.

When we mention air, many people will think about the external environment, looking to the sky as the source of air. They will follow the movements of the clouds and feel the wind. This air is not the elemental power but the element itself, which is a manifestation of the elemental power of air. This air can be pleasing and joyful to experience. However, air also can be threatening when the gentle breeze changes into a storm, tornado, or hurricane.

As much as air can give life, it can also destroy it. As we saw, the same is true for water and fire. Remember, the three mother elements are connected to both chaos (destruction) and creation as are their physical manifestations.

Earth

The elemental power of earth does not belong to the mother elements. As we have seen, it came from the three mother elemental powers. It seems that the elemental power of earth only belongs to the physical world. It is the energy of manifestation in physical form.

In our world, our reality, for most people, this refers to physical manifestations that can be seen and measured. That is the familiar world in which we function. It is the world that we study, define, and discuss. We are all part of these manifestations, sharing a common perception that allows communication. However, I believe that manifestation is more than that which is tangible.

What aspects of creation belong to the earth element? This question has always intrigued me. Is it indeed only connected to the manifested tangible world, or does it contain more? Is the physical world only the solid material? To answer this, I believe that we need to look at the different energy bodies of the human system. The problem is

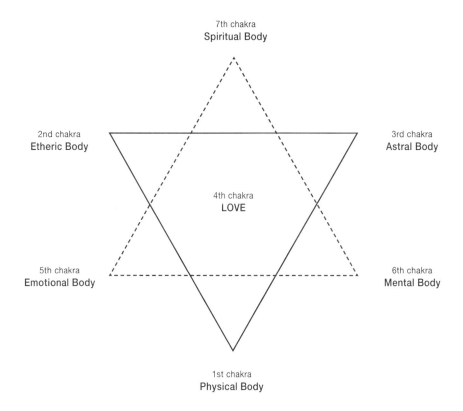

IMAGE 5.3. The human six-pointed star shows the seven basic chakras
with their corresponding energies.

that people's opinions differ as to the number of energy bodies that
form the human energy field. Also, the names that were given to these
bodies often differ, creating more confusion.

While I do not claim that the system I use is the correct one, it fits
all systems I have discovered and is in alignment with what Mother
Earth reveals. Therefore, I prefer to say that there are five energy bodies connected to the physical body. I presented reasons for this number in my book *Gifts of Mother Earth*.[6]

Image 5.3 shows the physical system with the etheric and astral
bodies connected to the physical triangle and the emotional and
mental bodies as part of the spiritual triangle. When people die,
the three bodies connected to the physical triangle stop functioning
and reintegrate into the physical systems of the earth. Therefore,

the physical system, the manifested system connected with the elemental power Earth, is more than the measurable world around us. It also includes the subtle energies connected with the two subtle, physical bodies.

We will never understand the manifested world in which we live if we do not include the energies that belong in the etheric and astral systems. That is especially true because the existence of the energy systems that we in the human system call etheric and astral bodies are present in all physical manifestation. There even are worlds and beings that only exist in these frequency systems.

All worlds and beings that exist outside the observable world are called subtle beings in subtle worlds, and they are an inherent part of the manifested world of Gaia. Based on the inclusion of the etheric and astral systems as part of the manifested world, we have to conclude that there are many forms of manifestation, far more than the ones of which we are aware.

In our way of perceiving this world, the key to the physical, visible reality is the electromagnetic energies. Every system that we encounter from a material perspective in our world has measurable electromagnetic frequencies. Therefore, many people associate the manifested visible world with the existence of electromagnetic energies. When energies cannot be measured, they fall under the term subtle energies. When something is not measurable according to the paradigms of science, it does not exist. As a consequence, science avoids spirituality, consciousness, and the subtle worlds.

The irony is that even the physical world has energies that cannot be measured directly; therefore, ignoring these energies prevents a complete understanding of the physical world in which we live. It seems that the other three elemental powers connect us to other energies, such as the subtle energies of life force or the energies of consciousness. However, this separation between the physical and nonphysical is flawed.

All energies exist in the physical reality, even subtle energies. We completely depend on the unmeasurable life force in our system. The electromagnetic energies make the manifested visible world manageable because we can measure and define it. The only aspects we measure are the activities within the densest system, which we need to do to understand our physical bodies. However, we also need to include the etheric and astral energies to understand our physical world more fully.

The manifested world gives us everything we need to function optimally within this physical reality. There is an abundance to fulfill our needs on all levels; unfortunately, not everyone experiences such abundance. In a practical sense, there are millions of people who do not have enough food or proper drinking water. In a world with so many resources, we have created a situation in which people have or do not have. Consequently, many people see the physical world more as a threat than as a place of infinite possibilities. As a species, we have lost our connection with our world, and as a consequence, we no longer care, thus we pollute indiscriminately and destroy.

All descriptions of the elemental power and the element of earth are based on the belief that the visible and measurable constitute the manifested world. However, we are now beginning to understand that the manifested world has both visible and invisible aspects. Many invisible beings and worlds are part of the manifested Earth system (Gaia). When we learn to work with dragons, we open ourselves to these invisible worlds. It is an opportunity to appreciate that these invisible aspects, brought into manifestation through the elemental power of earth, require the same four elemental powers for their creation and existence.

To work properly with the earth element, we have to be able to also work with the other three elements in a harmonious way. Because we have not learned to do so, we have created more challenges than most people realize. We must reform how this world operates, which we can only accomplish when we understand and work with the elemental powers and the elements themselves. Fortunately, we have the dragons as powerful allies who can and will help us to do so.

The Platonic Solids and the Fifth Element

The Platonic solids are named after the Greek philosopher Plato, who described these five solids extensively. They are part of sacred geometry and the Flower of Life.[7] Platonic solids are regular

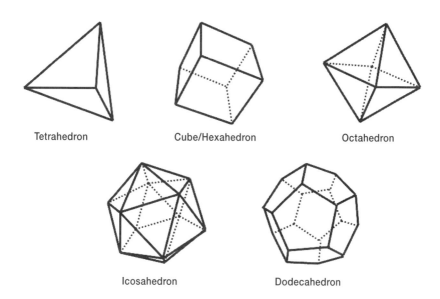

Tetrahedron   Cube/Hexahedron   Octahedron

Icosahedron   Dodecahedron

IMAGE 5.4. Drawings of the five platonic solids.

polyhedrons of which all sides, all angles, and all faces are identical. Their names reflect the number of faces that each of these five polyhedra has: tetrahedron (4 faces), hexahedron or cube (6 faces), octahedron (8 faces), dodecahedron (12 faces), and icosahedron (20 faces) (image 5.4). These five platonic solids are relevant for our work with the dragons because they also connect with the elemental powers.

According to Plato, the tetrahedron represents the element of fire; the cube, the element of earth; the octahedron, the element of air; the icosahedron, the element of water; and the dodecahedron represents Aether, the mysterious fifth element. This relationship between Platonic solids and the elements is accepted commonly. However, I do not agree with it. I believe that the tetrahedron and dodecahedron are not connected respectively to fire and Aether, but that it is the other way around.

The five Platonic solids form duals. Two polyhedra are duals when the vertices of one correspond one-to-one to the center of the faces of the other. Applying this to the Platonic solids, the cube and the octahedron are each other's dual (image 5.5), and so are the dodecahedron

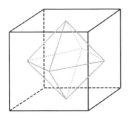

IMAGE 5.5. The dual of a cube and an octahedron.

IMAGE 5.6. The dual of a icosahedron and a dodecahedron.

IMAGE 5.7. The star tetrahedron; the tetrahedron is a dual to itself.

and the icosahedron (image 5.6). The tetrahedron has no dual (image 5.7). While it is geometrically correct, the combinations of the dual polyhedrons have always puzzled me. Yes, I am aware that understanding how things work will never be resolved with linear thinking. However, it does not make sense to me that the solid for the universe and Aether has a dual and the solid for fire does not.

Plato's idea that the dodecahedron is related to the universe seems to be confirmed by research.[8] Research suggests that if you measure the cosmic microwave background frequencies, which are the leftovers of the big bang, the shape from which the sound came is a dodecahedron or, more precisely, the shape of twelve dodecahedrons. There are several possible explanations. We need to consider Plato's explanation within the framework of the time in which he lived. Originally, he had found only four solids, which he related to the four elements. With the addition of the fifth, the dodecahedron, only one element remained: Aether. Therefore, Aether and the dodecahedron were connected.

Looking at the history of Aether, it is unclear what its function is. It is equated with the universe, with orgone and vril (life force), and with the fifth element as a secret and well-hidden force. It is called the source that binds us all. It is what drives the universe, what gives life and energy. Whether we call this vital spiritual energy prana, the force, or Aether, these names all refer to the same thing. Aether is the essential spiritual energy that enables life, in all its forms, to exist, function, and interact in harmony within all realms and dimensions.[9]

According to Wikipedia, Aether or ether (also called quintessence) is the material that fills the region of the universe above the terrestrial sphere.[10] I previously mentioned that four steps created the four elemental powers that make the creation of all manifestations possible. The next step, the fifth, indicates the power, the energy. It's the step that induces creation. The four powers to create are present, but they need direction, which the number five provides.

The five equates to humans, but also to any being who can direct the elemental powers into the act of creation. As the fifth element, Aether holds the energy field that directs creation. In that sense, we simply can call it consciousness. Because consciousness functions in many realities and dimensions, the fifth element can only be defined from the perspective and the context from which a consciousness looks at it.

The following descriptions and explanations may make it easier to understand the five Platonic solids and their relationship with the elemental forces. It makes more sense to see the dodecahedron as the symbol of fire. Fire is the intent that creates. The intent was made visible in the experiment that showed the shape of the universe is a dodecahedron. It is the matrix (energy, information, power — the dodecahedron) created by the overseeing consciousness from which creation is induced (fire).

However, the induction of the elemental power of fire into action is something beyond fire. What is beyond fire is a field that holds the information from which creation can take place — the fifth element, the Aether. I also call that field the morphogenetic field. That is to say, the active part of it. The representation of this field, the fifth element, is the tetrahedron.

Accepting the dodecahedron as the representation and symbol for fire makes it easier to understand why it is a dual of the icosahedron. As we will see when we look at the way dragons support the creation, the first step in any creation on any level is fire (intention). Water is the receiving system of this information. Water and fire form a unique combination (energy and intention).

The other unique combination is the octahedron and cube dual. The element of water creates. To enliven the creation, water needs air (the octahedron), so manifestation in physical reality (the cube) can live and function. These dual polyhedra systems explain creation perfectly without using the tetrahedron. The tetrahedron, however, induces the activity of all Platonic solids into the process of creation and manifestation. Also, geometrically, all Platonic solids can be created from the tetrahedron.

A few more considerations support the choice of the tetrahedron as the fifth element. In this reality, the tetrahedron is only a symbolic representation of the fifth element. The reality in which we live is physical; therefore the symbol for the Platonic solid that represents Aether has to have physical aspects. The tetrahedron has four faces, and each face has three sides.

As we have seen, there are three mother elemental powers. They are the first expression of consciousness. Together these three elemental powers created the fourth elemental power, earth. Therefore, in physical reality, all creation contains the four elemental powers, including the four elements as we see and experience them. The shape of the tetrahedron demonstrates this process. The three sides of each of the four faces show that the three mother elemental powers are an inherent aspect of all aspects of physical reality (the four elements).

For many years, I have doubted this. Could my idea that the tetrahedron rather than the dodecahedron representing Aether be wrong? Or do people tend to accept what they have been told as truth and do not dare to question? I have looked for confirmation of my idea, but I have been unable to find it. Working with the dragons means working with the elemental powers and the elements. The subject came up over and over again. I kept feeling that the dragons confirmed my feelings.

Recently, I read an article by Anders Sandberg discussing ideas similar to mine, pointing out that the traditional correspondences between Platonic solids and elements may be incorrect. He stated: "These solids naturally fall into three groups, based on their symmetries and duals. The Octahedron and Cube, which are duals of each other, form one group, while the Dodecahedron and Icosahedron form another. The Tetrahedron forms a third group with only itself as a member since it is its own dual. Note that the five elements are similarly divided: the spiritual elements are duals to the material elements (and a similar duality holds for actives and passives), and the fifth is left out o[n] its own ... Thus, from my mathemagickal standpoint, Quintessence belongs more naturally to the Tetrahedron, the Cube and Octahedron correspond as normal to Earth and Air while Fire and Water correspond to the Dodecahedron and Icosahedron respectively."[11]

Here's another thought: The four elements of fire, water, air, and earth are separated into two feminine elements, water and earth, and two masculine elements, fire and air. Based on the Platonic solid duals, there is a combination of the two opposite elements. Fire and water are respectively masculine and feminine — dodecahedron and icosahedron. Air and earth are respectively masculine and feminine — octahedron and cube. The idea of polarity is an inherent part of our reality.

When you replace the dodecahedron with the tetrahedron for the element of fire, the same duality no longer exists. The tetrahedron, being its own dual, forms the star tetrahedron. These two tetrahedrons point in opposite directions. The one with the point up forms the masculine aspect, and the one with the point down forms the feminine, creating a polarity again (see image 5.7).

The Great Pyramid of Giza and the Five Elements

In a monumental work, Willem Witteveen described in his book *The Great Pyramid of Giza*, the function of the pyramid as a monument that gives information about the way the universe works and also about the way our reality works.[12] He describes the pyramid as a power plant that uses all five elements. It is not within the scope of this book to summarize this extensive work. However, from my perspective, the pyramid shape has always been a representation of the five elements.

For a pyramid to function optimally, its orientation needs to be in alignment with the four directions. Also, the elemental powers align themselves with the four directions. Therefore, each of the sides of the base square represents one of the four elements: fire in the east, water in the south, air in the north, and earth in the west. The top is above the four elements and forms the fifth element: Aether. Does this sound far-fetched? Maybe. My reasoning is completely different from

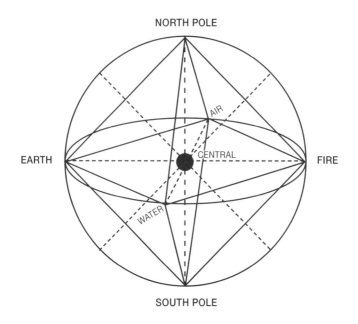

IMAGE 5.8. The octahedron in a sphere.

that of Witteveen. He explained his reasons convincingly through-out his book, demonstrating how all the elements are involved in the function of the pyramid. I use the pyramid more as a symbol. I will explain this symbol in several ways in the coming chapters, and here, I offer only a general overview.

In chapter 4 and this chapter, we have explored the image of the circle and the cross. The circle with the cross is a two-dimensional representation of a three-dimensional image. This image is, in fact, an octahedron within a sphere. The axis of the sphere that goes from the north pole of the sphere to the south pole represents aether, the fifth element. This fifth element is an aspect of the morphogenetic field expressed in different ways, depending on the specific dragon system. The sphere with the directions and the octahedron (image 5.8) are the images that form the basis of all the work with dragons. The octahedron is a shape that corresponds to two pyramids connected by their bases. Although the angles of the sides of the two pyramids of the octahedron are slightly different from those of the pyramid of Giza, they represent the same principle.

There is another interesting aspect that all pyramids have in common: They all have a basic frequency of 8.1 Hz, both inside and around them. This frequency has a very beneficial effect on all living beings.[13] The fact that it has such a beneficial effect has to do with life force. It stimulates life force that connects to the elemental power of air, whose corresponding Platonic solid is the octahedron. There are supporting correspondences everywhere.

Let us return to the dual regular polyhedrons. Given the fact that a pyramid has a basic frequency of 8.1 Hz brings up the question of whether the octahedron has the same basic frequency, and that turns out to be the case. The dual of the octahedron and the cube corresponds to this frequency. This correspondence is not very surprising if we realize that the cube resonates with the elemental power of earth, which connects to the manifested world.

The dodecahedron and icosahedron also form a dual, as we have seen. The frequency of this dual corresponds to 49.5 Hz. The tetrahedron is a dual by itself. Its frequency corresponds to 181.8 Hz. As you may notice, these three frequencies are each numerologically a 9. The number 9 represents completion and spirituality. All Platonic solids have a vibration that contributes to the completion of creation, reminding us that all manifestation holds inherent spirituality (represented by the number 9).

Nikola Tesla was fascinated with the numbers 3, 6, and 9. This fascination led to his statement: "If you only knew the magnificence of the 3, 6 and 9, then you would have a key to the universe."[14] Even today, people search for the deeper meaning behind this statement.

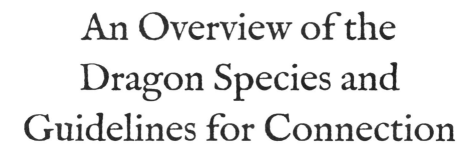

CHAPTER 6

An Overview of the Dragon Species and Guidelines for Connection

THE DISCOVERY OF THE DRAGON SPECIES HAS BEEN A LONG JOURNEY. In the first chapter, we discussed dragon species based on descriptions in literature. I do not believe that these, so described, species exist; however, they could be a reflection of subconscious connections with the beings I call dragons. When I first discovered dragon grids and, consequently, had to accept that dragons exist, I believed there was only one species with variable energy.

In chapter 3, I described the discovery of crystalline beings that led to the formation of what I thought to be one dragon species. As I connected with greater amounts of dragon energies, it became easier to feel differences. Also, from the beginning, I felt a guide that I named Drasil-air. At the time, I was unfamiliar with Drasil-air, but he felt supportive in all that I did in relation to dragon energies. I am now highly aware that Drasil-air has been guiding me along the entire journey and continues to do so.

I am also aware that Drasil-air has two counterparts and that he is part of a trinity. Although I now feel that this trinity guides me, I continue to feel that I connect and communicate mainly with Drasil-air. However, independent of whom I communicate with directly, I know that the trinity is the guiding principle in all my work with dragons.

The path of mastering all aspects of how to work with dragons to become a true master of the elemental powers may take a lifetime, and only very few will complete this journey. Most likely, this path is not for everyone. However, understanding and learning to work with elemental powers is helpful for everyone to function better in this physical world. To be able to master the elemental powers to the most optimal personal level is helpful in connecting, at least to some degree, with the different dragon species.

Once we discovered that crystalline beings could become real dragons, the question arose as to their function. Based on what you read in the previous chapters, you know that they are the guardians of the elemental powers, but at the time, this was unknown to me. Looking back, I realize that I could have constructed many beliefs that would have prevented me from discovering the dragon species. However, I was able to move forward, always following the guidance that led me one step closer to the discovery of the species, a process I wish to introduce to you.

I already explained that my way to connect with a species, visible or invisible, is through vortexes of their morphogenetic grids. It allows me to connect with information without being influenced by others' ideas. It allows for unbiased discoveries and establishing unique relationships with beings. I followed such a process with dragons and unicorns, other invisible beings, and visible beings with whom I sought to have a deeper connection and understanding.

I still remember vividly sitting on the first dragon vortex that I was guided to as part of my newly started research into dragon energies. I had no idea what to expect. Sitting in the hot sun on a spring day, I wondered what I was inflicting on myself. I still was not convinced that I wanted to study dragons, but at the same time, I was strongly attracted to the idea. Suddenly, I saw the circle and the cross that I described earlier. Because I was familiar with this symbol and also because of my understanding of the connection of crystalline beings with the four elemental powers, there was a confident knowing that I needed to find the four dragons connected to the four elemental powers.

The next question was simple: Which of the four dragons related to this morphogenetic grid? It was a simple question based on the idea that there were only four dragon species.

The first phase of the study of the four dragons led to the content of the first workshop I offered on dragons. It was about the crystalline being, crystalline life force, and the four dragons that are the guardians of the four elemental powers.

While I based this first workshop on a limited perspective, it was the beginning of a long journey of discovering more and more dragon species and energies. As limited as it was, this first workshop was important for many reasons.

First, the initial workshops ignited much excitement for the participants because of the birth of new dragons. Working with the crystalline beings and experiencing the dynamic of their splitting and merging was extremely stimulating and exhilarating. Even more exciting was the experience of the birth of real dragons, which felt as if we were engaged in something that made a difference. It also allowed a deepening of the connection with dragon energies.

Second, and even more important, the workshops activated the dragons' energies and their morphogenetic grids, thus making the energies of dragons more available for those who were open to receiving them. Despite the awareness that the knowledge about dragons and their roles were so limited, these early workshops were incredibly stimulating and exciting, opening the doors for further development.

Once the basic dragon energies were sufficiently established, the dragon guide Drasil-air guided me onward. The next step was the discovery that the four dragons were part of a group that we now call the duality dragons (see chapter 7). In the second workshop I developed, we worked with nine species. In retrospect, it is interesting to notice that at each stage when I was guided to present the available information on dragons that I had collected in a workshop, I believed that the dragons I knew about represented all the species that existed. I needed to feel confident to present this knowledge. Otherwise, I would have waited until I had learned more.

Undoubtedly, this was part of the dragons' plan — to awaken their energies one step at a time. The dragons' willingness to share more of their energies depended on our willingness and ability to connect with the energies as they were made available. The awakening of the dragon energies was truly a cocreation between dragons and humans. I am humbled and grateful that I was able to experience and participate in this important process.

At the end of the workshop with the nine dragon species, something happened that was extremely significant for the understanding of the duality dragons and all the other groups of dragons that were discovered later. In the workshop's final integration meditation, several participants and I were aware that there was another dragon energy that had become increasingly stronger. It had two colors: black and white. Later I discovered that it was not one but two dragons.

One was the species I called the black dragon. It is the guardian of the information and energy of the group of duality dragons that humans actively work with. It is the information present in the morphogenetic grids. The other species was the white dragon, the guardian of the information and energy of the full potential of duality dragons, the information that is present in the field. This discovery completed the understanding of the duality dragons. We had identified eleven species in the group of duality dragons. Finally, we had reached a point of full understanding of their composition.

Dragon Species Overview

At this stage of describing the discovery of the different species, it is worthwhile to review the information in image 6.1 (image 2.2 from chapter 2) as a foundation for a more detailed description of the species in general terms. In this overview, the large broken lines indicate the crystalline beings and the dragons that connect directly with Earth. All dragons within these lines have energies of crystalline beings. The morphogenetic system of Gaia uses crystalline being energies and Cassiopeia's energies (as mentioned in chapter 4) to create the different dragon groups and species. My guide, Drasil-air, and his trinity counterparts, Drasha-air and Draphi-air, are indicated in the image and are outside of the system of dragons connected directly to Earth.

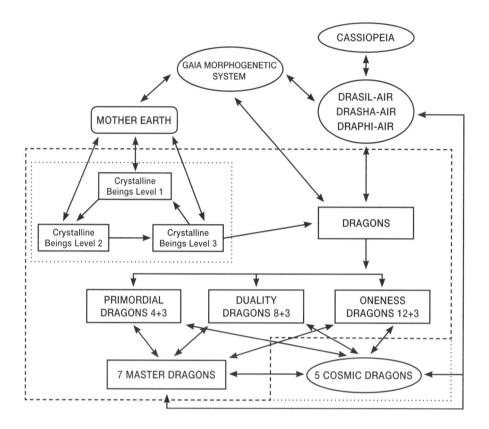

IMAGE 6.1. This is an overview of the existing dragon species connected with Earth. The dragons within the broken lines have grids and are connected with crystalline beings. The crystalline beings are within the dotted lines. The five cosmic dragons have grids but are not connected to crystalline beings.

In this overview, four dragon groups are the true Earth dragons because they also have the energies of the crystalline beings. We have only discussed the duality dragons, indicated as the 8 + 3 group; that is, eight dragons connected to the elemental forces and three to the central axis. In this group, the black dragons connect to the morphogenetic grids of that group and the white dragons connect to the morphogenetic field, and there also are the central dragons. The 3 of the 4 + 3 of the primordial dragons, the 8 + 3 of the duality dragons, and the 12 + 3 of the oneness dragons refer to similar dragon species: black, white, and central.

The primordial, duality, and oneness dragons have in addition to the three dragons of the central axis a number that is a multiplication of four: 1 x 4 = 4, 2 x 4 = 8, and 3 x 4 = 12. The numbers indicate that the primordial dragons connect to the four elements (the materialized elemental powers), the duality dragons to two qualities (or aspects) of the four elemental powers, and the oneness dragons to three aspects (or qualities) of the four elemental powers. We will look at all these energies and the dragon guardians connected to all these qualities in later chapters.

The master dragons integrate the six aspects of the four elemental powers and ultimately bring them to a level of mastery. Whether they are aware of it or not, all people need on their journeys a certain degree of ability to work with these aspects of the elemental powers. Otherwise, it will be difficult to fulfill their purpose in this world during this lifetime. The development of the ability to work with the elemental powers will hardly ever mean attaining a mastery over all four of them. For most people, this is highly unlikely and not needed for their journey.

Besides the four master dragons of the elemental powers, there are three other master dragons. These three help us to master the information held in the grids (the information that we as a collective are working with at this moment) and in the field (the total potential of the dragon information), as well as the information held by the central dragons.

The last group of dragons in the overview is in a different category than the earth dragons. Because they do not have the energies of the crystalline beings but only the energies that come from Cassiopeia, I have called them the cosmic dragons. Even though they are called cosmic dragons, they are an integrated part of the Gaia system because they have morphogenetic grids. They are committed to fulfilling a role within the Gaia system. This role is to make sure that all aspects of the energies that come from Cassiopeia maintain their purity to enable an optimal fulfillment of the role of dragons in the Gaia system.

Based on this overview, you may have tallied the number of dragon species. There are forty-five species in total, excluding Drasil-air, Drasha-air, and Draphi-air, who make it clear that they are not a separate species and that they do not have a grid connected to Earth. That is the reason I refer to them as guides. They seem to come directly from Cassiopeia. Their specific role is to guide people like me on our journey of connecting more deeply with the dragons that are active on Earth to help humanity with the process of increasingly mastering creation in physical reality.

Image 6.1 has changed many times over the years. Every time I thought the overview was complete (and Drasil-air allowed me to rest in that illusion for a while), something happened that made me realize I was incorrect. Participants of dragon workshops have seen over the years several different overviews. Occasionally, the question arises: "What makes me believe that this overview is complete?" I could easily have tricked myself into believing that these are all the species while it may not be true. After all, this has happened several times. There are several reasons:

- First, the most important reason is that Drasil-air gave me clear confirmation that the number of groups and the dragons in them are complete. (I know that my desire to complete the journey could have made me hear this answer.)
- Second, the groups and species cover all aspects of mastery over the elemental powers. I do not know what additional aspects could be added.
- Third, the total number of species is forty-five. In numerology, the number 45 reduces to 9, which is a spiritual number representing completion. When I realized that the number of dragon species was nine, I knew (besides hearing it from Drasil-air and besides feeling the truth) that I had completed this journey. At least I had reached the end of the first phase of the journey that focused on discovering the different dragon species and the powers of which they are the guardians.

Now the next phase starts, the phase of getting to know the different dragon species on a deeper level. This is the phase we can ask for their help in learning to work with the creative powers so that we can contribute to a world that functions more optimally, leading to the creation of the new fifth world. That is the journey toward ascension, the main reason why we human beings are here on this beautiful planet.

Based on the overview of the species, it is logical that the first group of dragons we will consider should be the primordial dragons, the 4 + 3 dragons. However, from the very beginning, Drasil-air was opposed, as he suggested starting with the duality dragons, then the oneness dragons, and only then, the primordial dragons.

It is important to learn to work with aspects of the elemental powers first before going into the connections and studies of the powers of the elements. Drasil-air knows that working with the duality and oneness dragons is preparation for working with the primordial dragons. The power of the elements is what destroyed Atlantis. Therefore, good preparation, awareness, and training with the different aspects of the elemental powers will help with the development of the ability to use these powers wisely and for the greater good of the Gaia system.

How to Connect with the Dragons

In the following chapters, we will connect with the forty-five dragon species. I mentioned that my way of connecting is by sitting on a vortex. I have formulated essences of the vortexes of the grids of the different species to allow people who do not have the skills to find these grids and vortexes or are unable to hike to these places to connect.[1]

Because you have only this book as a means of experiencing the different species, I felt that something was missing. I pondered a lot about a solution. When you set a clear intention to connect with a certain dragon, you will connect with that dragon. That in itself should be enough. However, I am very aware others might experience the various doubts I had during my studies. So I looked for an additional way to aid readers. The solution was to provide a picture of the location of the vortex of the grid system for each dragon. The combination of your intent and looking at the picture will — without any doubt — connect you to the species you want to work with.

Another important aspect of connecting with dragons is meditation. Dragons are not physical beings, so your normal five senses are not much help. You need to learn to feel and experience them. Initially, this might happen through energetic impressions and feeling differences between the different dragon species. Maybe you feel them in certain parts of your body. With more experience, you will build up information and reference points. That is the way to learn to work with subtle beings, including dragons.

I have given you guided meditations to help you connect with each of the forty-five species. Before going to the meditation to connect with the qualities and energies of each of the species, there is a general preparation to make sure you will obtain optimal results. To avoid repetition, I am providing here the basic introduction to the meditations to connect with each of the species. If you prefer, you can customize this general introduction. However, to work with dragons optimally, it is important always to include connecting with your heart in whatever preparation you choose.

—⟋⟍⟍⟍⟋—

INTRODUCTION TO ALL MEDITATIONS WITH DRAGONS

- Take a few deep inhalations and exhalations, and feel yourself relaxing.
- Bring your awareness as fully as possible to the present.
- Bring your awareness to your physical heart. Your heart is also the location of your spiritual (divine) essence.
- Imagine this essence as a sphere of white light. Allow this white light to shine through your entire physical body. Feel the unconditional love that is inherently connected with this light, and direct this love to yourself.
- Allow the love for yourself to permeate your entire physical system so that your frequency will increase. Feel this unconditional love for yourself, exactly as you are now, without the need to change anything.
- Allow the love to expand out of you and to fill the whole space in which you are seated. If you are with other people, animals, plants, or crystals, as well as invisible subtle beings in the room, also connect with them and together create a coherent field of unconditional love.
- Feel gratitude for all others present, knowing that they support you on this journey.
- From your divine essence, connect with the divine essence of Mother Earth. Feel love for Mother Earth, and

feel her love for you. Ask her to support you with her crystalline life force to enable you to optimally work with this energy, knowing that it will make your work with the dragons easier.

Sit in these created energies for as long as it feels good, and then move on to the specific meditation given to connect with the different dragon species and their energies.

—𝅊𝅊—

You can use this general introduction (with or without adaptations) for all types of meditations and even as a meditation itself. I strongly recommend doing this meditation regularly, maybe even as a morning routine. Connecting deeply with your essence is a very important aspect of raising your vibration and making a deeper connection with your life purpose.

CHAPTER 7

Journey with
the Duality Dragons

EVERY CREATURE ON EARTH, WHETHER VISIBLE OR INVISIBLE, is part of the total energy complex of Gaia — the consciousness of Earth — and all that lives on and in her. There is a morphogenetic field and grid system for every species, visible and invisible, that exists on Earth in the Gaia system. Gaia has her own morphogenetic field and grid system. We connect with every being, however small or big, through Gaia's morphogenetic field and grid system.

All beings contribute to each other's well-being in their unique ways. So every living being contributes to our well-being. However, we need to allow these beings to do so. We can do this when we reconnect with them, to some degree, and acknowledge our interdependence with them in the world in which we live.

Within this network of interconnected relationships, dragons play a special role. That is why or how Mother Earth created them in collaboration with the consciousness of beings from Cassiopeia. Mother Earth cocreated them with the purpose to be the guardians of the powers that play specific roles in all activities on Earth. When we master these powers, we will be one with Gaia and able to cocreate in a constructive and supportive way instead of the destructive way that is currently happening.

Through cocreation, it will be possible to fulfill our role as humanity: to increase the overall vibration of Gaia. We have accepted this role and promised to fulfill it. So far, it appears that we have done a poor job. Instead of increasing vibrations, we have decreased them, and we have prevented the expression of our potential as well as that of other creatures. Preventing the expression of the full potential of the species of plants, animals, and invisible beings is a consequence of the fact that we are all interconnected through the morphogenetic field and that our collective consciousness affects the expression of the potential of the morphogenetic field and, therefore, all morphogenetic grids.

We now live in a time when this can change. Therefore, it is important to understand that all beings, visible and invisible, are our allies. Among these allies, the dragons can help us to master the powers that govern this reality at every level. The first step is to master the powers that help us to become conscious cocreators in this physical dualistic world. Mastering these powers helps us to shift from duality to oneness. The dragons give us all the tools we need to be able to do so.

In the process of mastering these powers, we raise our vibrations and contribute to raising Gaia's vibrations as a whole. At the same time, we awaken more of our potential.

In a sense, dragons have functions similar to angels. However, angels work from the spiritual realms that affect the physical (helping us to become aware of our soul potential), and dragons work from the physical level affecting higher consciousness (helping us to become aware of our potential as stewards of Earth). We will look at the relationship of dragons and angels in more detail in chapter 12.

Dragons are more "home," seen from a physical human perspective and work more easily and directly with our human physical energies. Working with dragons is working with our mother. It is working within the realm that supports everything we do here on Earth. Without a balanced physical system, we cannot properly function in the physical reality, and consequently, we will be unable to bring our spiritual gifts into this reality.

From my perspective, we have come to Earth as souls with a purpose. That intent has locked us into this Earth reality. We have tried to complete this soul purpose over many lifetimes. Every time you are in a physical body, you can fulfill more of your soul purpose. The physical body is an extension of Mother Earth. To be able to fulfill our soul purpose in this lifetime, we need to align the physical body with Mother Earth so that the soul can finish its purpose. In this way, we form a trinity in which we can see our physical bodies as the masculine aspect, Mother Earth as the feminine aspect, and the soul as the child. When this trinity functions together in harmony, we will be able to fulfill our soul purposes. Once you have fulfilled this purpose, the soul will be unlocked from this realm and gain the freedom to choose to leave the Earth reality or to continue to support the ascension of Gaia.

We each have a different soul purpose; therefore it is important never to compare ourselves with others. We all need to find our unique purpose. Some souls will be ready when they fulfill their purposes in the three-dimensional, physical, dualistic reality, and others need to fulfill theirs in the fourth-dimensional physical reality of oneness. The dragons help to bring our physical systems in alignment with Mother Earth to make it possible for the soul to fulfill its purpose.

There is a tendency to romanticize dragons and perceive them in an anthropomorphic way. We also do that with angels and with many other beings such as unicorns and devas. This approach could prevent us from connecting with who they really are and what their role and function is in this world. To work with the powers of which dragons are the guardians, we need to be open and let go of preconceived ideas.

Every time we connect with dragons, we should do so as if we are considering a new subject. This perspective makes it possible to create a connection that becomes increasingly pure, no longer dictated by beliefs and preconceived ideas. When our connection is pure, the dragons can help us to master this reality, express our soul's purpose, and finally be free from the limitations of our minds. Then our minds can work for us.

The Types of Duality Dragons

There are eleven different types of dragons in the group of the

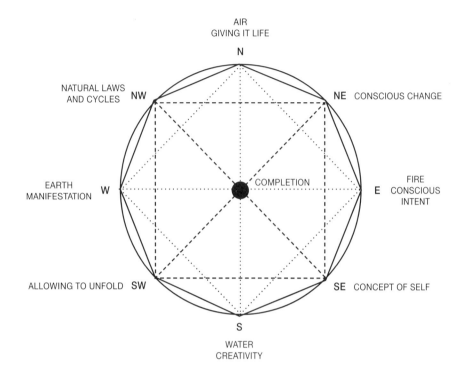

IMAGE 7.1. The circle with nine duality dragons; the eight dragons of the circle and the central dragon.

third-dimensional duality dragons. They are the guardians of the powers that help us to operate in this dualistic reality. Each has a morphogenetic grid system with lines and vortexes. Each represents a specific energy or power that we need to function optimally in this reality. The duality dragons are masters of the eleven energy systems, which hold the key energies to help us function optimally in this dualistic world, prepare us to shift into the fourth-dimensional reality of oneness, and ultimately, free us from this physical reality.

Image 7.1 is a representation of the eight main powers that can be seen symbolically as eight steps on a circle. The center is the place of the central dragons, the dragons of completion. Initially, we thought that these were all the powers that were guarded by the duality dragon species, but we later learned about two more dragons. When these two dragons emerged (became visible/noticeable to us), we realized

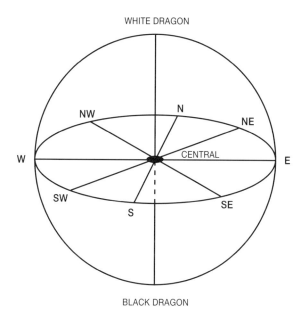

IMAGE 7.2. The sphere with all eleven duality dragon species.

that the system is more complex and can only be represented three-dimensionally by a sphere (image 7.2).

The three-dimensional reality we live in is based on duality. It is a general belief that we need to overcome duality and move into one-ness. However, duality is the result of polarity, which is an inherent aspect of creation. Overcoming duality does not come from denying it or imagining it as nonexistent. To overcome the problems of duality, we need to accept it, understand it, and learn to work with it.

It does not help us to deny that we live in a reality based on duality. We base our whole system of learning on experiencing polarity that shows us differences between what we can choose. Differences tell us what we resonate with and what we do not. It is a way to learn to understand who we are and to recognize our uniqueness. Therefore, there is nothing wrong with duality. On the contrary, it is a wonderful way to experience this beautiful physical reality, ourselves, and our way of functioning in it.

Because polarity is an essential aspect of and inherent in all creation, we can never escape it. Two, or duality, is polarity that came into existence when the All, the Infinite, became self-aware. We find this idea in almost all traditions from the Egyptians[1] onward and most likely from earlier traditions. It is also known as the fourth principle of the Hermetic philosophy and as such forms part of many religions and spiritual traditions.[2] The most important aspect of polarity is to see that they are the opposites of the same thing. The *Kybalion* states: "Opposites are identical in nature, but different in degree."[3]

Duality (opposites) and the consequent differences are not a problem unless we choose a side and make it into something that we call truth. It especially creates problems when we judge and become afraid of those who do not share the same view or values that we have chosen. Fear seems to be the underlying energy that plays a role in the lives of many people in our society. Fear creates withdrawal or aggression and survival strategies. We see a lot of aggression in our world, but we also see many people who are passive because they are afraid to share their point of view.

Although learning through differences may accentuate differences, duality is nonetheless the way to learn how this three-dimensional reality works. It helps us to feel differences from which we learn to make choices. It is therefore not surprising that the powers represented by the duality dragons are also based in dualistic energies. We are invited to master the energies so that we can transcend the dualistic aspects and move into oneness. We need to overcome the negative feelings of dualism, of opposites, to see that they are only different in degree and not in absolute value. Then we see everything as an aspect of the whole, of oneness.

When we look at image 7.2, we see a sphere with a central plane (equator) and a central axis. The eight dragons on the equator of the sphere form two groups of four (image 7.1). The two groups of four represent the duality in physical reality. The number 4 is the number of the earth, of physical reality, and it represents the four elemental powers that create this reality. The fact that there are two squares is the reflection of the duality of these powers. At the same time, the number 8 represents a higher vibration of 4 (the earth). The number 8 stands for self-replication, creating a new unity and a deeper understanding of the mysteries of the manifested world. It corresponds to the physical world as we experience it.[4] The number 8 also is needed

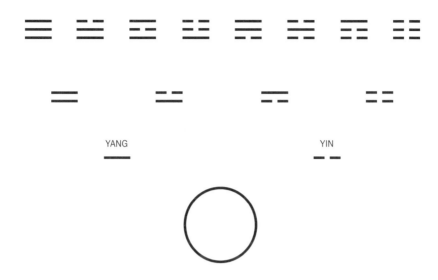

IMAGE 7.3. Pictured are yin and yang as they are represented in the eight trigrams.

to bring the creative powers of the four into motion to make creation a process instead of potential.

As we have seen, initially there were only three elements (fire, water, and air). Consequently, there was no duality, only oneness. Bringing the three elements into the world of manifestation created the fourth elemental power, and that created duality. Instead of three unique elements that represented the trinity, we now have two elements that are considered masculine (fire and air) and two that are feminine (water and earth). We no longer include the third aspect of this system directly. Even the indigenous traditions do not mention the child or neutral aspect. These traditions use the four directions or, in certain traditions, the eight directions.

We see a similar system in the way the Chinese look at reality. They base everything on duality — yin and yang. When they create four in their philosophy, we see that combinations of yin and yang form the four aspects, creating two opposing forces. When we add another yin or yang to the two, we get eight combinations in total (image 7.3), which have a correspondence to the eight duality dragons. In the Western way of thinking, these eight are related to four elements, and in the Eastern philosophy, they are related to five elements (Wu Xing).

To use the term "element" for the Chinese system is incorrect and confusing. Whereas the classical Greek elements (the system we use) are concerned with substances or natural qualities or powers, the Chinese *xing* are "primarily concerned with process and change," hence the common translation as "phases" or "agents."[5]

The Primary Directions

In our three-dimensional reality, the four elemental powers are a reflection of duality. They form two axes that show polarity. Let us look first at the four primary directions and the connected elemental powers (image 7.1). There are two axes connected with these four elemental powers: the east-west axis and the north-south axis. They form the basic qualities needed for creation. The two ends of each axis represent the masculine and feminine aspects of that axis. For the east-west axis, it is the dynamic of the physical (feminine force, west) and the spiritual (masculine force, east).

On this axis, we learn to find the balance between these two aspects (being in a balanced way in both the physical and the spiritual). This balance is unique to each person, and its location is somewhere on this axis. In the New Age movement, there's a tendency to be too much on the spiritual side. In the health food movement, the emphasis can be too strong on the physical. It always is about finding the balance so that we no longer see them as opposing forces but as one system.

However, we can never find the balance if we are not aware of the powers or forces themselves. I call this the creation axis. You also can call it the results axis. It shows the results of what you want to create. If the result is identical to your intent (your desire), you have success (east). If the result is something that you do not desire, you fail (west). This system can be applied on different levels and in different ways.

The same applies to the north-south axis. Here, the feminine aspect is emotions and creativity (the south), and the masculine aspect is thinking (the north). Again, we have to find our unique point of balance on the axis. The key is not to use thoughts to control emotions or allow emotions to dictate the way we think. This axis is the mind — the combination of thoughts (beliefs) and emotions that rule our lives.

As we will see, the dragons help us to separate thoughts and emotions in such a way that we can step out of the habit of the mind to link thoughts to emotions and emotions to thoughts. These activities of the mind create a continuous stream of thoughts and emotions that rule our lives and are often not in alignment with what we wish.

We cannot find the unique point of balance on these two axes if we do not embrace both aspects of each axis fully. Only when we connect with the opposites and recognize the polarity will we be able to find this balance. However, we often are only partly connected to those aspects. The dragons help us to connect fully to the aspects to allow us to find our new balance.

The Secondary Directions

While there is a certain familiarity with the four elemental powers, the energies represented by the other four (often called secondary) directions are less well known. While the four elemental powers connect to the four main, or cardinal, directions, these additional powers connect to what some people call the additional, or intermediate, directions. However, the powers connected to these additional directions are equally important and are in no way secondary. They represent the more dynamic elements of the circle.

Adding the additional four directions creates the eight and changes creation from a potential to an active state, setting the previous four powers into motion. Based on the directions of east, south, west, and north, the directions of the second square can be called southeast (SE), southwest (SW), northwest (NW), and northeast (NE).

In this system, the pair NE–SW also has a point of balance somewhere between the masculine NE (conscious change) and the feminine SW (feeling and allowing the direction in life to unfold, also called unfolding the creative process). This polarity also has a more personal aspect. When we are too much in the NE, the tendency is to control the process. The SW is the opposite. You trust the process because you know that you have done everything you could. However, it also can lead to passivity. Again, we need to find a balance.

We are responsible, and therefore, we have to make choices. We need to know when to let go and allow the process to unfold. I call this axis the trust axis. We need to trust the creative process to be able to allow the process to flow naturally based on where we are in our journeys. We always will learn from the process, despite the outcome.

The second pair is NW–SE, which has a balance point between the masculine SE and the feminine NW. The masculine SE represents our true selves instead of what we believe about ourselves. We can also call this the self-concept. The feminine NW represents the process of allowing your internal and external rhythms or that of your creations to flow in alignment with natural laws and flows (natural rhythms and cycles). Here the polarity is the individual versus the whole. We learn to be aware of our needs and to balance them in alignment with the whole Gaia system or, on a smaller scale, with your partner or the company for which you work.

Being at the extreme of the poles will not bring balance. By understanding the balance, the powers of the poles will optimally support the process of creation. I call this the focus axis. Are you focused on personal gain (self), or do you choose to benefit the whole with your creation? However, working for the greater good of all can never mean that you exclude yourself.

Now we can understand that the eight qualities of the circle are not absolute but relative qualities that differ for each person and situation. However, they tell an important story about the levels of awareness and consciousness from which a person functions.

There is another duality that is an inherent aspect of this circle. We can look at the four elemental powers of the four main directions as the essences of the powers. As we mentioned, they are the basic powers that make creation possible. They are the powers that receive their inherent quality from a higher perspective and will always connect to that higher source. This receiving aspect is why we define them as feminine qualities. When we use these qualities, they become dynamic, as we can see with the other four energies or powers.

Those four dynamic energies force us to set things into motion, and consequently, they are masculine. Therefore, each of the four elemental powers presents itself in the circle as a feminine and a masculine quality, being dualistic. The rhythmic variation of feminine and masculine aspects will make even more sense when we go through the cyclical movement of all eight powers.

The movement through the circle is a flow that goes clockwise, as all natural systems on Earth, dictated by the way we perceive the Sun to move. When we move through the energies presented in the circle, we move through the mentioned eight powers and energies, and we give form to our lives. If we are balanced, we will always use each of the eight powers to the degree that is most optimal for each situation. It is an endless cycle of giving form to our reality.

However, every time we go through the circle, we are meant to do that from a slightly higher energetic vibration, forever evolving. That is the quality of the number 8, which refers to renewal. Unfortunately, many people are stuck, and there is not much of an increase in vibration every time they go through the circle. Thus, people see no improvement in their lives and become unmotivated, so the vibration may even decrease every time they go through the circle due to disappointment and frustration that once again things did not go as the person had intended.

It is also important to realize that all these eight points (powers and energies) are in action at the same time. We are not in just one creative process. There are many processes, small and large, taking place at the same time. To understand the essence of these creative processes, we will go through each step of the circle two at a time. We will use the two directions connected to a particular elemental power, for example, the east and southeast, which are both fire energies. Next, we will look at the dragons that hold the powers connected with the north and the south poles of the sphere. Finally, we will integrate the whole with the support of the central dragon: the dragon that unites the powers in the circle and the poles in such a way that we will integrate all aspects of the sphere into a dynamic whole. Working with these eleven powers ultimately leads to mastering the creative processes in the world of duality.

Initially, it may seem as if these powers are outside of us. That is the way we get to know them, to recognize them. Once we know and recognize them, we may realize that they are inside of us, and by working with them, they become integrated parts of us. Once we become these powers, we can integrate them with the help of the central dragon and function more optimally in the world of duality. When we can see that duality looks at the whole from opposing perspectives, we can move from duality to oneness, which is the ultimate goal.

When we work with dragons from the three-dimensional physical perspective, everything is about the powers and the cycles — understanding, working with, and mastering them. When we integrate these powers, the central dragon will help us to bring them to different levels of expression. That will lead us to mastery of the dualistic world and free us from the bonds of the illusion of this reality.

Connect with the Fire Dragons (Steps 1 and 2)

We begin at the east, fire. For us, being spiritual beings while having a human experience, all beginnings are supposed to emerge from a spiritual perspective. Therefore, the intention for creation needs to come from the highest possible level of consciousness, preferably from the higher self or the soul or from higher dimensions that work through the soul. We need to learn to feel whether an intention is in alignment with our soul and its purpose in this physical reality.

Fire in the east is the power of the beginning, the passion for life and for what we came here to do. Fire is also the element of energy. This direction, based on intention, will create the energy, the passion, to move through the circle. If there is not enough energy — enough passion — you will never complete the circle. In summary, every intention needs to come from the higher self or soul, which means from our hearts. The fire energy and the dragons of the east and the SE help us and support us.

The dragons of the southeast, as the dragons of the east, are connected with the element of fire. They invite us to look actively at who we are to form a concept of self — the way we see ourselves. This concept is, of course, not supposed to be based on what others have told us. The connection with the fire element indicates that our concept of self is not supposed to come from a mental or an emotional perspective but a spiritual one. We need to connect with consciousness, with the higher self or soul, to be able to feel who we are (as seen from this incarnation's perspective) instead of what we think we are supposed to be based on rules and ideas we have taken from others.

The beliefs about who we are based on our experiences and from what others have told us form the personality, or ego. By connecting with consciousness through our higher selves or souls, we can feel the essence of who we are. The ego needs to surrender to the soul and come into alignment with it so that it will not object to the soul's intention. The ego needs to surrender to the soul to be its support system. Without being aware of how we see ourselves and how much that is in alignment with what our hearts say, we can never create our reality in alignment with our soul's purpose. The true self is the ego in its purest form — the ego that is in alignment with the soul's purpose.

All eight qualities of the equator of the duality dragons' sphere constantly interact with each other through forward movements as well as feedback loops. Our concept of self feeds back to the intention we set, and based on our concept of self, it will allow the purity of the intent to be passed on to the next step of the creation cycle, the water of creation, or diminish its power due to lack of belief in self. Low self-esteem will diminish the power of intent considerably.

The dragons of the east hold the wisdom of consciousness. In that sense, it is the feminine aspect of the two fire dragons. The concept of self is the active application of our spiritual essence based on what this concept is, and it induces the expression of our intent in this world. The southeast holds the masculine aspect because it passes on the intent to the next step, the south. The east, the feminine aspect of fire, and the southeast, the masculine aspect of fire, are the duality aspects of the fire element in third-dimensional reality.

In chapter 6, I described the preparation for each meditation to connect with the different dragon species. I provided a general introduction that functions as the starting point of each meditation. I will include it again here, but for future meditations in this chapter, please refer back to this. I also mentioned that I would present a picture of a vortex of the grid of each dragon species with whom we are going to connect. In this case, there are two pictures. See image 7.4 for a vortex of the grid of the east fire dragons, and see image 7.5 for the southeast fire dragons. Look at these two images to prepare yourself so that you can relax and feel comfortable.

—〰—

GENERAL INTRODUCTORY MEDITATION

- Take a few deep inhalations and exhalations, and feel yourself relaxing.
- Bring your awareness as fully as possible to the present.

- Bring your awareness to your physical heart. Your heart is also the location of your spiritual (divine) essence.
- Imagine this essence as a sphere of white light. Allow this white light to shine through your entire physical body. Feel the unconditional love that is inherently connected with this light, and direct this love to yourself.
- Allow the love for yourself to permeate your entire physical system so that your frequency will increase. Feel this unconditional love for yourself, exactly as you are now, without the need to change anything.
- Allow the love to expand out of you and to fill the whole space in which you are seated. If you are with other people, animals, plants, or crystals, as well as the invisible subtle beings in the room, connect with them and together create a coherent field of unconditional love.
- Feel gratitude for all others present, knowing that they support you on this journey.
- From your divine essence, connect with the divine essence of Mother Earth. Feel love for Mother Earth, and feel her love for you. Ask her to support you with her crystalline life force to enable you to optimally work with this energy, knowing that it will make your work with the dragons easier.

FIRE DRAGONS MEDITATION

- Look at the pictures (images 7.4 and 7.5) of the locations for grid vortexes of the east fire dragon and the southeast fire dragon. Both are connected to the elemental power of fire. Connect with the energies of the two vortexes through the pictures. This will allow you to connect with the essence of the elemental power of fire.
- Expand the connection you made with the elemental power of fire to an optimal state, and ask the two fire dragons (the east and the southeast) to help you. Allow some time to allow this process to unfold.
- When deeply connected with the elemental power of fire, focus on the east, on your spiritual essence, your higher

IMAGE 7.4. This is a picture of the location of a vortex of the morphogenetic grid of the duality fire dragons of the east. The little bottle (highlighted) marks the center of the vortex.

IMAGE 7.5. This is a picture of the location of a vortex of the morphogenetic grid of the southeast duality dragons. The bottle marks the center of the vortex.

self, your soul. Fill yourself with your spiritual essence to always be able to set the purest intent whenever you choose to create. Ask the fire dragons of the east to help you in this process.

- Feel the intent to fulfill your soul's purpose to the best of your ability and to be clear so that you choose always to set intentions that are in alignment with your soul's purpose.
- Feel passion for your life and your soul's purpose. If you cannot connect with that passion, set a clear intent to choose to be passionate about fulfilling your soul's purpose. Feel energy generating through your whole system. Sit in this energy for as long as feels right for you.
- From your optimal connection with your spiritual essence, make contact with your perception of self. How do you see yourself? How do you feel about yourself?
- Connect again with the element of fire, and use the power of this element to set the intent to choose to see yourself, to the best of your ability, from the perspective of and in alignment with your divine spiritual essence. Ask the dragons of the southeast to support you.
- Set the intention to bring your spiritual essence and your concept of self into alignment as much as is possible and to make this your daily goal. Sit in this energy for as long as feels good.
- Take a deep breath, and bring your awareness back to the place you are sitting. When you are ready, open your eyes.

Reflect on your experiences. This reflection helps you to become increasingly aware of your journey and that the dragons are allies supporting you. Forgetting this reflection is easy; however, the benefits are great. You could choose to write down your experiences as a way to follow your development and to build on your experiences.

Connect with the Water Dragons (Steps 3 and 4)

The main qualities of the elemental power of water are emotions and creativity, which are located in the south and southwest.

The energy of the intention, filtered and changed through what we believe about who we are (our concept of self as we see ourselves at that moment) is integrated with the creative process. The south is the location of the feminine aspect of water and is the source of creation. The feminine aspect of water receives the information of the intention from the southeast. Water is the creative elemental power, and we see that reflected in our physical world, where the creation of all life takes place.

However, because this direction also refers to our emotional state, our emotional condition functions as a second filter that influences how the creation process, based on the intention, will unfold into a manifestation. In that sense, both the southeast and the south affect the purity of our intention, possibly diminishing its power and affecting the outcome. Also, our emotional condition at the time of creation informs us about the way we see the self. It also influences the energy of the southeast which, in turn, affects our emotional state. This feedback loop diminishes the creative power in many people.

The dragons of the southwest connect with the elemental power of water. Through intent, our self-perception, and emotional state, creation is set in motion. The next step (the southwest) allows the process to unfold. In this phase, we need to trust that we have done everything possible to the best of our ability. The outcome cannot be changed anymore, as we have done all we could do. However, we still are responsible for maintaining the correct circumstances to make it possible for the process to unfold properly. From the perspective of the mind, this seems to be the most passive step of all eight powers. However, it is a creation in action determined by the need to maintain the proper conditions actively. Therefore, in comparison to the south, this is the masculine aspect.

Realize that our emotional state in the south affects the way we allow the unfoldment to proceed. It also affects the way we create the proper conditions during this unfoldment. An optimal unfoldment can only occur when we trust that what we have done was in alignment with our soul purpose and for the greater good of all. Therefore, trust is a key aspect of the process in the southwest.

We have to actively maintain a state of trust along with the optimal conditions that allow unfoldment to proceed. It is similar to a mother being pregnant. She needs to allow the process to unfold while she maintains the optimal conditions for the child's growth. Without trust, the emotions of the water element will interfere with manifestation (which is the next element: the earth element). Alertness is crucial because for most people this is the weakest and most difficult phase. It is a quality that our society does not stimulate very well. Collectively, we are impatient and controlling people. We can compare this process with shooting an arrow from a bow:

- We need to be clear about our aim (intent).
- We need to be aware of our abilities concerning the art of shooting an arrow (self-image).
- We need to bring ourselves into the proper emotional state to create the most optimal condition (creation).
- Finally, we need to let go (unfoldment).

We cannot run after the arrow because we do not trust ourselves. After we have created the most optimal conditions based on our goal, the arrow will land where it lands without our being able to change that result (manifestation).

The following meditation helps you connect with the energies of the dragons that are the guardians of the direction of the south (creativity) and the southwest (unfoldment). Remember to look at the pictures (image 7.6 for the water dragons of the south and image 7.7 for the southwest dragons). The energies of the locations in the pictures will help you to prepare for or deepen your connection. (Remember to begin with the introductory part of the meditation.)

———※※———

WATER DRAGONS MEDITATION

- Look at the two pictures of the locations for grid vortexes of the water dragons of the south (image 7.6) and the southwest (image 7.7). Both vortexes are from grids of dragons connected with the elemental power of water. Connecting through the pictures with the energies of the two vortexes will allow you to connect optimally with the essence of the elemental power of water in the dualistic reality.
- Bring in the energies of the elemental power of water as

IMAGE 7.6. This is a picture of the location of a vortex of the morphogenetic grid of duality water dragons of the south. The bottle marks the center of the vortex.

IMAGE 7.7. This is a picture of the location of a vortex of the morphogenetic grid of the southwest duality dragons. The bottle marks the center of the vortex.

fully as is possible at this moment, and ask both species of water dragons to help you.

- In this state, call the water dragons of the south, and ask them to help you feel your emotional and creative powers. Feel that you can create everything you choose to create. Fill yourself with your creative powers.

- Feel your enthusiasm for creating a life in alignment with your spiritual purpose and with the essence of who you are. Sit in this energy for as long as it feels good.

- Now bring in the powers of the southwest as fully as possible to allow what you set into motion to unfold. Ask the water dragons of the southwest to help you.

- In this state, trust that you have set things in motion to the best of your ability and that you can now allow it to unfold.

- Feel yourself surrender to the unfoldment of what you have created without judgment and in total trust, unwaveringly maintaining the conditions needed for this unfoldment. Sit in this energy for as long as it feels good.

- Take a deep breath, and bring your awareness back to the room. When you are ready, open your eyes.

—⚬⚬⚬—

Remember to reflect on your experiences. Focus on what feels different in comparison to the previous dragons to learn to recognize and work with the energies of the different dragon species. Feel your connection deepen with dragon energies in general and with these two species in particular.

Connect with the Earth Dragons (Steps 5 and 6)

Earth is the element of manifesting form in our physical reality. The element shows us whether we can create what we say we want to create. Also, it shows us how well we have been able to realize the intention we set in the east and whether that came from a clear intent and alignment with our soul purpose. We also see the results of our ability to connect with our true selves with our creativity and whether we can allow things to unfold by maintaining the proper conditions.

The west is the place of harvesting the results of the previous

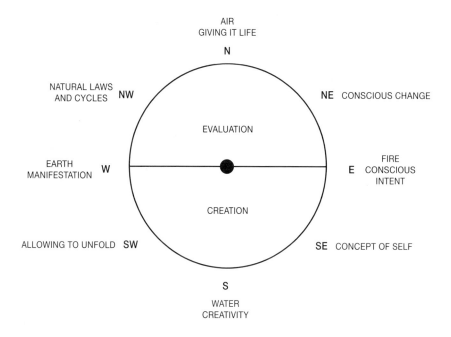

IMAGE 7.8. The circle of the eight duality dragons can be divided into two halves. The lower half represents creation, and the upper half represents evaluation.

steps. The results show us how well we can keep each of the steps in an optimal state. It tells us what works well and what does not. It is interesting that the west is also the direction of harvest in our yearly cycle because this is the place of autumn, which is the time of harvest.

The location of the west is opposite the east. The east-west axis is the axis of creation: intention and the resulting manifestation. The three directions that are below this axis (southeast, south, and southwest) represent the creative elements that determine whether we will accomplish the results we desire. In fact, with the element of earth in the direction of the west, we have completed the creative process.

How alive this creation is and how well it fits within the reality we wish to live will be determined by the next three directions. This aliveness has to do with the way we evaluate the results. Thus, the next three directions are steps of evaluation that determine the aliveness and functionality of our creation (image 7.8).

The dragons of the northwest also connect to the elemental power earth. It is the place where we begin to understand the manifested world and how it operates. It is the place where we learn to see that all manifestations have to be part of the natural laws and rhythms of the world and the universe in which we live. In the energies of the northwest, we experience the degree our manifestation is aligned with natural laws and cycles. If the intention truly comes from a connection with our soul and is not deformed by our self-concept and emotional state, the result will be in alignment with natural laws and rhythms.

The northwest is also the place to learn to accept the flow of natural rhythms and universal laws and the place to understand and work with them. These rhythms can be external (day, lunar month, solar year, and life cycle) as well as internal, such as the twenty-four-hour rhythm of meridians and the rhythm of melatonin production. Acceptance is a critical component of this process.

Cycles are part of the manifested physical world, and we cannot change their laws. By connecting more deeply with these natural laws and cycles, we will understand them better. That will make it possible to see whether we live and create in alignment with them. Animals naturally live in alignment with the cycles and laws of this reality, and they accept and surrender to it, as do plants. However, humans always fight the cycles because of the ideas (mental concepts) we have about how life should be.

The dragons of this direction help us to accept and work with the natural systems of the earth and the universe. The northwest is a strongly active direction and therefore is masculine. It is the direction for understanding cycles and also to align our manifestations with the cycles, rhythms, and laws of the world in which we live to the highest degree possible.

Use images 7.9 and 7.10 to make your connection deeper and more attuned. (Remember to prepare yourself using the general introduction of the meditation.)

—⟋⟍—

EARTH DRAGONS MEDITATION

- Look at the two pictures of the locations for grid vortexes of the duality west dragons (image 7.9) and northwest dragons (image 7.10). Both vortexes are from grids of dragons

IMAGE 7.9. This is a picture of the location of a vortex of the morphogenetic grid of duality earth dragons of the west. The bottle marks the center of the vortex.

IMAGE 7.10. This is a picture of the location of a vortex of the morphogenetic grid of the northwest duality dragons. The bottle marks the center of the vortex.

connected to the elemental power of earth. Connecting with the energies of the two vortexes through the pictures will allow you to connect optimally with the essence of the elemental power of earth.

· Activate the vortexes of the two earth dragon grids to allow you to connect with the essence of the duality earth dragons.

· Invite the elemental power of earth, as optimally as possible, to help you to manifest all that you intend, and ask the duality earth dragons to help you.

· In this state, feel your ability to exactly manifest what you intend and the conditions that support your creation. Feel the power and trust that you can truly manifest whatever you have chosen to manifest.

· Feel the joy of having the power to manifest what you have set into motion. Sit in these energies for as long as feels right for you.

· Now bring in the powers of the northwest, the understanding as well as the ability to work with the laws and rhythms of life. Open yourself to these energies so that you can more easily accept and work with this aspect of physical life. Ask the northwest dragons to help you.

· Feel your willingness to work in harmony with the natural laws and rhythms of life.

· Feel yourself accepting and working with all natural laws and rhythms, knowing that it is the right thing to do.

· Set the intention to bring all that you manifest into alignment with the natural cycles, laws, and rhythms of the world in which we live. Sit in these energies for as long as it feels good.

· Take a deep breath, and bring your awareness back to the room. When you are ready, open your eyes.

—〜〜—

Realize that feedback mechanisms are in play here too. The southwest — the unfoldment — co-determines the manifestation that feeds back to the process of unfoldment and the connected emotions. "Can

I trust the process better, or am I frustrated and doubt myself?" The manifestation affects the natural laws and cycles, whereas these laws and cycles have a feedback effect on the manifestation. Everything in the circle affects everything else through constant feedback loops.

Again, remember to reflect. Are you beginning to feel and better understand the dynamics of the creation process?

Connect with the Air Dragons (Steps 7 and 8)

The north and the northeast are the directions of the elemental power of air, which relates to the breath of life and thus to life force and love. The breath of life is the love of the Creator for the creation. For us, it is the elemental power that connects our thoughts. Our thoughts are ruled by fear or love. It is intended for love to rule, thereby helping us to have clear thoughts.

Thoughts affect and determine the quality of life. When that quality is high, we will breathe properly and have abundant life force to support us. Our thoughts draw, or do not draw, attention and thus life force to the creation. In general, north connects with a mental state, which in turn connects mostly with the mind. However, the mind is the whole N–S axis and is the combination of thoughts and feelings. The north is about thoughts and the process of making the thoughts as pure as possible without the interference of fear-based emotions that often are part of the south.

North is the direction in which we analyze the creation and whether this creation is in alignment with natural laws and rhythms. Here is where we gather insights into how well we have done in the cycle. This process is not about judgment. It is about learning more about yourself by seeing your creation in a way that we can look at it with love and appreciation.

The dragons of the northeast also work with the elemental power of air, and they are the last step of the circle of the eight powers. This final step is realizing through our mental clarity (clarity of thoughts) of what has happened in this circle of creation and how well the creation is in alignment with our souls' purpose.

The northeast is the direction where we apply what we know through the mental clarity of the north to determine what we would like to change. The experiences of the steps through the circle tell us what worked and what did not so that we can change what we want to change. This change, of course, needs to happen in alignment with consciousness, the highest level of awareness. The experiences we have when we move through the circle provide the information that helps us to create the conscious change of this direction: the change we want to bring into the intention of the next cycle of creation.

Again, be aware of the feedback process. The degree of alignment of the manifestation with the natural laws and cycles will influence the way we think about the manifestation. Our thoughts influence the energy of the natural harmony of this world. The way we think about the manifestation also affects the idea of what to change. The idea of what to change, in turn, affects the conscious intent in the east, where we start a new cycle. If we do not change our way of thinking based on our experiences, we could repeat the same way of doing things that result in similar or even less desirable outcomes, creating demotivation. Repeated demotivation may lead to depression.

As was mentioned, the number 8 is an invitation for active creation and renewal. It invites us to do things differently so that every cycle is a contribution to the process of raising our vibration. We have forgotten the meaning of the power of 8. Thus, we do not use the creation cycle properly, and as a consequence, the results are often not good for us. Working with the dragons and understanding this cycle makes it possible to turn the process around so that we create a life of joy, happiness, abundance, and love.

Let us connect with the dragons who can help us with the two directions of the elemental power of air. Use images 7.11 and 7.12 to make a deeper connection. (Remember to prepare yourself with the introductory part of the meditation.)

—ɯ—

AIR DRAGONS MEDITATION

- Look at the two pictures of the locations of grid vortexes of the air dragons of the north (image 7.11) and the northeast (image 7.12). Both vortexes are from grids of dragons connected to the elemental power of air. Connecting with the energies of the two vortexes will help you to connect optimally with the essence of the elemental power of air.

IMAGE 7.11. This is a picture of the location of a vortex of the morphogenetic grid of duality air dragons of the north. The bottle marks the center of the vortex.

IMAGE 7.12. This is a picture of the location of a vortex of the morphogenetic grid of the northeast duality dragons. The bottle marks the center of the vortex.

- Now connect with the energies of the vortexes of the air dragon grid to allow you to connect with the essence of the elemental power of air as optimally as possible.
- Call on the powers of the elemental power of air (the north), and ask the air dragons to help you.
- In this state, feel your ability to use your mental abilities from a clear and loving place. Trust that you will be able to be in this state in every situation to the best of your ability.
- Feel the joy of having this clear and loving way of thinking. Sit in this energy for as long as feels comfortable.
- Now call on the powers of the northeast to support your mental clarity to make the change you have chosen. Ask the northeast dragons to help you.
- In this state, feel the clarity of what you want to change in your life, especially those aspects that you learned during this past creation cycle.
- Feel your willingness to make these changes and apply them in your life. Sit in these energies for as long as feels good.
- Take a deep breath, and bring your awareness back to the room. When you are ready, open your eyes.

—∭—

Reflect on your experiences, feelings, and insights. You have completed the cycle. Feel proud that you have made a deeper connection with the elemental powers that can help you to function and to create more efficiently and harmoniously with your soul's purpose.

To connect even more deeply with the eight powers of the circle, to expand and optimize them, we need to include the three dragons of the central axis.

The Dragons of the North and the South Poles

I've described the discovery of the black and white dragons (chapter 6). The black dragon is the dragon of the south pole, and the white dragon is the dragon of the north pole of the sphere of the duality dragons (image 7.2). The black dragons connect you with all the grids of the duality dragons. In these grids, we find those aspects from the morphogenetic field of the duality dragons that we actively use or have used. Consequently, what is in the grids is only a part of what is in the field. The energies and information in the grids depend on our consciousness because we collectively determine with which part of the field we work.

The white dragons connect you with everything held within the morphogenetic field of the duality dragons, which holds their full potential. This morphogenetic field is a subfield of the total dragon morphogenetic field, which in turn is a subfield of the Gaia morphogenetic field. The purpose is to master the gifts of the duality dragons in such a way that the information found in the grids increasingly matches what is available in the field. The white and the black dragons are part of the central axis and directly connect with the central dragon.

To connect with the black and the white dragons, focus on the pictures of the vortex of their grids (images 7.13 and 7.14). Remember to prepare yourself with the introductory part of the meditation, and continue with the following.

—∿∿—

THE BLACK AND WHITE DRAGONS MEDITATION

- Focus on the pictures of the vortex of the grids of the black dragons (image 7.13) and the white dragons (image 7.14). Connecting with the pictures allows you to connect with the energies of the grids of the black and the white duality dragons.
- In your imagination, connect even more fully with the vortex of the duality black dragons grid to experience the energy of these dragons to the most optimal level possible.
- Feel the energies, and be aware of your connection with all the information from the duality dragons available in the grids. Sit in this energy for as long as feels good.
- Now, in your imagination, connect with the vortex of the grid of the white dragons of the duality group to the most optimal level possible.
- Feel the energies, and be aware that you are now connected with the full potential of all the duality dragons.

IMAGE 7.13. This is a picture of the location of a vortex of the morphogenetic grid of the duality black dragons. The bottle marks the center of the vortex.

IMAGE 7.14. This is a picture of a vortex of the morphogenetic grid of the duality white dragons. The bottle marks the center of the vortex.

- Set the intent that you bring more information from the field into the grids to the level that is most optimal for the Gaia system and all beings within it. Sit in this energy for a while.
- Take a deep breath, and bring your awareness back to the room. When you are ready, open your eyes.

—ᵐ—

The meditation and the connection with these two dragon species help you to connect deeper with the energies of the duality dragons, with those that are already available as well as their full potential. Be aware that no one can connect with all the energies of the duality dragons. However, we all make unique connections, and in that process, we can be channels for energies from the field that we can bring into the grids. Only when we open ourselves are we able to fulfill such a function.

This requires training and dedication. However, that is true for everything we choose to do in our lives and wish to master.

The Dragons of the Center: Completion

The dragons of the center are more than an addition to the energies of the powers of the duality dragons. They have a unique function. We have not yet reached oneness, and that is not the function of the central duality dragons. However, when you have mastered the powers of the duality dragons sufficiently and can align with them harmoniously through the central dragons, you move in the direction of oneness.

The function of the central duality dragons is to steer the progression through the cycle and ensure that it is completed optimally. The size of their grid reflects the importance of the central dragons. All eight dragons of the circle and the dragons of the north and south poles have grids with lines and vortexes about the same size. All eleven networks are based on irregular rectangles. However, the grids of the central dragons are larger and therefore different from all others.

Connecting with the central dragon is not only a completion of the steps to optimally create in the third dimension but also can enable the completion of your connection with the existing duality dragon species. You may call on the central dragons to feel whether you completed the cycle. It is important to connect regularly with these dragons to feel the degree of completion. These dragons can help you determine which of the elemental powers is unbalanced during the creation process and whether it is the feminine or masculine aspect that does not function optimally. You then can call on the aid of the dragons of the unbalanced or weaker power.

You should work with the central dragons daily. They are also the bridge between the black and the white dragons. They regulate your connection with these two dragons based on the degree of connection you have with the eight duality dragons of the circle.

To summarize: The central dragons help us to complete our creation optimally in this reality. In other words, they help us to fulfill our life purpose as far as it relates to third-dimensional reality. Finally, they help us to master all powers connected with creation in third-dimensional, physical reality by connecting us to the grids and the fields supported by the black and white dragons.

Imagine that the black dragons draw information from the grids into each of the eight powers (the circle of eight), and they draw the white dragons' information from the field. Then imagine the energies of the eight powers flowing into the central dragons, who bring it all together into one, completing the mastery of the powers of creation in the third dimension. Realize that you determine the power of each of these flows.

To prepare yourself for your connection with the central duality dragons, look at the picture (image 7.15) of a vortex of the grid of these dragons. Remember to prepare with the introductory meditation, and continue with the following.

—〜〜—

CENTRAL DRAGONS MEDITATION

- Look at the image of a vortex of the grid of the central duality dragons (image 7.15). Connect with these energies through this picture to the best of your ability.
- Now connect with the vortex of the central dragons' grid more fully to promote the most optimal connection.

IMAGE 7.15. This is a picture of the location of a vortex of the morphogenetic grid of the duality central dragons. The bottle marks the center of the vortex.

- Call on the powers of the central dragons and the energies of completion to integrate the elemental powers of the circle, the energies of the grids, and the field of the duality dragons into one dynamic, harmonious flow. Ask the central dragons to help you do this optimally.
- Feel your ability to complete whatever you want to complete. Feel the increase in ability to integrate and master the powers of creation in the three-dimensional physical reality.
- Feel yourself accept everything this completion brings and that you will always use these increasing powers and abilities for the greatest good of all. Sit in these energies for as long as it feels right.
- Take a deep breath, and bring your awareness back to the room. When you are ready, open your eyes.

Reflect on the completion of your connection with the duality dragons. Feel the power of your ability to complete and to always go to the most optimal situation for you in each creation cycle. Feel your gratitude for all the dragons' support.

Become the Full Power of the Sphere of the Duality Dragons Energies

After having connected with all the duality dragons, most people want to function as the central dragon. The central dragon reflects our mastery over the powers of creation in our dualistic, physical reality. To possess such mastery, we need to be able to connect with all the powers of the sphere. Otherwise, we cannot resonate optimally with the energies and function of the central duality dragon. Even when we are not yet resonating optimally, it is possible to imagine that you are in the center of the sphere. Seeing yourself in the center of the sphere will bring you closer to functioning as the central dragon. You can do this process daily.

Also realize that although we can separate the different powers that play a role in the way we function in this reality, the truth is that it is one dynamic flow. We make many decisions/choices each moment, and these choices all have a circle of activity. That means all the powers/energies of the duality dragons are in action continuously. Understanding, feeling, and experiencing these energies allow us to bring them to a more optimal state and in alignment with each other. Consequently, everything in our lives flows better.

You Are the Sphere

In the final meditation of this chapter, we will bring more aliveness to the sphere of creative power and potential. It will help you to realize that as a cocreator in this reality, you are the sphere. All energies of the sphere are within you. However, you determine how well it functions and how well you have mastered the potential that this sphere offers you.

If you like, you can prepare yourself for this meditation by looking again at the eleven pictures of the vortexes of the grids of the duality dragons. Then remember to start with the introductory part of the meditation and continue with the following.

—∿∿—

SPHERE MEDITATION

- Be aware, in a general sense, of the sphere with its equator, the eight powers, and the central axis with its north and south poles and center (image 7.2).
- Be aware of the vortexes of the grids of the eleven dragons (review the photos) that you have connected with, and set the intention to connect with all their energies to support the journey you are about to start. Trust that you are now fully connected with all their energies.
- Bring your awareness to the east — the elemental power of fire, the duality fire dragons, and the place of spirituality and conscious intention. Feel your decision to always set the clearest intention from the highest possible state of consciousness. Use the energy and passion of this direction to set this intention into motion. Do this with the intention to be in full alignment with your soul's purpose. Ask the duality fire dragons of the east to help you. Feel the energy inside of you.
- Move one step clockwise to the southeast, and open yourself to the second fire direction, which helps you to connect with your concept (your idea) of yourself to be able to give form to the intention, to hold all aspects of the purity of that intention. Call in the southeast dragons to support you to align your self-concept as optimally as possible with your spiritual essence. Feel the energies in motion inside you.
- Move one step to the south — to the elemental power of water, the duality water dragons, and the place of emotionality and creativity. Feel your ability to create an emotional state that will optimally support the creation of your intention. From this emotional state, allow the creativity to flow through you. Become the creative power. Feel that you can trust that you can create anything based on your intention as long as it is in alignment with your true self. Ask the duality water dragons to help you with this process. Feel the energies you have set into motion.

- Move to the next point on the circle, which is the southwest — the next direction of the elemental power of water and the place of unfoldment. This direction represents the moment where you are asked to trust that what you set into motion is all that you can do. Therefore, this is the moment of letting go of any control.
- At this moment in the process, you need to trust that all is perfect and just allow the process to unfold. Feel the willingness to allow this unfoldment under the most optimal conditions and that you will do everything to maintain these conditions in that optimal state. Feel your trust and your willingness. Ask the southwest dragons to help you with this trust and willingness. Feel the energies that belong to this direction.
- The next point of the circle is the west — the place of the elemental power of earth and the duality earth dragons. This direction is the place of manifestation, the place of seeing and experiencing the result of the intention you set in the east. In this direction, you can experience joy as well as disappointment. In the west, you are invited to fully accept the result of your creation. Feel the acceptance of your creation. Ask the duality earth dragons to help you. Feel the energies this direction has set into motion for you.
- Now move to the northwest — the direction of the next earth elemental power and the place of the natural laws and rhythms. Feel the acceptance of these laws and rhythms as a natural aspect of who you are and of the environment in which you live. Feel your willingness to always check whether the manifestation is in alignment with the natural rhythms and cycles and supports you and the Gaia system as a whole. Also feel your connection with these cycles and rhythms and feel your willingness to live and create in alignment with them to allow the flow of creation to move unhampered. Ask the northwest dragons to help you. Feel what is set into motion by this power, by this direction.
- Move to the next point, the north — the place of the

elemental power of air of the duality air dragons. This direction holds the mental energy. This direction is the place where the thoughts about your creation ignite aliveness or something that will be forgotten soon. It is the place where you bring life force into your creation through its mental acceptance so that it can establish its place in the whole. At this place, it is important to accept all your thoughts about your creations and make them supportive. Feel that your thoughts determine the amount of life force that will connect with the manifestation. Ask the north duality air dragons to help you. Feel what this has set energetically in motion within you.

- Now move to the last step of the circle, the northeast — the place of the northeast dragons, the place of the next air elemental power, and the location of conscious change. Here, you decide to change what you want to change based on the experiences of the previous seven steps. In this direction, you prepare for the new intention. This change can only become clear with mental clarity and connection to our spiritual essence, our souls. Feel your decision to make changes only from this perspective. Ask the northeast dragons to support you. Feel what happens with energies of this direction as fully as possible.

- Now bring your attention to the south pole of the sphere, the place of the black duality dragons. Here, you can connect with the energies of the grids of all the duality dragon species. Feel that your ability to connect with these energies has increased, and ask the black dragons to make this connection even fuller.

- Now bring your attention to the north pole of the sphere, the place of the white duality dragons. At this location, you can connect with the morphogenetic field of the duality dragons, which holds their full potential. In collaboration with the white dragons, you can bring those energies from the field into the grids that create the most optimal situation for the greatest good of all. Ask the white dragons to help you with this process.

- Finally, bring your awareness to the center of the circle — the place of the central dragons: integration and completion. Feel for yourself whether having gone through the cycle and making the connections with the black and white dragons results in a feeling of completion. If not, feel to the best of your ability what is incomplete. Do this without judgment, because it all is part of your growth and development. If you have a feeling of completion, ask for joy and happiness to fill you. That will make it easier to complete things in the future. Ask the central dragons to help you with this process.
- You have now made a connection with all the duality dragons. Feel that you have taken an important step on your path to mastering the duality reality. Know that you always can invite the dragons to help you further master the creation process in the third-dimensional reality.
- Trust that you have reached the most optimal state for now. Sit in these energies for as long as feels good for you to allow them to integrate.
- Take a deep breath, and bring your awareness back to the room. When you are ready, open your eyes.

—⟋⟋⟍—

You have completed your journey with the duality dragons. Know, however, that this journey is only complete to the level that is optimal for you at this moment. Through a deep connection and collaboration with the elemental powers and their guardians — the dragons — you will be able to master the creative process. Once you see that your intention and the consequent manifestation are in complete alignment, you truly understand the creation process. A way to support this process is by looking at the correspondence of the duality dragons with the chakras.

Duality Dragons and Chakras

It was mentioned in chapter 4 that the chakras correspond with many systems. Correspondence does not mean that they are identical; rather they resonate with each other to various degrees. It was also mentioned that the different dragon groups correspond with the chakra system. As will become apparent, these correspondences result in seemingly contradictory connections. However, while going through the correspondences with the different groups, the pattern may become clearer.

Also, remember that the chakra system resonates with the earth, and the dragons are also part of the earth. It would be almost illogical to believe that there is no resonance. Earth's chakra system and our chakra system have a wide range of frequencies.

Different groups of beings (we will look at some of them in chapter 12) resonate with different chakras or different aspects of chakras. Also, the order may not always seem to be in alignment. Table 7.1 gives a summary of the correspondences and relationships between the duality dragons and the chakras.

DUALITY DRAGONS	CHAKRA(S)
Fire, East — Intent	8 and 9 (etheric and astral bodies)
Fire Southwest — Self-Reflection	7 (crown chakra)
Water, South — Creativity	6 (brow chakra, third eye)
Water, Southeast — Allowing to Unfold	5 (throat chakra)
Air, North — Thoughts, Life Force	4 (heart chakra)
Air, Northeast — Conscious Change	3 (solar plexus)
Earth, Northwest — Cycles, Rhythms	2 (sacral chakra)
Earth, West — Manifestation	1 (root chakra)

TABLE 7.1. Listed are correspondences between duality dragons and human chakras.

The correspondences may confuse you in two ways. First, the order does not seem to fit. Second, there are only nine chakras involved. To understand correspondences, you need to release linear thinking. We talk about vibrational systems that resonate with each other. Each of these systems has different aspects, and these aspects resonate with each other regardless of the order in which we believe they need to function. You might remember that all eight steps of the creation circle are working at the same time; thus it is with the chakras.

When we examine correspondences, we look at the systems that most optimally resonate with each other, and at the same time, we are aware that both systems are always fully operational. Correspondences are meant to help us understand aspects of the functioning of systems to obtain an idea of what does and does not work, helping us to choose what and how to change. If you return to the table, the correspondences may now make more sense.

Duality dragons help us to function in the three-dimensional physical world. The chakras involved at this level of functioning are the chakras connected with the physical (chakras 1 to 7), etheric (chakra 8), and astral (chakra 9) bodies. The bodies of the soul are not directly involved in the way we function in the three-dimensional world. They are only involved to the degree that they can reach and affect the etheric and astral systems.

When we function more optimally, the eighth and ninth chakras will become a better bridge between the physical and the spiritual. The connection with the bodies of the soul (emotional, mental, and spiritual — the tenth, eleventh, and twelfth chakras respectively) will become more open and increasingly will guide us into functioning in the fourth-dimensional physical world, the world in which the oneness dragons function.

Also, note that the energies of the central axis are not directly connected to the chakras. They can make working the eight steps more efficient, and in that way, they contribute to the chakras functioning more optimally. If you can release linear thinking and learn to feel the energies of the corresponding systems, they can be very helpful on your journey of expansion and development.

The Sixty-Four Frequency Systems

Initially, I did not want to include the following information. However, this book is a collaboration with the dragons, and they have a say about content. They prefer that I include it even though I have not grasped the fullness of the meaning of what I am about to share.

The information about the sixty-four frequencies started when I discovered that the way the duality dragons function and relate is best represented by a sphere (image 7.2). One day I was playing with the images. I drew lines from the north pole to the eight powers on

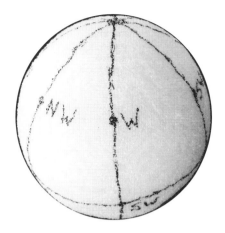

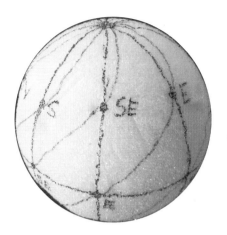

IMAGE 7.16. A Styrofoam sphere showing that the eights points on the equator
of the duality dragon sphere are part of
eight circumferences that each holds the
same eight qualities. In this way, sixty-
four qualities are created.

IMAGE 7.17. A Styrofoam sphere showing that when you connect the same
eight qualities, eight wavy lines are
created.

the equator and the south pole. That created eight different circumferences that went through two of the eight powers. That led to a
flash of insight: Each of these eight circumferences also have all eight
elemental powers. That means that there are sixty-four powers.

Each of the eight powers has eight expressions that are in complete resonance with all eight elemental powers. Image 7.16 presents
this information. When you connect all eight points on the sphere
that represent the same power, for example, the northeast, a wave-
form (image 7.17) is produced. Image 7.18 provides another overview
showing all the lines involved.

The full implication of these sixty-four energies is still unknown.
It shows that the creative powers in three-dimensional reality form
a dynamic system that is more complex than was initially described.
When we make a deeper connection with the eight elemental powers
and connect more deeply with the information in the grids and the
field, we will fine-tune the energies and flow in our creative expression in ways that we cannot yet imagine.

The interesting aspect of this description is that it corresponds

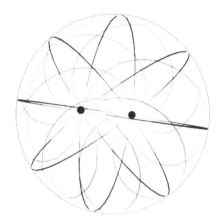

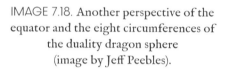

IMAGE 7.18. Another perspective of the equator and the eight circumferences of the duality dragon sphere (image by Jeff Peebles).

IMAGE 7.19. The Chinese bagua with the eight directions marked by trigrams, as used in feng sui.

to the Chinese system of the bagua and the I Ching (image 7.19). The bagua (the literal meaning in Chinese is "eight symbols") is eight trigrams used in Taoist cosmology to represent the fundamental principles of reality, seen as a range of eight interrelated concepts. Each consists of three lines, and each line is either broken or unbroken, representing yin or yang, respectively. Due to their tripartite structure, they are often referred to as trigrams in English. There is a strong correspondence with the eight dragons of the equator as we described in this chapter.

The eight symbols, or trigrams, can be combined to form hexagrams. The total number of hexagrams you can create with these eight trigrams is sixty-four. These sixty-four hexagrams form the basis of the *I Ching*, or *The Book of Changes*. The *I Ching* is a classical text that is estimated to be over two-and-a-half millennia old. People use it as a divination text. The interpretations and translations vary considerably. The parallel between the sixty-four elemental powers and the sixty-four hexagrams is striking. As interesting as it is and as much as it may help us to understand these energies and powers and how they influence our lives and our ability to change reality, it is something that is a study in and of itself and falls outside the scope of this book.

CHAPTER 8

Create with
the Oneness Dragons

THE DRAGONS THEMSELVES HAVE DIRECTED the order in which to consider the different dragon groups. In the previous chapter, we discussed the duality dragons and their connected elemental power. In this chapter, we will discuss the oneness dragons. In the overview of dragon species (image 6.1, chapter 6), this group has twelve species, seen at the equator of the sphere, and three species located on the central axis: the group of the 12 + 3 dragons.

These dragons guide us to a state of oneness in physical reality. They are a logical and automatic follow-up to the duality dragons. Mastery of the duality dragons is not a precondition to working with the oneness dragons. However, it is easier to connect with them when at least some work has been undertaken with the duality dragons.

Oneness is a requirement in ascension and also a state of being leading to awakening and enlightenment. For most people, achieving the state of oneness is a challenging process because it necessitates letting go of all concepts established from life in a world of duality and the world of five senses. The world of the senses is a world of

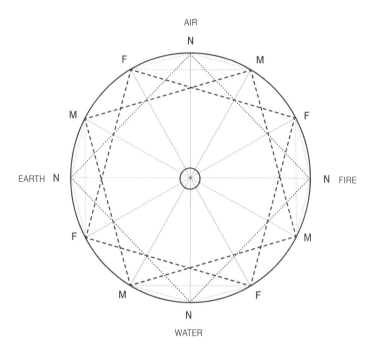

IMAGE 8.1. This sphere shows the twelve dragons of the equator of the oneness dragons assembled in three groups of four: neutral/child (N), feminine (F), and masculine (M).

illusions. The oneness dragons will help us with the shift required to perceive the world as it really is.

In a dualistic world, we see a world with opposing forces demanding a choice of one force. The first step in moving into oneness is to abandon seeing the 12 + 3 dragon system as a system of opposites that works separately. However, because we still live mostly in duality, we can begin by looking at the powers connected with the oneness dragons with dualistic eyes: seeing three groups of four (image 8.1). By understanding the energies of these powers, we will be able to shift our awareness into four groups of three, each holding oneness within each elemental power (image 8.2). The approach is the way out of duality into oneness. There no longer is a need to choose between opposing forces because the opposing forces are part of a trinity. In a trinity, there is no separation; all three aspects are always active at the same time. This is the subject of this chapter, and the oneness dragons help us to achieve this way of functioning.

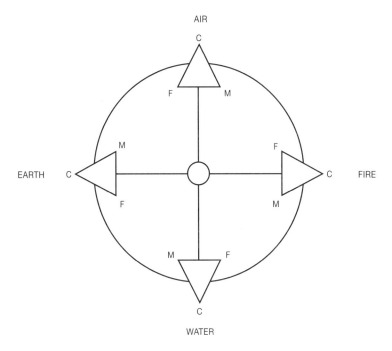

IMAGE 8.2. This sphere shows the twelve dragons of the equator of the oneness dragons assembled in four groups of three: feminine (F), masculine (M), and child/neutral (C).

In the previous chapter, we considered dragons as beings who represent powers that we need to function and create in the dualistic physical world. We were invited to internalize these powers. Nevertheless, we still tend to see the dragons as outside us. This perspective is not surprising given that the duality dragons are part of living and experiencing duality.

Through the central axis of the sphere of the duality dragons, we opened the door to train ourselves to internalize the duality aspects of the elemental powers. This internalization is a preparation for working with the oneness dragons. This step was essential because by working with the duality dragons, we overcome duality and begin to experience and ultimately be in a state of oneness.

True oneness means that we are one with the dragons. We are truly becoming one energy system, one being. This state is similar to what is portrayed in the movie *Avatar*[1] in which there are two groups of beings, the Na'vi and the dragons. However, as soon as they connect (in the movie, the connection is physical), they function as one. Such unity is the purpose of working with the oneness dragons. We are invited to connect so deeply that we become the dragons completely.

When we connect with the oneness dragons, we continue to work with the four elements. Although these aspects connect us with physical reality, we are working at a much higher vibration. In other words, these fifteen oneness dragons help us to increase our vibration and prepare us for supporting the process of Gaia's ascension. As we work with the oneness dragons, we learn to feel the essence of these elements. **It is no longer about working with energies of the elemental power but rather becoming the elemental power.**

Working with the oneness dragons will also lead to an ability to work with the elemental powers as part of creating a balanced world. Working optimally at this level with an elemental power means not only being the elemental power but also feeling and working with all aspects of it. You only can work optimally with an elemental power when you work with the triad, the trinity, of it. There is a trinity for each of the four elements. Consequently, there will be twelve powers; thus, there are twelve dragons in the circle of the equator of the sphere (image 8.1). The central dragon helps to harmonize the four trinities into a balanced form of functioning in a state of oneness. The north pole and south pole dragons bring in the aspects of the twelve energies from the morphogenetic field (north pole) and the morphogenetic grid (south pole).

In the previous chapter, we looked at creation as a progression of paired steps connecting with one of the elemental powers. The movement was circular. In our world, we see that this circular motion leads easily to becoming stuck in the creative process. We circle, without progression, repeating the same patterns. The circling pattern is a consequence of the way the mind operates. As we tend to function from certain similar emotional patterns and similar belief structures, we keep circling at more or less the same level. A perfect path to mastering duality is being willing to earnestly look within and make changes in the northeast, the place of the dragons who support conscious change, which is the key to growth.

Another challenge in the dualistic world is the tendency to look mainly at the four elemental powers and not at the eight, the dualistic expressions of these four elemental powers. The consequence is that most people mainly work with three steps (see image 4.12 in chapter 4).

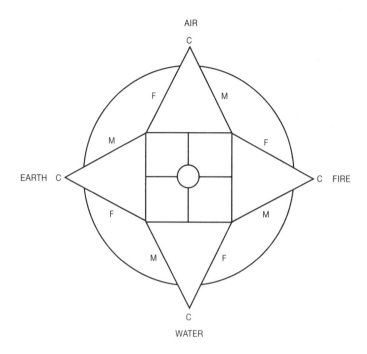

IMAGE 8.3. This sphere shows the four trinities of the twelve dragons of the equator of the oneness dragons represented as a pyramid folded open.

They have an idea, and then they add to that idea some creative elements from their emotional states, and then they manifest it. In this way, they use creation entirely from the physical perspective.

We have discussed that we also need to consider spiritual aspects in creation. When we include the spiritual aspects, the intention does not come from the mind but the spiritual intent. Ultimately, we bring the emotions from the physical and spiritual systems into alignment. We do the same with thoughts. We create from the spiritual triangle and manifest in the physical. That is the teaching of the oneness dragons, explaining the reason there is a trinity for each of the four elemental powers. In this way, we include the spiritual aspects (the higher aspects) of each of the four elements, leading to the state of oneness.

There are some powerful aspects of this system. Built into the four triangles of the oneness dragons is a deeper understanding of other aspects of our growth. When we bring the four triangles of image 8.2 together, they form a square on the inside, and with the four triangles, we get a pyramid folded open (image 8.3). The square

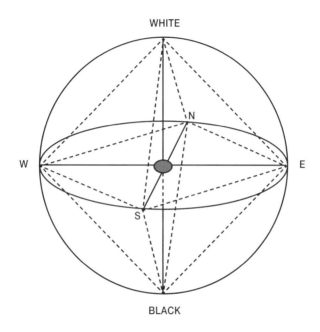

IMAGE 8.4. This shows the pyramid and its counterpart,
creating an octahedron in a sphere.

forms the base and together with the four triangles, when folded up,
forms a perfect pyramid.

So much can be said about a pyramid. Within this context, it is
important to realize that when there is a pyramid, there also is its
counterpart, its mirror image. You can fold the four triangles up as
well as down. Together, they form an octahedron (shown by the dotted lines in image 8.4). The octahedron is a Platonic solid that assists
to move beyond space and time as we know it. This functional aspect
of an octahedron is interesting since going into a state of oneness
changes our perception of space and time.

It is not very surprising that the dragon systems are based on an
octahedron. Astrophysicists have discovered that the structure of the
universe is based on the shape of the repeating octahedron, which led
to the description of the universe as an egg carton.[2]

There are a total of four triangles. When you group the four triangles in a certain way (image 8.5) and fold them, you produce a
tetrahedron (image 8.6). The tetrahedron is a three-dimensional

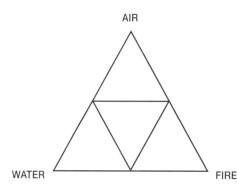

AIR

WATER   FIRE

IMAGE 8.5. The four trinities of the twelve oneness dragons form a triangle that can be folded into a tetrahedron (see image 8.6).

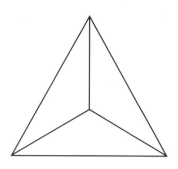

IMAGE 8.6. A tetrahedron.

representation of the twelve, reflecting the four elemental powers (four sides) and the trinity (the triangles).

We looked at the tetrahedron previously and mentioned that it is also the building block of all Platonic solids. Platonic solids are the basis of the matrix through which creation of physical reality takes place. It may become clear that there are many correspondences within the system of the oneness dragons. Also, the tetrahedron represents the universe that holds the consciousness from which everything is created. Consider the tetrahedron as the consciousness where creation begins.

The original crystal skulls, the information system of the Star Nations, is also based on the number twelve (plus the one in the center).[3] The original crystal skulls and the ones that people carved in their image in a later phase are all made of quartz. The basis of the molecular structure (matrix) of quartz is the tetrahedron. Quartz is a material that helps us to connect with universal consciousness beyond our current limitations and helps us to connect more deeply with our spirituality.

We previously mentioned that the number 4 represents the four elemental powers required for creation (the number 4 represents the potential of creation). We need eight to continuously renew and create through time and in space (9 represents the dynamic of creation). However, only twelve makes it possible to use all potentials and possibilities.[4] You need twelve to work out the full potentialities by including the numbers 2, 3, and 4. The number 12 is the first number that can do so. When we look at image 8.2, we see six meridians representing polarity (the number 2 [6 x 2 = 12]). We see the trinity of the four elemental powers (the small broken triangles [4 x 3 = 12]), and we see three sets of the elemental powers (the three squares [3 x 4 = 12]).

Twelve gives us a world of potentials and possibilities to express through the simultaneous action of the numbers 2, 3, and 4. We see a similar phenomenon in the zodiac, which is intended as a system to understand the universe, similar to the oneness dragons. Unfortunately, over time people diluted this wisdom.

The Journey to Oneness

In our dualistic world, people are increasingly open to the idea of oneness. However, oneness is an idea that has many levels and expressions. Most people long for it but lack a clear understanding of what it is. We can easily understand duality because we experience it daily. We learn through differences, and as such, it is a useful tool to understand the world and to learn what you do and do not resonate with. However, many people have come to a sufficiently clear understanding of the principles of duality to feel ready to move on to oneness.

One view of oneness is that opposites are two sides of the same coin. We can also say that opposing forces are different degrees of the same phenomenon. However, this does not provide a clear enough tool with which to work. To master duality and move on to oneness, a third factor is needed: the coin or the phenomenon. The third factor creates a trinity, which offers a basis for many systems to facilitate the understanding of oneness.

Oneness is inherent in all higher dimensional systems beyond the physical. The whole idea of our incarnation is to bring that oneness into physical reality. The dragons help us to do so. It is only through bringing oneness into the physical that the whole system will ascend. We need to master duality sufficiently before we can understand oneness.

Duality works within the three-dimensional, physical world as most people perceive it. The duality dragons help us to function while we perceive the world from this perspective of duality. Oneness works within the whole of Gaia, the third and fourth dimensions, the visible and invisible. The oneness dragons help us to function in a way that we become one with all of Gaia. The duality dragons help mainly with creating the physical and emotional aspects of life. The oneness dragons cover the higher mental and spiritual aspects of our lives. They teach us to be in the physical from a spiritual perspective (fourth dimension).

In oneness, the elemental powers work together at the same time. If one of these powers, or the way we work with them, is inharmonious, it can throw us out of the state of oneness into duality. In duality, the powers seem to work in separate steps with different functions. In the state of oneness, we use the elemental powers through a connection with what they do and how they contribute to giving form to this world. In both cases, we have the opportunity to master aspects of the elemental powers.

The Trinity of the Elemental Powers

At the level of oneness, each of the four elemental powers expresses itself through the trinity, indicating that each power has a feminine, masculine, and child/neutral aspect. As mentioned previously, all four elemental powers are working at the same time, as are the trinity aspects of each of the four elemental powers. Based on our connection, and following the guidance of the soul, each of the twelve energy qualities of this system will function in alignment with what we need in each moment and contributes to the ever-unfolding expression of our consciousnesses.

This process is not something you need to analyze because it is part of the way things function on the oneness level. On the level of duality, the third-dimensional level, we need to know, understand, and work with it. As we do, our connection with the elemental powers develops and reaches such a level that we begin to function on the level of oneness. Through this awakening, we will again know how to connect and work with these powers on the oneness level. It is no longer about thinking what to do but rather about connecting and allowing things to unfold. In the duality dragon system, allowing unfoldment is one step of the process. With the oneness dragons, it is an inherent part of the whole process.

In the first phase of functioning in oneness, we connect with the trinity aspects of each of the four elemental powers to awaken the connection and the knowledge. We can only do this when our vibration is high enough. A willingness to continuously raise our vibration is essential to awaken our potential of working optimally with the energies of the oneness dragons and of connecting permanently without falling back into the energies of duality.

In the same way we worked with the two dragons of each elemental power in the previous chapter, we will work in this chapter with the three (trinity) dragons of each of the four elemental powers. See it as a continuation of the process of awakening. However, be aware that we may tend to see the three aspects of the trinity as separate powers, or forces. To understand the principles, we will describe these powers separately. However, as I mentioned, you cannot separate them. The dragons who are the guardians of the four trinities each have their own morphogenetic grid.

The fact that guardians are separated means we can define them in separate ways, but they function as one system. To experience the three aspects of the trinity as one may be the most difficult thing to grasp in working with the elemental powers. At the same time, it offers the opportunity to train ourselves to understand that although we may think they are separate systems, we work with one dynamic, interactive, and interwoven system.

There are fifteen morphogenetic grids for the oneness dragons. However, as with the duality dragons, there is only one morphogenetic field, a subfield of the total dragon morphogenetic field. The consciousness of Gaia expressed through the oneness dragon morphogenetic field creates the fifteen dragons and their respective morphogenetic grids.

The Three Oneness Fire Dragons

The three oneness fire dragons assist you to become one with your soul (spiritual essence); that is, to act together in optimal alignment. The passion, purpose, and love of the soul are the guiding forces in this world, and the degree to which you can allow your passion (purpose) to come through into your physical system determines the level of consciousness from which you work and create in this physical world. When we refer to spiritual essence, we are talking about the divine spark that exists within every being. In the case of humans, we call it the soul, higher self, or soul fragment. The soul is the key aspect of our spiritual essence from which we are invited to work in this physical reality.

As mentioned previously, the challenge in understanding the oneness dragons is that we describe a trinity as separate forces, but we must realize that they are not separate and never will be. The neutral, or child, aspect represents the aspect that gives life to the spiritual essence in this physical world through unconditional love, inducing the experience of oneness in the human mind. Love from the soul for the physical world results in love for your physical life. The child aspect helps to connect to the purity of consciousness, the love aspect of consciousness. This love determines the quality of your spiritual essence and thus consciousness, which comes through in your physical system.

The energy of the feminine oneness fire dragons helps us to feel and experience the conscious intent that comes from the spiritual essence. While the neutral aspect is the intent, the essence of the intent — the feminine aspect — helps us to feel the intent in such a way that we become the intent energetically. This feeling and experience are needed to be able to set the energy of the intent into motion on the level of oneness.

The masculine is the induction, the activation of the intent, the setting into motion of the intent. The feminine aspect feels the intent in such a way that the energy flows (feeling the passion as well as the passion for the passion). The totality of this trinity is the power of Divine intent. This approach leads to cocreatorship in the physical world in its fullness. The duality aspects help us to understand how to function in the physical reality in daily life. The oneness aspect of the physical world creates in the physical reality with the purpose of changing, transforming, enhancing, and ascending. At this level of creation, you remain connected with spirituality throughout the whole creation process. Creating in a state of oneness is not taking one step at a time but rather having all aspects fully active and continuously creating while you are in full connection with all of them.

In the physical world, your intent can come from your mind as a reaction to the world around you (duality). When it comes from you being an integrated part of the world, you create at the level of oneness. Everything reflects you, and you are an integrated part of everything. Oneness means doing everything from a complete connectedness and consciousness, knowing that what you do to the world, you do to yourself.

All the oneness fire dragons support you with the purification and the transformation of your consciousness to bring you to increasingly higher levels of oneness consciousness. It is imperative to allow them to do so. In this phase, it is no longer about what the dragons look like or whether you can see them. This process is about connecting with the consciousness, which is the foundation of your being a cocreator of this reality. From what level of consciousness do you choose to create, act, think, feel, and speak? Let the oneness fire dragons guide you.

Do these meditations as you did previously with the duality dragons. First, look at the pictures, which are now three instead of two. Image 8.7 shows a vortex of the neutral/child aspect of the oneness fire dragons, image 8.8 shows the feminine aspect, and image 8.9 shows the masculine aspect. The general part of the meditation will be included in the first meditation of this chapter and will be referred to in the following meditations.

—⟵ɯ⟶—

GENERAL INTRODUCTORY MEDITATION

- Take a few deep inhalations and exhalations, and feel yourself relaxing.
- Bring your awareness as fully as possible to the present.
- Bring your awareness to your physical heart. Your heart is also the location of your spiritual (divine) essence.
- Imagine this essence as a sphere of white light. Allow this white light to shine through your entire physical body. Feel the unconditional love inherently connected with this light, and direct this love to yourself.
- Allow the love for yourself to permeate your entire physical system so that your frequency increases. Feel this unconditional love for yourself, exactly as you are now, without the need to change anything.

IMAGE 8.7. This is a picture of the location of a vortex of the morphogenetic grid of the child oneness fire dragons. The bottle marks the center.

- Allow the love to expand out of you and to fill the whole space in which you are seated. If you are with other people, animals, plants, or crystals, as well as the invisible subtle beings in the room, connect with them, and together, create a coherent field of unconditional love.
- Feel gratitude for all others present, knowing that they are supporting you on this journey.
- From your divine essence, connect with the divine essence of Mother Earth. Feel love for Mother Earth, and feel her love for you. Ask her to support you with her crystalline life force to enable you to optimally work with this energy, knowing that it will make your work with the dragons easier.

ONENESS FIRE DRAGONS MEDITATION

- Use the picture (image 8.7) to help you connect with the energies of the vortex of the grid of the child oneness fire dragon to allow you to connect with the essence and love

IMAGE 8.8. This is a picture of the location of a vortex of the morphogenetic grid of the feminine oneness fire dragons. The bottle marks the center.

of the elemental power of fire at the level of oneness as an aspect of setting an optimal intention.

- Be fully aware of the consciousness of oneness, and allow the energies to awaken the fullness of this consciousness in you. Become the consciousness that can induce the most optimal intention, and ask the child oneness fire dragons to help you.

- Allow the energies to unfold, and sit in this energy as long as it feels good.

- Take a deep breath, and shift your awareness to the picture (image 8.8) of the vortex of the grid of the feminine aspect of the oneness fire dragons. Connect with the energies of this vortex as fully as possible.

- Be aware of how the state of oneness consciousness feels for you. How do you experience this state of consciousness? Can you allow the energies of conscious intention at this level to flow through you?

IMAGE 8.9. This is a picture of the location of a vortex of the morphogenetic grid of the masculine oneness fire dragons. The bottle marks the center.

- Ask the feminine oneness fire dragons to help you feel and experience this state of consciousness to connect with its energies to create as optimally as possible.
- Allow your feelings to flow freely, and sit in these energies as long as it feels comfortable.
- Take a deep breath again, and now shift your awareness to the picture (image 8.9) of the vortex of the grid of the masculine aspect of oneness fire dragon energies. Connect with the energies as fully as possible.
- Feel your ability to work actively from the state of the oneness consciousness, and feel the ability to set the energies of the conscious intention into motion. Ask the masculine oneness fire dragons to help you to reach the most optimal connection at this moment.
- Allow the energies to unfold, and sit in this energy for as long as it feels good.
- Take a deep breath again, and bring your awareness to

all three oneness fire dragons at the same time. Feel how you have deepened your connection with the oneness consciousness and the elemental power of fire at the level of oneness. Feel how you have increased your ability to set intentions from this state. Sit in these energies for as long as feels good.

- Take a deep breath, and slowly bring your awareness back to where you are seated. When you are ready, open your eyes.

—⁓—

The Three Oneness Water Dragons

The duality water dragons help us to create based on the fulfillment of needs, which results in feeling that we function optimally in this physical reality. The oneness water dragons help us to create to support the world in which we live (Gaia). The trinity of the oneness water dragons helps us to create in oneness from the perspective that we live in an interconnected world. Each of the trinity aspects and each of the dragons connected to those aspects do so in a unique way. Again, realize that we are describing them separately, but that they do not function separately.

The child oneness water dragons invite us to be creative while we are in alignment with the Gaia system. Being in a natural state of pure joy, happiness, and love of being part of Gaia enables us to be in an optimal creative state. This state also leads to a state of total connectedness with access to the total creative potential, experiencing that nothing is impossible. The child state is the state of full creative potential in the physical world of the fourth dimension.

The feminine state receives the intent (from the fire trinity) and feels whether it is in alignment with the state of oneness. Realize that the feminine aspect of water at this level needs to be fully active to be able to receive the full intention, which is true for every level. The training of openness that began at the duality level continues and expands on this higher vibrational oneness level. If we cannot be open due to unprocessed emotions, we cannot function from oneness; rather, we will operate from the level of duality.

Even when we can set an intention at a oneness level, our

emotional states determine whether we can remain in oneness when we connect with the elemental power of water and our emotions. The emotional state determines the level at which creation occurs.

The masculine energy sets the energy of creation (of the intent) into motion and maintains the proper creative state enabling creation in oneness. Although water is considered to be a passive feminine quality, it also has a masculine aspect. That is the power of water, the power of creation. Realize that creation on a oneness level is a creation in harmony with all aspects of Gaia.

The trinity forms a triangle at each of the four directions. For water, the field of creativity is formed by love for creation (child), receiving information (intent) for creation (feminine), and setting creation into motion (masculine). To connect with the three aspects of the oneness water dragons, look at the pictures of vortexes of the grids of the child (image 8.10), the feminine (image 8.11), and the masculine oneness water dragons (image 8.12). Remember to start with the introductory part of the meditation, and continue with the following.

—〽—

ONENESS WATER DRAGONS MEDITATION

- Focus on image 8.10, the picture of a vortex of the grid of child (neutral) oneness water dragons. Connect with the energies of this vortex, and sit in this vortex energy. Feel unconditional love for creating in a way that supports the whole Gaia system.
- Ask the child oneness water dragons to support you and help you to integrate these energies within your system in the most optimal way.
- Let the energies unfold, and sit in these energies for as long as it feels good.
- Take a deep breath, and let go of the previous energies. Through image 8.11, connect with the energies of the vortex of the grid of the feminine oneness water dragons. Sit in these energies and experience your openness to receive the Divine intent.
- Feel that you can receive this intent fully without alteration. Feel the power of this ability.

IMAGE 8.10. This is a picture of the location of a vortex of the morphogenetic grid of the child oneness water dragons. The bottle marks the center.

IMAGE 8.11. This is a picture of the location of a vortex of the morphogenetic grid of the feminine oneness water dragons. The bottle marks the center.

IMAGE 8.12. This is a picture of the location of a vortex of the morphogenetic grid of the masculine oneness water dragons. The bottle marks the center.

- Ask the feminine oneness water dragons to help you connect with this power and to awaken it in you so that you can integrate it within your system.
- Let the energies unfold, and sit in these energies for as long as it feels good.
- Take a deep breath, and release the previous energies. Focus now on image 8.12, a vortex of the grid of the masculine oneness water dragon. Connect with the energies, and sit in this vortex energy. Connect with the ability to set the received intention into motion to start the creation process.
- Feel the power to be able to create all that you have intended. Ask the masculine oneness water dragons to help you integrate this energy within your system.
- Let the energies unfold, and sit in these energies for as long as it feels good.

- Take a deep breath, and bring your awareness to all three oneness water dragons at the same time. Feel the creative power within you — your ability to receive every intention clearly and to set the creative process optimally in motion from a place of unconditional love for the world in which you live.
- Let the energies unfold, and sit in this energy for as long as it feels good.
- Take a deep breath, and bring your awareness back to the place you are seated. When you are ready, open your eyes.

―⟋⟍⟍⟋―

The Three Oneness Air Dragons

The focus of the oneness air dragons is on the purity of thoughts. Your thoughts reflect your state of consciousness: either duality or oneness consciousness. In oneness, thoughts do not support ego but reflect the awareness of being one with the system in which we live. At the level of oneness, thoughts support the creative process and bring life to the creation and the resulting manifestation.

Pure thoughts are possible only when we function from the purity of our hearts, reflecting a state of unconditional love. The oneness air dragons guide us to this state of being. Pure thoughts draw pure life force and love into each manifestation. The air dragons also help us to breathe properly, drawing in the life force that supports being in oneness in physical reality.

The energy of the oneness air dragons is unconditional love and a higher frequency of life force. This higher frequency truly gives life to creation. Every thought supports giving life to a creation based on unconditional love and gratitude. This gratitude is not only a result of feeling but also a consequence of our thoughts about the creation.

The purpose of oneness is to raise the vibration of the manifested world and to create all that supports ascension. This support comes from the oneness dragons. The oneness air dragons contribute by helping us to hold thoughts that reflect our unconditional love for the world in which we live for every creation. We can attain a state of pure supportive thoughts for the greater good of all by working actively with life force and breath. When the oneness air trinity functions well, we bring life to the Gaia system, which raises its vibration as a whole.

The mind induces thoughts. For most people, their minds keep them in duality. To have a mind that works from a state of oneness, we need to have control over our minds, which means over our thoughts and emotions. The masculine oneness air dragons help us to keep our thoughts actively in alignment with oneness thinking. They also help us to breathe in the life force that has the vibration of oneness. This life force also represents the energy of energy healers.

The masculine oneness air dragons support us to think regarding oneness, contemplating only thoughts relevant to the present based on love. For example, when you fantasize, you move away from the present and oneness, separating from reality. Fantasizing or daydreaming as an escape from reality can easily become an addiction, pulling you away from the present and from who you are. Long retreats are popular as a means of learning how to deal with the mind. When you do not accept yourself, your thoughts are impure — not based on love. The purity of thoughts leads to purity of actions, and the masculine oneness air dragon can help with holding pure thoughts.

What you are thinking is a choice. Although this choice is supposed to emanate from the heart, often it comes from the mind, mostly the subconscious mind. Choosing what to think (giving direction to thoughts) in oneness is the masculine aspect of the oneness air dragons.

The feminine oneness air dragons help you to feel the quality of your thoughts and can signal when thoughts are impure. The feminine aspect and quality of your thoughts guide you toward creative thoughts that infuse life that nurtures and supports oneness. The feminine aspect of the oneness air dragons is the energy of people who care for others through pure thoughts and wisdom.

The child aspect adds love to ignite pure aliveness of your thoughts. The child aspect sparks the breath of life in each new beginning.

To make a connection with the energies of the three aspects (trinity) of the oneness air dragons, use the pictures of the vortexes of their grid systems. Image 8.13 shows the picture of the child aspect, image 8.14 shows the feminine aspect, and image 8.15 shows the masculine aspect of the oneness air dragons. Remember to start with the general introduction meditation, and then continue with the following.

IMAGE 8.13. This is a picture of the location of a vortex of the morphogenetic grid of the child oneness air dragons. The bottle marks the center.

IMAGE 8.14. This is a picture of the location of a vortex of the morphogenetic grid of the feminine oneness air dragons. The bottle marks the center.

IMAGE 8.15. This is a picture of the location of a vortex of the morphogenetic grid of the masculine oneness air dragons. The bottle marks the center.

ONENEƧƧ AIR DRAGONƧ MEDITATION

- Bring your awareness to the picture of the vortex of the grid of the child oneness air dragon (image 8.13), and connect with its energies. While sitting in these energies, feel love for your positive thoughts, which give life to the creation and contribute to the oneness within Gaia.

- Ask the child oneness air dragons to help you connect most optimally with these energies. Allow the energies to unfold, and sit in these energies for as long as it feels good.

- Take a deep breath, and let the energies subside. Bring your awareness to the picture of the vortex of the grid of the feminine oneness air dragons (image 8.14), and connect with its energies.

- While sitting in these energies feel how the positive thoughts about your creations cause a deeper understanding (wisdom) and feeling of oneness.

- Ask the feminine oneness air dragons to help you connect

with these feelings. Let them unfold, and sit in these energies for as long as it feels good.

- Bring your awareness to the picture of the vortex of the grid of the masculine oneness air dragons (image 8.15), and connect with these energies. Use these energies to emit only positive, supportive thoughts regarding your creations — and creation as a whole — to bring them into harmony with the Gaia system, supporting oneness.
- Ask the masculine oneness air dragons to help with that process to achieve the most optimal result. Let these energies unfold, and sit in them for as long as it feels good.
- Take a deep breath, and bring your awareness to all three oneness air dragons at the same time. Feel your ability to stay in a state that creates loving thoughts that contribute to giving life force to creations that lead to oneness within the Gaia system. Ask the oneness air dragons to support and stimulate that ability.
- Take a deep breath, and bring your awareness back to the place where you are seated. When you are ready, open your eyes.

—ɯ—

The Three Oneness Earth Dragons

The oneness earth dragons help us to manifest within the energy and consciousness of oneness. When fully connected to oneness, every manifestation is in alignment and harmony with the entire Gaia system. That is only possible when we function from oneness consciousness and from a creative power supported by emotions that are pure and aligned with love, joy, happiness, and respect. The oneness manifestations are, by definition, in harmony with the laws and cycles of the Gaia system, fitting into the energy of Gaia. It is the result of egoless creation, of creation meant to support the whole.

The energies of the oneness earth dragons help us to experience manifestation from our higher vibrational essence to feel how it contributes to oneness, how it is one with all that exists in the physical realm, and how it aligns with the subtle realms connected with the earth. It is the ability to feel whether your manifestation fits within the totality of Earth/Gaia and, consequently, in All That Is. In other words, you look at manifestations from a higher perspective that contributes to the whole.

In the world of duality, we develop our ability to manifest our beliefs, desires, and needs as individuals or as a group in order to function in this world. In the world of oneness, the joy of manifesting is the contribution to the whole. We move from manifesting for ourselves or our group to manifesting for the greater good, for the total system of Gaia, of which we are an intricate part. In duality, we learn to manifest. In oneness, we ensure that our unique contribution supports the whole.

In duality, we manifest things that support our journeys. In oneness, we manifest that which supports the Gaia system on her journey. In duality, we must learn to create and manifest in alignment with our physical needs. In oneness, we manifest and create in alignment with our souls. As a species, we have created clouds of emotional, fear-based energies that permeate our world. There are areas where light is increasing and the cloudiness is beginning to lift, but there is still a long way to go. We need to move forward, clear the cloudiness, and see the light of oneness once again. To achieve this, we need to raise our vibrations and help others to raise their vibrations. That will make it possible to connect with our spiritual essence to set intentions that result in manifestations that are in alignment with Gaia.

We are continuously manifesting. These numerous, subconsciously induced manifestations are based on survival strategies, creating these clouds in the collective human energy field. It is all about awareness. Awareness of dragons and their powers may motivate us to change so that we contribute positively to the whole.

The feminine oneness earth dragons help us to feel the manifestation and whether it is in alignment with the Gaia system. The masculine oneness earth dragons activate the manifestation process, and the child oneness earth dragons help us to love and respect all aspects of manifestation.

To connect with the three oneness earth dragons, we again have three images. Image 8.16 shows a vortex of a child oneness earth dragon grid, image 8.17 shows a feminine oneness earth dragon

IMAGE 8.16. This is a picture of the location of a vortex of the morphogenetic grid of the child oneness earth dragons. The bottle marks the center.

IMAGE 8.17. This is a picture of the location of a vortex of the morphogenetic grid of the feminine oneness earth dragons. The bottle marks the center.

IMAGE 8.18. This is a picture of the location of a vortex of the morphogenetic grid of the masculine oneness earth dragons. The bottle marks the center.

grid, and image 8.18 shows a masculine oneness earth dragon grid. Remember to start with the introductory part of the meditation, and continue with the following.

—⁓〴〴〱—

ONꟾNꟾꟾ EARTH DRAGONꟾ MꟾDITATION

- Bring your awareness to the picture of the vortex of the grid of the child oneness earth dragons (image 8.16), and connect with the energies. Sit in these energies and feel your ability to receive all that is needed to optimally manifest your intention.
- Feel your ability to fully receive this impulse to manifest without losing anything in the process. Ask the child oneness earth dragons to help you to connect with these energies as fully as possible.

- Let the energies unfold, and sit in them for as long as it feels right.
- Take a deep breath, and allow the energies to subside. Bring your awareness to the picture of the vortex of the grid of the feminine oneness earth dragons (image 8.17), and connect with these energies. Sit in these energies, and feel the power of your ability to manifest all that you have intended.
- Feel that you always can manifest your conscious intentions fully when you set them at the oneness level. Ask the feminine oneness earth dragons to help you.
- Let the energies unfold, and sit in the energy for as long as feels good.
- Take a deep breath, and allow the energies to subside. Bring your awareness to the picture of the vortex of the grid of the masculine oneness earth dragons (image 8.18), and connect with these energies to their optimal level. Sit in these energies and connect with the love and respect for the manifestation.
- Feel this love as part of your love for the whole, and feel how each manifestation becomes part of the whole because love connects all. Ask the masculine oneness earth dragons to help you to connect with these energies optimally.
- Let the energies unfold, and sit in them for as long as it feels right.
- Take a deep breath, and bring your awareness to all three oneness earth dragons at the same time. Feel your ability to always fully manifest every intention in a way that it becomes a harmonious part of Gaia, contributing to the experience that all are one and that your manifestations contribute to and strengthen oneness.
- Allow the energies to unfold, and sit in them for as long as it feels right.
- Take a deep breath, and bring your awareness back to where you are seated. When you are ready, open your eyes.

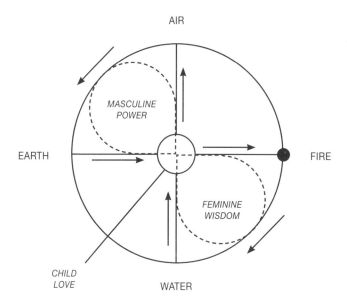

IMAGE 8.19. The flow of creation in the oneness creation cycle
forms an infinity symbol.

The Energy Flow when Working with Duality and Oneness Dragons

You may have noticed that with the oneness dragons, we proceeded through the four elements in a different order than we used with the duality dragons. In duality, we use the four powers in a circular motion. We move from fire (intent) to water (creation) to earth (manifestation) and then to air to give life to our manifestation through positive thoughts. The order differs for the oneness dragons. The first two steps are similar. We set an intention and then create. However, in the oneness system, we then give life force to the creation and manifest this creation into the physical reality. This motion is not circular but moves in the form of an infinity symbol (image 8.19). It indicates an infinite creative motion, creating two circular motions.

The circular motion in the lower right quadrant is clockwise, which means that it is feminine. The motion in the upper left quadrant is counterclockwise, which is masculine. There also is the neutral, or child, aspect, which is the central point, the place where the directions shift.

Given that we always start in the east, with conscious intent, these aspects tell us that when we create in oneness in the physical world, the feminine wisdom comes first. Then we add love (the child), and only then do we add the masculine power to complete the creation process.

In the world in which we live, many people try to the best of their ability to live from a higher, or oneness, perspective. They start with clear, conscious intent, often during a powerful meditation. They know which direction is right. However, they have sidetracked to their minds, to their beliefs, instead of their feelings and emotions, based in love. Consequently, they go north, then south, and then west. Thus, the first step takes place in the upper right quadrant, and the motion is counterclockwise. Then they move into the lower left quadrant in which the motion is clockwise. In this infinite motion, the power comes first. It often overrules love and wisdom. Consequently, instead of a oneness creation, it becomes a deformed duality creation that leads to unbalanced situations.

In our society, we usually have positioned the feminine wisdom as secondary. If we look at the well-intended but misguided way people function in our society, we see how this approach has led to severe imbalance. The training from the duality dragons, which prepares us for balance, is missing. I believe that this step is required before we are ready to create from oneness.

The Oneness Dragons
of the North and South Poles

The role of the oneness south pole (black) and north pole (white) dragons is similar to that of the duality black and white dragons. In the system of the oneness dragons, the black dragons at the south pole are the guardians of all the energies the oneness dragons hold in the morphogenetic grids. The white dragons hold the information of the elemental powers in the oneness morphogenetic field.

The flows of the energies of the oneness black and white dragons are similar to those of the duality dragons. The energies from the grids come in from the south pole and flow to the twelve powers and then to the central dragon, and they also flow directly to the central dragon. The energies from the morphogenetic field flow in from the north pole into the twelve dragons of the equator and then to the central dragon. The central dragon also receives information directly from the morphogenetic field from the white dragons at the north pole.

The energies the white dragons draw from the morphogenetic field represent the potential of the highest vibrations in physical reality. These energies also feel like a doorway into the oneness consciousness that people call Christ consciousness. This doorway may be the entrance used by ascended masters, such as the Buddha and Jesus, and also by high-dimensional ETs that support our evolution. They all help to acquire the purity, love, and joy of oneness.

This feels like a powerful and important point. At first, I wanted to call the energy of the oneness white dragons "Buddha-hood," but I then realized that Buddha-hood corresponds to the oneness central dragon.

One day while I was meditating about the sphere of the oneness dragons, suddenly, it seemed that I could see from the perspective of the oneness black dragon. It was as if I was looking from underwater to the surface. From my perspective, being the oneness black dragon, the energy was flowing to the four times three (4 x 3) points (dragons on the equator of the sphere) and the central dragon. I could not see beyond the equator; it was as if there was a ceiling beyond which I, as the black dragon, could not see.

It was fascinating to see that the black dragons connect only with the energies of the lower half of the sphere, the information connected to the morphogenetic grids. I realized that the same is true for the oneness white dragons. They connect with the upper half of the sphere that corresponds to the morphogenetic field. I also realized that the dragons of the equator, the twelve dragons, and the central dragon can see in both directions. This situation is similar to that of the duality dragons as well as all other dragons groups.

For a deeper connection with the oneness black and white dragons, look first at the pictures of a vortex of their grids (image 8.20 for the oneness black dragons and image 8.21 for the oneness white dragons). Remember to start with the introductory meditation, and then continue with the following.

IMAGE 8.20. This is a picture of the location of a vortex of the morphogenetic grid of the oneness black dragons. The bottle marks the center.

IMAGE 8.21. This is a picture of the location of a vortex of the morphogenetic grid of the oneness white dragons. The bottle marks the center.

—⟋⟍—

ONENEƧ BLACK AND WHITE DRAGONƧ MEDITATION

- Bring your awareness to the picture of the vortex of the grid of the oneness black dragons (image 8.20), and connect with these energies. Sit in these energies and feel the energies of the oneness dragon complex available in the grids. Ask the oneness black dragons to help you to connect as deeply as possible with these energies.
- Allow the energies to unfold, and sit in them for as long as it feels good.
- Take a deep breath, and let these energies dissipate. Bring your awareness to the picture of the vortex of the grid of the oneness white dragon (image 8.21), and connect with these energies. Sit in these energies, and connect with the morphogenetic field of all the oneness dragons. Ask the oneness white dragons to help you to do so.
- Let the energies unfold, and sit in them for as long as it feels comfortable.
- Bring your awareness to both the energies of the oneness black and white dragons. Set the intention to allow energy to move from the field into the grids to the most optimal level for the greatest good of all.
- Let the energies unfold, and sit in them for as long as it feels comfortable.
- Take a deep breath, and bring your awareness back to where you are seated. When you are ready, open your eyes.

—⟋⟍—

The Oneness Central Dragons

The central dragons truly are the dragons of balance and oneness. They integrate the energies of the twelve dragons plus the black and white dragons who all support creation from the state of oneness. These are the dragons that help us to master creation and function in the oneness consciousness of physical reality. They help to complete the creation within physical reality on the levels of duality and oneness. The central dragons present a higher aspect of completion: the completion of creation within the Gaia system on all levels.

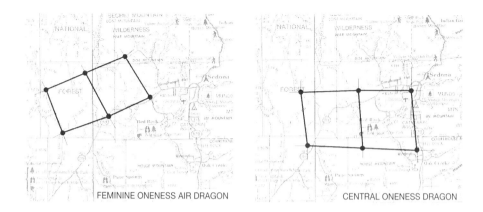

FEMININE ONENESS AIR DRAGON   CENTRAL ONENESS DRAGON

IMAGES 8.22 A AND B. These images show the difference between the size of the morphogenetic grid of a oneness dragon (the feminine oneness air dragon) and the oneness central dragon. The maps have the same scale.

The function of the oneness central dragons is to steer the creation process as represented by the infinity symbol. It is invaluable to ensure that the creation process is completed and that the result contributes to the creation of oneness, establishing the balance between the physical and the spiritual aspects of the physical reality.

The central dragons' importance is reflected in their grid. All twelve dragons of the cycle, as well as the black and white dragons, have grids with lines and vortexes that are roughly the same size. The grids from the central dragons are larger and therefore different from the others, which is also true with the central duality dragons. The increase in size is not only reflected in the distance between vortexes (see images 8.22 a and b) but also in the size of the vortexes and the lines.

Connecting with the central dragons does not only support completion of the steps of creating in the fourth dimension (oneness) but also the completion of connecting with the existing types of dragons that function in oneness reality. You call on these dragons to feel whether you have completed a creation cycle. You can do that for any cycle in your life. It is important to connect regularly with these dragons to feel how complete you are, and if you are not, to determine which of the elemental powers/energies is off balance as well as within that elemental power which of the three aspects (feminine, masculine, or child) is not functioning optimally. Then call in the

IMAGE 8.23. This is a picture of the location of a vortex of the morphogenetic grid of the oneness central dragons. The bottle marks the center.

dragon of the power that is off balance or too weak to help you. Like the central duality dragons, you can work with the central oneness dragons daily.

We can call the oneness central dragons the masters of the powers of creation in oneness reality. Connecting with these dragons helps you to live optimally in this physical reality on all levels. They also guide you to the power you need most in your life in each moment.

To connect optimally with the oneness central dragons, first view the image of a vortex of their morphogenetic grid (image 8.23). Remember to start with the introductory meditation, and then continue with the following.

〰〰

ONENESS CENTRAL DRAGONS MEDITATION

- Bring your awareness to the picture of a vortex of the grid of the oneness central dragons (image 8.23). Connect with these energies of the vortex of the oneness central dragons grid to experience their essence.

- Feel that you can complete what you want to achieve to support oneness in the Gaia system, contributing to raising the vibration of the whole Gaia system. Ask the oneness central dragons to help you to connect with the feeling of completion of every step on your journey in physical reality on both the duality and the oneness levels.
- Feel yourself accepting everything that completion brings.
- Allow the energies to unfold, and sit in this energy for as long as it feels comfortable.
- Take a deep breath, and bring your awareness back to the place you are sitting. When you are ready, open your eyes.

―――∿∿―――

Become the Powers of the Sphere of the Oneness Dragons

The oneness central dragons reflect mastery over the powers of creation in the physical reality. This mastery requires that we be able to connect with all the powers of the oneness sphere. Otherwise, we cannot resonate optimally with and ultimately become like a central dragon. Even when we do not yet resonate optimally, we can imagine ourselves in the center of the sphere.

Seeing yourself in the center of the sphere will bring you closer to functioning as the central oneness dragon. You can do this visualization daily. We will close the journey of connecting with the oneness dragons with a meditation that can help you to be the sphere of energies and powers of the oneness dragons to the highest degree possible and to be able to always create for the greatest good of all.

―――∿∿―――

BE THE SPHERE OF ENERGIES MEDITATION

- In your imagination, sit in the center of the sphere, the location of the central dragons. While in the center, connect first with the equator of the oneness sphere, the circle around you.
- Move to the east and connect with the dragons of the

masculine, feminine, and child aspects of the oneness fire dragons. Feel your ability to become the power of the consciousness connected with this trinity. Feel also the unconditional love that is an inherent part of this consciousness. Feel your ability to set intentions based on unconditional love, and be in total alignment with the Gaia system.

- Move to the south and connect with the dragons of the masculine, feminine, and child aspects of the oneness water dragons. Feel your ability to receive the conscious impulse that comes from the fire trinity. Feel that your love can fully receive and accept this intention and feel the power that induces creation based on the energies (information) received from it.

- Move to the north and connect with the dragons of the masculine, feminine, and child aspects of the oneness air dragons. Feel how your thoughts contain love for what is created, and give it the life force it needs to contribute optimally to the Gaia system.

- Move to the west and connect with the dragons of the masculine, feminine, and child aspects of the oneness earth dragons. Feel the power of the manifestation and the gratitude for the manifested addition to the whole, and through your love, feel it integrate and contribute optimally to the Gaia system.

- Bring your awareness to the south pole (below) to connect with the oneness black dragons. Feel your ability to connect fully and work with the energies of the oneness dragons that are available in the grids.

- Bring your awareness to the north pole (above) to connect with the oneness white dragons. Feel your ability to connect with the morphogenetic field of the oneness dragons. Feel also that you are increasingly able to bring information from this field into the grids, contributing to the increase of energies and information available for all to work and live in oneness.

- Now feel that you are not only the central dragon but that you are the whole sphere, connecting with all the dragons of this sphere at the same time. Become one with all of them and with the powers of which they are the guardians.

- Let the energies unfold, and sit in them for as long as it feels good.
- Take a deep breath; feel that you are truly empowered, living more fully in a state of oneness. Feel that you can create more clearly what you want for the greater good of all.
- Feel your body and feet on the ground. Bring your awareness back to where you are sitting. When you are ready, open your eyes.

—⟳—

You have completed a journey of making connections with the elemental powers that will allow you to create optimally within the total physical (third- and fourth-dimensional) world in which you live. This completion is an impressive achievement. However, we all have tendencies that prevent us from using these powers optimally, such as the many fear-based emotions and belief structures to which we are attached even though they limit us.

The task of the dragons is not to help us with the transformation of these emotions and belief structures. However, as our connections deepen with the elemental powers, the dragons can help us to see the world differently. Consequently, we change our neural pathways, which in turn changes us, our emotions, and our beliefs. These changes will inevitably lead to experiencing our reality in new ways. These experiences will make it easier to be even more open to connecting with and using elemental powers. It is the path of mastery of creating in the physical reality.

Oneness Dragons and Chakras

In chapter 4, it was mentioned that there is a relationship between dragons and chakras. This relationship was considered in more detail while discussing the duality dragons in the previous chapter. The relationships between chakras and dragons are, as mentioned, not necessarily linear. However, the dragon group that portrays a direct linear relationship with chakras most clearly is the group of the oneness dragons.

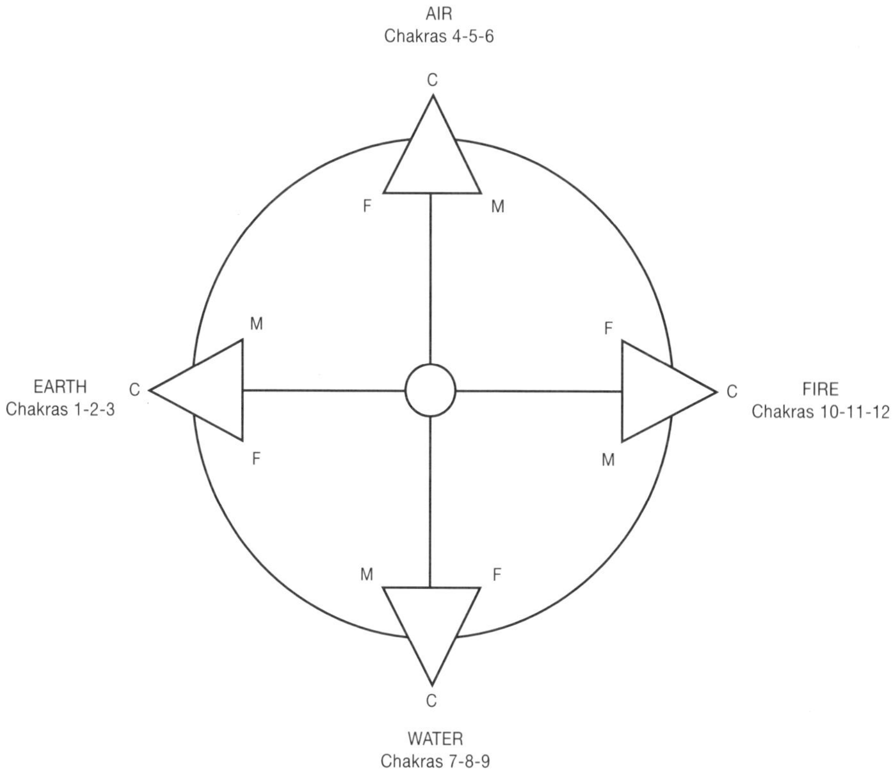

IMAGE 8.24. Here are the twelve chakras separated in four elemental groups.

Although this image was presented in chapter 4, let us consider it once more (image 8.24). This image shows that we can separate the chakras into four groups of three, similar to the twelve oneness dragons of the equator of the sphere of the oneness dragons. For some people, this relationship may prove challenging. However, image 8.25 goes one step further, correlating each of the twelve oneness dragons that connect to the twelve aspects of the elemental powers on a oneness level to the chakras. This observation may prove even more challenging for you because, again, there is no linearity.

Feeling into this relationship may require some time and effort. First, let go of preexisting ideas. Second, let go of what seems to be logical. Feeling into the relationship of the oneness dragons and the chakras is a great way to learn to feel the energies instead of thinking about what you think you know.

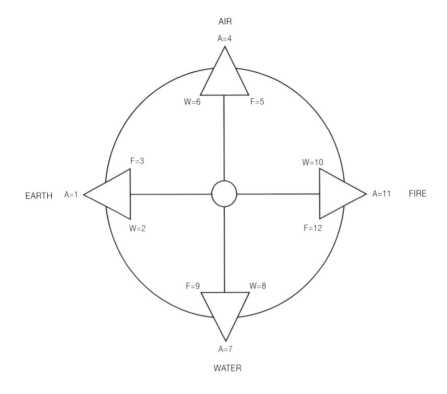

IMAGE 8.25. This shows the relationship between the twelve oneness dragons and the chakras.

Explaining the rationale for the presentation of image 8.25 would require a whole chapter. To prevent a focus on chakras instead of dragons, consider this an invitation for you to explore the topic more deeply on your own. Such an inquiry will help to understand the oneness dragons and the chakras on a deeper level.

144 Energy Qualities

In the previous chapter, it was mentioned that each of the eight elemental powers of duality had all eight elemental powers within it, creating sixty-four different energy frequencies. We find a similar situation with the twelve oneness dragons of the equator. Image 8.2 shows these twelve points on the equator. Like we did with the duality dragons, we also can draw twelve lines (circumferences) through each of the twelve points of the equator and the north and south poles. Each of the twelve circumferences we produce holds all twelve elemental powers of the oneness system. In this way, we create 144 (12 x 12) different energy qualities.

In chapter 4, the numbers 3 (trinity) and 4 (elemental powers) were discussed. In relation to chakras, each of the twelve chakras possesses a trinity, creating thirty-six different chakras that are present as vortexes in the landscapes of Mother Earth. Each of these thirty-six chakras resonates at four different frequency levels, representing the four elemental powers and creating 144 chakra frequencies.

There is a direct correspondence between the oneness dragons and the chakra energies. When we work with the oneness dragons, we contribute to an improvement of the functioning of our total chakra system, leading to enlightenment. That confirms that working with dragons not only improves our ability to create in this world optimally but also confirms our functioning in all areas of our lives.

CHAPTER 9

Primordial Dragons

OF ALL THE DRAGON GROUPS, THE PRIMORDIAL DRAGONS have been the most challenging for me. As may become clear in this chapter, we have such a limited understanding of the powers of the elements that it is difficult to comprehend their fullness. I am aware that my descriptions are limited and maybe sometimes even awkward. Nonetheless, the dragons found it's the right time to share what can be shared as a basis of the process of deeper understanding and learning to work with these powers. As mentioned, to make it possible to work with each dragon group independently, you might encounter some repetition.

The duality and the oneness dragons have been discussed in the previous chapters. These two groups are connected and are masters of certain aspects of the four elemental powers. The duality dragons help us to master two aspects of these elemental powers, and the oneness dragons help us to connect with three more. Therefore, we have worked with five of the six elemental powers. In this chapter, we will work with the sixth aspect of the elemental powers: the primordial aspect, which connects us with the power of the elements.

We need to connect deeply enough with each of the six elemental powers to be able to master each of the four elements. Once we have worked sufficiently with all six aspects of each of the elemental powers, we are ready to work with their master dragons (which will be the next chapter).

My dragon guide, Drasil-air, provides a clear description of the duality and oneness dragons and the group with whom we will connect in this chapter, the primordial dragons: "The duality and oneness dragons help you to understand yourselves and how you function in this world. The primordial dragons help you to understand the manifested world in which you live and the powers that govern it." Everyone can learn to work optimally with the powers that govern the manifested world. However, it requires dedication and perseverance because the process takes time. Nonetheless, every step helps us to expand and function more optimally in this world.

To prevent confusion, we need to realize that when we speak about the elements as we experience them on Earth, we are talking about four expressions of the manifested world. Manifestation is an aspect of the elemental power of earth. The four physical elements all belong to the elemental power of earth, which is responsible for the manifestation of all four elements. That means the elements earth, water, fire, and air are all manifestations, and you need all four elemental powers to make their creation possible. Therefore, each of the four elements always has all four elemental powers functioning within their manifested forms.

It is important to understand this clearly. There is much confusion about this subject, and without a deeper clarity, you can't utilize the actualized potential of the four elements, the physical manifestations, fully. So each element has all elemental powers of which one is dominant. The elements have many of the characteristics of their dominant elemental power and are consequently the sixth aspect of the elemental powers. They are the densest, physical form and consequently hold the lowest vibration of the six aspects of the elemental powers.

Drasil-air has always been clear that it is not advisable to work with the energies and powers of the primordial dragons until there are understanding and mastery of the elemental powers of which the

IMAGE 9.1. This is the cave of the primordial earth dragon KashMaRi.

duality and oneness dragons are guardians. Working with these latter dragons is preparatory to connecting with the primordial dragons. Drasil-air offered guidance for working with their energies.

Meeting KashMaRi

When I started my research of the primordial dragons, I had no idea how to begin. Often it is a matter of trust that guidance will bring me to the right starting point. One day while researching, I was so strongly attracted to a cave in the distance that I was compelled to go to it. The cave was in the red rocks northwest of Sedona, Arizona. It turned out to be much deeper than I thought. The ceiling had a lot of soot, suggesting that people had used this cave over long periods. About three-quarters of the way into the cave, I found a vortex of the root chakra. However, I felt something else.

Because I had worked with dragons for a couple of years, I recognized their energies; however, they felt different from what I had encountered before. After a meditation to connect more deeply with the energies, I realized that I had stumbled across my first vortex of the primordial earth dragon grid (image 9.1). The energies made me feel that I was fully in the manifested world. When you are in the manifestation, you can feel it, understand it, and work with it. It enables you to master it and to work with it so that you can keep it in balance, in harmony. This statement is true for all manifestation — visible and invisible. However, it takes time and training to feel into these manifestations because we are not used to doing this.

Besides energies, I also felt an extremely powerful presence, almost uncomfortable. It brought me into full contact with my body as well as all that my emotions and thoughts have done to my body. If you are fully in this energy, you can feel all aspects of the physical earth and, consequentially, your physical body. In the developmental state that I was in at the time, it felt too much for me. Feeling deeper, I realized that I was in the presence of a primordial earth dragon.

Connecting with KashMaRi, the name the primordial earth dragon gave me, was extremely powerful and profound. She shared how in the past people tried to control the primordial dragons so that they could manifest whatever they wanted (power and wealth). According to KashMaRi, there are only eight primordial earth dragons in the whole world: two in the Himalayas and one each in the Andes, the Alps, Sedona, Australia, the Rocky Mountains, and New Zealand.

Every time I visited KashMaRi, I learned much from her. One of the most surprising things she shared was that dragons could be either a field or a being. It is somewhat like the wave/particle story in quantum physics. In this case, the being itself can shift consciously from field to being and from being to field, independent of the observer. The field of a dragon will always stay within the energy system of Gaia and will remain coherent. It is a being but more spread out.

Maybe it is better to say that these dragons can spread their energies over large areas or concentrate their energies into something perceptible as a being. It would be like us going from a physical system into a widespread energy field and, by choice, having the ability to go back to our form at will. In theory, it seems that we can do that. If that is true, we are far from having that ability.

Every time I talked with KashMaRi, I felt her as a being. When my connection with her deepened, she offered to help me work with the primordial powers and the connected dragons. KashMaRi emphasized that the primordial dragons are here to assist the functioning of physical reality. Humans and primordial dragons are supposed to work together. While initially it worked well, this collaboration changed over time. People wanted to use the powers for personal gain, and the dragons did not want to support that. This growing tension between humans and dragons is the basis of the many negative stories about them. When the tension became too much, the primordial dragons withdrew from humans.

KashMaRi believes that we may be able to work together again. She refers to times before humanity fell deep into the lower vibrations of physicality. She said that we have fallen so deeply that from now on we can only grow and expand. At this moment, we may be at a starting point for a renewed collaboration that will be different from what it has ever been before. This collaboration needs to develop gradually. We are already separated, so there is nothing to lose and everything to gain.

She told me that our working with the other groups of dragons helps us to function better and gives us power and control over our lives. She said, "Working with the primordial dragons will give you power over the physical world in which you live. You can only develop this power when you work from a place of wisdom and love." She then asked me: "Are you ready?"

Overwhelmed with emotions, I could only say, "Yes." While the intensity of the emotions has subsided, the answer still is an unwavering yes.

I realized how different my journey with the primordial dragons was compared to the dragons of the previous two groups. The connections with the duality and oneness dragons were the result of my connections and growing understanding of the elemental powers. The connection with the primordial dragons was not because I had studied the elements. It was because I met a dragon who is an inherent part of the earth, an ancient being.

Connecting with KashMaRi helped me to better understand how the stories about dragons originated. The stories did not originate from connections with the duality or oneness dragons but from the connections with the ancient primordial dragons.

Knowing the Primordial Dragons

The primordial dragons hold the powers inherent in all manifestation. These powers are also able to transform and change manifestation. The primordial dragons connect us specifically with the manifestation of the elemental powers as they function in the four elements: earth, water, air, and fire. For example, the primordial water dragon can teach us everything about water as a physical manifestation (element) and master the elemental powers of water within the physical. As such, they can help us to learn how to direct water. A bit like what the *Avatar* boy did in the movie based on the animated series.[1] The boy worked with the powers of the elements in the physical manifestation. These are the powers of the primordial dragons.

Ultimately, if you truly want to contribute to the creation of a harmonious world, you need to know enough about the powers of the elements to let them support you in the manifested world. Only then can you contribute to a new world in which the elements are in balance for the greater good of all who live within the Gaia system, as seen in these examples:

- In growing plants and trees on the earth and working with stones and crystalline energies, we work with the primordial earth dragons consciously or unconsciously. They can help to prevent earthquakes (or diminish their power). Primordial earth dragons can help us levitate stones and even help to change stone and crystal composition. More importantly, they can help improve the quality of the soil to improve the quality of our food.
- Water as part of all living beings and as part of the earth system is influenced strongly by our emotions and consciousness, and water itself affects emotions, awareness, and creativity. The system receives information and holds it. The information is the basis for creation and for supporting life. Water is considered by many to be the dominant element in our lives because life depends on it. The primordial water dragons help us to work with all qualities of water.
- Air is the life force and also the power of thoughts. Both can support creation (give life to creation) but can also destroy it. We need to transform chaotic collective thoughts because they can induce, or at least contribute to, storms, tornadoes, and hurri-

canes. The primordial air dragons help us to balance these energies and powers.

- Fire transforms, which means that energy/consciousness dictates, directs, and determines the transformational process. Fire is the end and the beginning (the phoenix). It is a way to choose what to continue. Primordial fire dragons also work with all the energetic aspects of life forms and the energies of the earth. Therefore, they relate to volcanoes, the electromagnetic fields of the earth, and our neurological systems.

These short descriptions are only a small indication of the forces of which the primordial dragons are the guardians. These forces are so powerful that we can only imagine what we can do once we have mastered them. That is one of the reasons that Drasil-air suggested to work first with the other dragons.

I was surprised that Drasil-air opened the door for us to work with these powers. I am far from being a master of all the powers with which we have worked in the previous chapters. I am not saying that I have not made progress, but that is much different. I also see that people who have followed the dragon workshops have made progress, but they have much to learn. When I felt invited to write this book, I realized that many people who will read this chapter might have very limited training. So I asked Drasil-air what has changed that makes it possible that we are ready to work with these powers. It was important for me to know, especially given the fact that these powers can have such positive as well as destructive effects, as history has proven.

According to Drasil-air, when dragons and humans were working together in the past, there was no restriction on the use of the elemental powers and the powers of the elements. The dragons were the guardians of these powers, and they simply made them available. During that time, there were only five primordial dragon species who were the guardians of the four elemental powers and the central dragon. These five dragon species made all aspects of the elemental powers available. When humanity increasingly disconnected from their world and from the beings who shared their world, they wanted to use the powers of the elements for their personal use.

In this world of free will, that was the experience they had chosen, so that was the experience they had. In this process, they used the power of the elements and elemental powers in such a way that, ultimately, they destroyed the existing world. You are familiar with the stories and legends, such as the story of Atlantis. The tendency is to blame a few, especially those in power, but actually, it is the result of the ways of a whole civilization and its collective consciousness.

To prevent the repetition of destruction, dragons and their guides (such as Drasil-air, Drasha-air, and Draphi-air) cocreated a system in which each of the elemental powers was split into six aspects. This makes it much more difficult to master and use each of the elemental powers in a destructive way. Although it is still possible, it has become highly unlikely, especially because the consciousness of humanity has decreased to such a low level that the integration of the six aspects of the elemental powers takes a long time.

Some of you are now learning to work with the different aspects of each of the elemental powers, and that may lead to mastery for some. However, because it is very difficult to attain that level without using your heart and being in a state of love, misuse is highly unlikely. Drasil-air said that the dragons invite us to use the potential of the energies of the elemental powers wisely.

Throughout the work I have done with the primordial dragons, I have felt Drasil-air and later Drasha-air and Draphi-air as the overall guides, and KashMaRi's guidance augmented and supported the process. She reminded me that I have chosen in this lifetime to work with the element of earth as an entrance into this reality and as a basis to understand it. That is why she of all the primordial dragons functions as my teacher and guide. I felt that I needed this support because I find working with the primordial powers challenging and a bit scary, especially after realizing their powers, even though I can oversee only a small part of it.

KashMaRi told me that it was not surprising that I felt uncertain. She told me that I do not understand these energies because I cannot fully connect with them. Also, there is fear connected with these powers in the collective due to past misuse and destruction. Therefore, it is better not to go directly to the powers connected with the earth as a whole but to connect with the powers in our bodies first and create balance in our system.

Realize, however, that what happens inside you will be reflected outside you. This statement is based in the second Hermetic principle, the principle of correspondence: as above, so below; as below, so above; as inside, so outside; as outside, so inside.[2] You can use certain tools in your attempt to understand yourself. You know them: crystals and stones for the physical atoms and molecules in your body, water for your water systems, air for your breathing and life force, and fire for the energy as well as consciousness and awareness.

For example, when you work with water, you will understand it both inside and outside of you. Once you understand air, you understand life force and the movement of air (the air movement on Earth also has to do with life force). Once you understand fire, energy, and consciousness in yourself, you will understand the fire, energy, and consciousness of the earth.

While it is important to understand the elements and their inherent powers, the focus of this chapter is to connect with the primordial dragons. That will give you a basis from which you can start your work with the elements. All the chapters are about reconnecting with the dragons and what they represent to further your studies to the degree that feels right for you.

You will notice that if you do not come from a place of love and respect, the primordial dragons will not support you. In this chapter, we will connect with the primordial dragons and only touch on the powers inherent in the elements. It is not the time for anybody to fully understand these powers. For those who are guided to do so, understanding these powers will be a lifelong study, leading to increasing mastery.

The Morphogenetic Grids

As with every species we connect with and want to better understand, it is important to study the morphogenetic grids. Therefore, an important aspect of working with the primordial dragons is the study of the energies of the vortexes of their grids. I will mention some of the discoveries of these studies under each of the seven primordial dragons. However, I discovered an interesting aspect of these grids.

Based on the size and the distances between the vortexes, the energies do not cover the whole Earth, as is the case with dragon grids of the previous two groups. You must look for the energies to be able to connect to the grids; it is not present everywhere.

Once connected, you need to learn to interpret it. The interpretation of the energies of the primordial dragons is for the determined. I have learned that the help from the primordial dragons only comes when your intention is clear and pure. For a deeper connection with the primordial dragons and the exploration of their gifts, we will use pictures of the vortexes of their grids and meditation.

Primordial Earth Dragons

In the previous two chapters, we started the discussion with the elemental power of fire. In this chapter, we will start with the element of earth. Earth as an element refers to all manifestation in solid form in the universe. However, we will restrict our discussion to the manifested world in which we live, Gaia. As was mentioned, all four elements are part of the manifested world, resulting from the creation process. Therefore, all primordial dragons help us to function optimally in this manifested physical world. Each of the seven primordial dragons will do so in their unique way.

KashMaRi reminded me that what looks solid is a vibration that consists of a coherent energy field that we perceive as a form because that is what our senses tell us. This form is never constant even though it may seem so. Therefore, it is not about understanding form in and of itself but rather the reason for this energy field that we perceive as a form. When we understand that it is all energy, it will be easier to understand how to work optimally with these forms and support the whole system we call Gaia.

Understanding and creating form is not about technology. Unfortunately, so often technology is valued as a goal when it is supposed to be a tool to assist us in becoming conscious beings. Technology is an aspect of the manifested world. However, it is the result of manifesting from the physical triangle discussed in chapter 4 (see image 4.12), and rarely does it include spiritual aspects. Therefore, for most people, technology has the opposite (negative) effect of what manifestation is supposed to accomplish. When we make technology a goal, we might destroy the process of understanding consciousness and our role in the Gaia system.

The primordial earth dragons work with the whole range of manifestation in physicality, whether manifested through the elemental powers on the level of duality or oneness. Mastering the physical world can only mean being a master in working with all manifestation in physicality. We can do this only with unconditional love and from the point that all is one and interconnected.

You cannot master the full power of manifestation while in duality because there must also be harmony with the consciousness of oneness. You can only possess full power when you operate from oneness consciousness, realizing that Gaia is one dynamic, interactive system. That may help you to understand why we first needed to connect with the elemental powers that help to create and manifest in both the third- and fourth-dimensional worlds before we learn to work with powers within the manifested systems.

What we manifest is only a small part of the total manifestation. Nonetheless, the understanding of the manifestation process helps us to comprehend the powers inherent in the manifested universe. However, to do so, we need to understand the sixth aspect of the elemental powers.

When we work with the element of earth at the primordial level, we deal with the structure of the manifested forms, understanding the structure and working with its inherent power. Through understanding the manifested world, we contribute to awakening the full potential of the manifestation. For example, we learn to do so by activating crystals and stones. However, we need to activate (connect to the full potential) all physical forms as fully as possible. We can only reach such a state when we connect through our hearts. When we connect and awaken the full potential of all aspects (all four elemental powers) of the manifested world, we will create a tremendous shift in energy within the manifested world. When a manifested form reaches an optimal state, we can do more with its potential by exploring the nature of possibilities available through working with it.

The last step is the connection with the matrix of an object in such a way that you can change that object at will. You can choose to develop this ability with ordinary stones. Changing the matrix is a process similar to spoon bending. As in the movie *The Matrix*, when Neo asked how the boy could bend the spoon, he responded: "There is no spoon."[3] What he meant is that there is only an energy field that holds the atoms together and that what we see as the spoon is the vibration of the molecules in that coherent energy field.

In chapter 5, we discussed that the key to the manifested world is the frequency 8.1 Hz.[4] That is the basic frequency required to be in harmony with earth as an element. Everything physical resonates with this frequency. It is the undertone of the frequency that resonates with the golden mean: the golden frequency of 16.2 Hz (based on its resonance with phi: 1.61803398, which is 1.62). The golden mean is the basis of harmony within all manifested forms. The 8.1 Hz allows us to become one with the earth and with all creation on Earth.

In summary, we can say that there are three main steps in working with the manifested world: activation, exploring the potential, and the ability to change things to their optimal form in each situation. When we master the powers and energies connected with the manifested world, we can move mountains. Having such a power requires unconditional love and deep respect for all that exists so that we act only in alignment with what is optimal for the Gaia system.

KashMaRi possesses a wide variety of frequencies; however, her ground tone is 8.1 Hz, which is the same as ours (not the 7.83 Hz). The concept of 7.83 Hz comes from measurements of the Schumann resonance frequencies, whose bandwidths differ slightly in different locations. KashMaRi suggested that it is important to meditate regularly inside a pyramid that has roughly the proportions of the Great Pyramid of Giza.

Let us now connect with the energy of the primordial earth dragons. To prepare, you can use the picture of a vortex of the primordial earth dragons grid (image 9.2). Prepare yourself by doing the introductory meditation, and then continue with the following. The introductory meditation is provided for this first mediation and can be referred back to for the subsequent meditations in this chapter.

IMAGE 9.2. This is a picture of the location of a vortex of the morphogenetic grid of the primordial earth dragon. The bottle marks the center.

—⟋⟍⟍—

GENERAL INTRODUCTORY MEDITATION

- Take a few deep inhalations and exhalations, and feel yourself relaxing.
- Bring your awareness as fully as possible to the present.
- Bring your awareness to your physical heart. Your heart is also the location of your spiritual (divine) essence.
- Imagine this essence as a sphere of white light. Allow this white light to shine through your entire physical body. Feel the unconditional love inherently connected with this light, and direct this love to yourself.
- Allow the love for yourself to permeate your whole physical system so that your frequency will increase. Feel this unconditional love for yourself, exactly as you are now, without the need to change anything.
- Allow the love to expand out of you and to fill the whole space in which you are seated. If you are with other people,

animals, plants, or crystals, as well as the invisible subtle beings in the room, connect with them and together create a coherent field of unconditional love.

- Feel gratitude for all others present, knowing that they are supporting you on this journey.
- From your divine essence, connect with Mother Earth's divine essence. Feel love for Mother Earth, and feel her love for you. Ask her to support you with her crystalline life force to enable you to optimally work with this energy, knowing that it will make your work with the dragons easier.

PRIMORDIAL EARTH DRAGONS MEDITATION

- Focus your awareness on the picture of a vortex of the grid of the primordial earth dragons (image 9.2). Connect with the energies to such a degree that you are seated within the energies.
- Feel the energies of this vortex, and take in the energies that will bring you to the most optimal state possible at this moment.
- Ask the primordial earth dragons, especially KashMaRi, to help you to connect as optimally as possible with the energies of the vortex and to support the process of connecting with, understanding, and working with the powers inherent in all manifested forms. Also, set the intention to connect with the frequency of 8.1 Hz to support you in connecting optimally.
- Sit in this energy for as long as it feels good, and allow the process to unfold.
- Notice what has changed for you.
- Take a deep breath, and bring your awareness back to where you are seated. When you are ready, open your eyes.

—〜〜—

Primordial Water Dragons

Water receives information and passes it on. It takes on the energy through contact to a certain degree, but water is especially very sensitive and susceptible to conscious intent. Therefore, physical water can be programmed in whatever way we choose, both positive and negative. We have considered many aspects of water already in a previous chapter.

We can work with water in many ways. First, we understand more about water in general — its cycle and its optimal structure. It is important to learn more details about the role water plays in our physical system and that of Gaia as a whole. Second, we can program water. In chapter 2, the process of programming water to hold essences of energy systems, such as vortexes or crystals, was explained. We can program water in many ways through understanding it and how it functions.

Third, we can clear water everywhere in the world. Understanding that water is important makes it obvious that water needs to be clean without pollution to fulfill its optimal role in supporting all life on Earth. There is a lot of information brought into the water from polluting chemicals that produces negative effects in every living being who consumes it. And the water itself can thereby become a negative, lower-vibrational energy field.

Fourth, we can communicate with water to understand its role, its cycle, and its movements underground. Collaborating with water and the water devas could make it possible to distribute water in a new way to benefit all who live on Earth.

Water holds information and creates an environment in which to create life. Water holds the wisdom that reflects the fire (the morphogenetic grids and fields). Our consciousnesses codetermine what information from the fields will be in the grids (we are the cocreators). We have a connection with the morphogenetic system that through water creates the manifestation that will be given life through life force (air).

The primordial water dragons support the function of physical water, which is a manifestation in fluid form. They help us to work with water to create the most optimal physical reality possible. The elemental power of water is in everything physical. It expresses itself most strongly in the form of water. Connecting with physical water, understanding its properties, and working with it for the greater good of all creates a world that will support all that exists — both visible and invisible.

There is no such thing as the ideal molecular structure of water. Circumstances, for example, vibration, determine at each moment the most optimal structure of water. The form of snowflakes and water crystals is the basis for the concept that hexagonal structures are the most optimal and natural form. It is in alignment with the concept that inorganic molecular structures are based on hexagonal forms and organic molecular structures are based on pentagonal forms. Water aligns itself with the most powerful energies or consciousness. Some of these qualities of water were discussed in chapter 5.

Humans consist of 70 to 80 percent water and develop in water when in utero, substantiating the critical importance of water. Although it is still unclear how communication through water takes place, it happens extremely quickly. Water plays a fundamental role in our internal communication system. When we have strong thoughts and emotions, they affect our internal water, determining the nature of the information that flows through us. Our internal water affects the outside world. First, we remove water from our bodies that then enters the environment. Second, water communicates with other water in ways we do not yet understand. Could that be the reason we affect people, organisms, plants, and animals so strongly?

Although we do not know all aspects of the role of water, recent research shows that a 2 to 3 percent reduction of bodily water (mild dehydration) negatively affects cognitive performance. Some research indicates that even just 1 percent dehydration affects cognitive performance.[5]

Water connects us to creativity and emotions. In earlier chapters, it was said that the word "emotion" means "energy in motion." Water receives energies and passes them on, setting them into motion. Because water receives energies and knows what to do with them, we can define water as the elemental power of wisdom. It is the feminine quality of being receptive to energies and creating with those energies.

Learning to work with water and understanding its gifts is a process. We have forgotten so much. The primordial water dragons can help us remember and reconnect with water's power and potential. While learning to work with water is a journey, we can begin immediately with some important actions.

First, we can set the intent to clear water whenever we meet it. We can do so by connecting with our hearts and with unconditional love to set the intention to optimally clear water. Second, we can become aware of what products we use and release into the water in our homes. We should solely use biodegradable products to prevent further pollution. Third, it is important to become aware of our thoughts and emotions, realizing that they will affect the quality of water. Everyone can commit to these three steps every moment of their lives without much effort.

Some people will feel guided to explore the qualities of water on a deeper level. When you feel this guidance, follow it, and know that the primordial water dragons will support you.

Water is primarily a receiver and holder of energies and information. The key, however, is that water can use the information to create and to gather all that is needed to create life. Water alone cannot accomplish these results; rather it requires collaboration with the other elemental powers.

An aspect of water that is more difficult to understand is its ability to instantly pass on information, even over distances, when intent (consciousness/fire) is involved. When there is no conscious intent, the communication happens within the body of water. Therefore, the oceans contain the same information instantly everywhere. Of course, circumstances in different parts determine how that information is used and expressed. It acts as the grid or the field that connects us all, but each of us will take something different from it.

Water is the element that can receive all information from Mother Earth. However, certain thoughts and emotions prevent our water from linking in total communication with all water. When our water is in an optimal state, it is able to resonate with all information in water. Imagine what knowledge would be available if we could receive this information undisturbed and translate it into awareness. Is this how we are supposed to function?

The reason that ancient civilizations talked about primordial water and creation was that they were aware of the instant communication and consequent creation in water. From the very beginning, dragons were associated with this primordial water, which holds all four elemental powers (see chapter 1).

IMAGE 9.3. This is a picture of the location of a vortex of the morphogenetic grid of the primordial water dragons. The bottle marks the center.

Primordial water dragons live in water most of the time. However, they are not the giant water snakes in the ocean or Nessie. But they are similar in appearance (if they were visible). At this moment, there still are seven primordial water dragons on Earth. I am not familiar with all the locations, but I am aware of one living close to the California coast near Santa Barbara and the Channel Islands.

To connect deeper with the primordial water dragons, look first at a picture of a vortex of the grid of the primordial water dragons (image 9.3). Then prepare yourself with the introductory meditation, and continue with the following.

—⟋⟍⟍⟍⟍—

PRIMORDIAL WATER DRAGONS MEDITATION

- Focus your awareness on the picture of a vortex of the grid of the primordial water dragon (image 9.3). Connect with the energies to such a degree that it feels as if you are sitting on this vortex.

- Feel and take in the energies that will bring you into the most optimal state possible at this moment.
- Ask the primordial water dragons to help you to connect as optimally as possible with the element of water to help you understand its gifts and its powers and to support the process of optimally working with the potential and the powers of this element. Ask them to help you to contribute to clear water from everything that does not support life on Earth.
- Sit in this energy for as long as it feels good, and allow the process to unfold.
- Feel what has changed for you.
- Take a deep breath, and bring your awareness back to where you are seated. When you are ready, open your eyes.

—⟋⟍⟍—

Primordial Air Dragons

We can study the element of air from a larger perspective to learn its dynamics. We can learn to communicate with air to understand its role, its problems (pollution), the way air flows, and how to work with these flows to prevent storms. It is especially important to learn to understand the relationship between air movements and the collective thoughts of humanity. Currently, Earth seems to be experiencing more air disturbances. Because there is a relationship between air movement and the collective mind, it is important to understand these dynamics.

Air brings life as it holds life force (prana). Part of understanding air is to understand prana. What factors cause an increase and decrease of prana? What is dead orgone (DOR)? ("Orgone" is another word for prana.) What is its role in air movement? These are important questions, and the primordial air dragons know the answers and, therefore, can help us to obtain them.

All living beings use air in one way or another. For animals (including us), air and breathing are essential. Understanding breathing is part of becoming healthy. Breathing exercises help us to learn to breathe optimally and bring balance and health into our systems. Life force and love are connected intricately. Therefore, it is important to understand the effect of love and prana within the element of air.

As mentioned, our thoughts strongly affect air. Thoughts are an aspect of the elemental power of air, and they play an important role in the atmosphere of our planet. It is important to understand the role of our thoughts on the quality and dynamic of air. The quality of thoughts is a factor in determining the quality of all created life. Once while viewing a documentary, I heard that thoughts are our biggest problem. However, I believe that it is the mind — the combination of the thoughts and their associated emotions. Thoughts create emotions, and emotions induce thoughts.

Proper thoughts make things more alive. We also see this with water. Thoughts determine the quality of water, and so do emotions. In our world, the mental part has taken over. Unfortunately, our thoughts are influenced strongly by fears and by the need for cheap and quick satisfactions, which always only last a short time. So we should, as much as possible, have only thoughts that contribute to raising our vibrations to raise the quality of air and life force and also the quality of water. As much as possible, we should prevent or stop the thoughts that lower our vibration and affect the quality of air and life force negatively. We have this responsibility even though most people have forgotten this or may never have been aware of it.

As with all elements, there are two main aspects to consider: the elemental power of air and the translation of that power in what we call air. All dragons work with the elemental powers, but the primordial dragons also work with the manifestation of that element in a physical, noticeable form. In this case, the reference is to air, which is a manifestation in gaseous form. All gaseous forms belong to the element of air.

When we talk about the air and the life force in the air, we might not realize that this is needed by all life forms whether they are visible or invisible. That is why it is so important to look beyond our lives when we talk about pollution of air, water, soil, and energy because it affects all life. When we consider the condition of planet Earth, it is obvious that all elements and manifestations are out of balance and that the condition of both our water and air is reaching a state of irreparable harm. We notice this mostly with water and air because they cover so much surface area and are pervasive. We cannot help but recognize that they reflect humanity's collective mind.

In physical reality, air and life force are strongly interconnected. As

IMAGE 9.4. This is a picture of the location of a vortex of the morphogenetic grid of the primordial air dragons. The bottle marks the center.

Earth/Gaia is also a living system, she needs life force. The atmosphere is comparable to our lungs. It makes sure that life force is distributed sufficiently to all parts of Earth. Life force is more active in certain areas than in others. Air movement is meant to balance the life force on the planet. Due to their thoughts and emotions, humans diminish the life force of the area in which they live. This diminishment is stronger in certain areas. Therefore, air needs to move, sometimes in a very powerful way. Air movement often also includes water (rain) movement. In many cases, excessive air movement, needed for the redistribution of life force, can also cause excessive rain and consequent flooding.

To connect deeper with the primordial air dragons, first look at the picture of a vortex of the grid of the primordial air dragons (image 9.4). Then prepare yourself with the introductory meditation, and continue with the following.

—ɯ—

PRIMORDIAL AIR DRAGONS MEDITATION

- Focus your awareness on the picture of a vortex of the grid of the primordial air dragons (image 9.4). Connect with

the energies of the place in the picture to such a degree that you feel as if you are sitting there.
- Feel and take in the energies that will bring you to the most optimal state possible.
- Ask the primordial air dragons to help you to connect as optimally as possible with the element of air in general and especially with life force and air movements in such a way that you contribute to supporting Earth and all that lives on her. Ask the primordial air dragons to support you in this process.
- Sit in this energy for as long as feels good, and allow the process to unfold.
- Feel what changes in you.
- Take a deep breath, and bring your awareness back. When you are ready, open your eyes.

―――\\\―

Primordial Fire Dragons

In physical reality, fire relates to energy. Energy is induced by conscious intent, thoughts, and emotions. It also relates to burning, whether it is the visible fire that keeps us warm or the physiological process of burning to create the energy we need for all our physical and internal activities. The energies and their qualities provide us with information about how the element of fire functions in that system. In living animals, it also determines their mobility, health, and functionality.

To fuel the fire, air (or life force in living beings) is needed. It is important for us to better understand the relationship between life force and energies. Energy is everywhere, and everywhere is energy. There are different types of energies: electromagnetic energies, subtle energies (immeasurable), and scalar energies (standing or longitudinal waves). We do not understand all aspects of the interactions of these energies, which would be very helpful in understanding the role of the fire element.

The primordial fire dragons are also the guardians of the energetic aspects of the morphogenetic fields and grids. These fields and grids are aspects and expressions of consciousness, and consequently, they have a connection with the elemental power of fire. The primordial fire dragons help us to work with the energies in the morphogenetic grids to the degree that we or any other consciousness can set them into motion.

We need to understand that we have a strong impact on these grids and fields. Through these fields and grids, we can bring in energies and make changes for the greatest good of all. To be able to receive the information from the morphogenetic system, water needs to be in an optimally pure form to hold the purity and accuracy (without deformation) of the information from this system to enable the most optimal creation.

From my perspective, fire can be the most challenging primordial element. When the element of fire is out of balance, all is out of balance. Fire is the beginning, the induction. It also keeps things going (energy). People believe that the Sun is the life giver to our planet, and many civilizations have honored the Sun. The Sun has the information, consciousness, and energy needed to induce and support life. Because consciousness is the starting point and consciousness is fire, we define fire as the first elemental power, and we place it in the east to honor the rising of the Sun.

As was mentioned, in our current reality, most of what we create does not come from a spiritual intent but from thoughts that are based on real or imagined needs. Therefore, we create a world with a lack of the elemental power of fire. Lack of fire means lack of energy and spirituality. It is important to bring the energy of fire into all aspects of the manifested world, harmonizing and raising the vibration of the world. The primordial fire dragons help us bring that balance back into this world.

When we talk about primordial fire, we are referring to the energies that are part of the Gaia system. Part of that is the consciousness of Gaia herself and, of course, also that of the Sun, the planets, and the star systems and other celestial bodies. However, the sources of incoming energies are not of primary importance but rather what happens with these energies once they are part of the Gaia system. That is the area of the primordial fire dragons. They are responsible for the energies as they flow through the Gaia system and all the systems within it. This energy is strongly influenced by human beings —

their thoughts, feelings, and actions — as is everything else on this planet. Within the human collective, there is a lot of violence, and you see that reflected in all primordial elements.

Starting with your body, you will see that your intentions and choices have a strong influence on your energy system in all its aspects. There are places with too much fire (energy) and with not enough. Fire affects your health, functionality, joy, and happiness. It affects your motivation. When our inner fire is diminished, we grow tired and become burned out. When we have too much fire, we can become hyperactive, and that also can lead to becoming burned out or even lead to chronic fatigue. Learning to work with fire creates the balance needed for our functionality and helps us to work with the other elements.

Fire is the transmutational and transformational element. It maintains our temperature, but when our system is out of balance, we might produce a fever to bring back balance. We see something similar on Earth with the natural fires caused by lightning. They are a functional part of ecosystems, which changed when we started to "regulate" them, changing the role of fires considerably. Instead of being a transformational aspect in a natural system, we see them as a threat that needs to be controlled.

While there seem to be eight primordial earth dragons, seven primordial water dragons, and seven primordial air dragons, there are only six primordial fire dragons on Earth.

To connect deeper with the primordial fire dragons, do the following meditation. Remember to prepare yourself with the introductory meditation. Then use the picture of the location of a vortex of the primordial fire dragons grid (image 9.5), and continue with the following.

— ⁓𝟙𝟙𝟙⁓ —

PRIMORDIAL FIRE DRAGONS MEDITATION

- Focus your awareness on the picture of a vortex of the grid of the primordial fire dragon (image 9.5). Connect with the energies of this vortex so that you feel as if you are sitting there.
- You are now seated within this vortex. Feel and take in the

IMAGE 9.5. This is a picture of the location of a vortex of the morphogenetic grid of the primordial fire dragons. The bottle marks the center (barely visible in the window).

energies that bring you to the most optimal state possible at this moment.

- Ask the primordial fire dragons to help you connect with the element of fire and its powers to activate consciousness, support energy systems, destroy what no longer is needed, renew, and activate. Ask them also to support the process.
- Sit in this energy for as long as it feels good, and allow the process to unfold.
- Feel what has changed for you.
- Take a deep breath, and bring your awareness back to where you are seated. When you are ready, open your eyes.

Primordial Black Dragons

It seems all the black dragons have a similar task. They help us to connect with the morphogenetic grids of the group to which they belong. All these grids help us to work with all the dragon energies people have worked with throughout time. Working with the grids is (with very few exceptions) the first step in our deeper connection with the dragons. The black dragons of this group help us to connect with the morphogenetic grids of the primordial dragons.

In the past, people have worked extensively with the gifts of the primordial dragons. This information is available in the grids. A lot of this energy and information has become dormant because people no longer work with these energies. Now, as people are beginning to awaken spiritually, they are also opening again to dragon energies. These energies, of course, also include the primordial dragon energies. Once we have made a sufficient connection with the information and energies in the grids, we also might be able to connect with the field.

When you start working with one of the primordial dragons, it is helpful to ask the primordial black dragon to help you to connect with the information and energies in the grid of that dragon species. We have forgotten so much about the powers of the elements that we are like children just beginning to learn. As we still have a long way to go, we can call on the primordial black dragons for support.

To connect with the energies of the primordial black dragons, a picture of the vortex of their morphogenetic grid is available (image 9.6). Prepare yourself with the introductory meditation, and then continue with the following.

---⌁〰⌁---

MEDITATION

- Focus your awareness on the picture of a vortex of the grid of the primordial black dragon (image 9.6). Connect with the energies of the vortex in such a way that you feel as if you are sitting there.
- Feel and receive the energies that will bring you to the most optimal state possible at this moment.
- Now ask the primordial black dragons to help you to connect as optimally as possible with the information of the primordial dragons in the grids that allow you to most optimally work with the available energies of the elements. Ask them to support this process.
- Sit in this energy for a while, and allow the process to unfold.

IMAGE 9.6. This is a picture of the location of a vortex of the morphogenetic grid of the primordial black dragons. The bottle marks the center.

- Feel what has changed for you.
- Take a deep breath, and bring your awareness back. When you are ready, open your eyes.

Primordial White Dragons

Similar to what we have seen with the white dragons of the duality and the oneness dragons, the primordial white dragons help to connect with the morphogenetic field of the group to which they belong. The morphogenetic field contains information about the optimal state and functioning of each of the dragon species in the group. Therefore, we need to connect with white dragons to help us connect optimally with the specific energies of the dragons in the group we choose to work with. That will succeed only after we have sufficiently connected with the primordial dragons through their grids.

As far as I can understand, the potential powers connected with the primordial dragons exceed those that humans have used even in

IMAGE 9.7. This is a picture of the location of a vortex of the morphogenetic grid of the primordial white dragons. The bottle marks the center.

the past. However, these powers are available in the field. Even though it is better to connect with the primordial black dragons and work with them first, it is possible for some people to bring new information from the field into the grids.

Again, a picture of a vortex of the morphogenetic grid is available to help you to connect with the energies of the primordial white dragon (image 9.7). Start with the introductory meditation, and then continue with the following.

—⟍⟍⟍—

PRIMORDIAL WHITE DRAGONS MEDITATION

- Focus your awareness on the picture of a vortex of the grid of the primordial white dragon (image 9.7). Set the intent to feel the energies of this vortex as if you are seated there.
- Feel and receive the energies that will bring you to the most optimal state possible at this moment.
- Ask the primordial white dragons to help you to connect

with the morphogenetic field of the primordial dragons and its information to bring as much energy and information from this field into the grids as is optimal for our world. Ask them to support the process.

- Sit in this energy for a while, and allow the process to unfold.
- Feel what has changed for you.
- Take a deep breath, and bring your awareness back to where you are seated. When you are ready, open your eyes.

―――ᘯᘯ――

Primordial Central Dragons

All central dragons fulfill a powerful role. They help us feel and become aware of how well we can work with all the powers of the group. They can help us become aware whether our connection with the dragons of the group is balanced properly. They also can help us become aware whether we can finish the work with the dragons of the group. Finally, they can tell the extent of whether we correctly use the powers.

After we have worked with the individual primordial dragons, it is always important to connect with the primordial central dragons. Such a connection will contribute to integration and an increasing mastery of the energies and powers connected with the primordial dragons.

Again, a picture of a vortex of the morphogenetic grid of the primordial central dragons is available to connect with the energy (image 9.8). Prepare with the introductory meditation, and then continue with the following.

―――ᘯᘯ――

PRIMORDIAL CENTRAL DRAGONS MEDITATION

- Focus your awareness on the picture of a vortex of the morphogenetic grid of the primordial central dragons (image 9.8). Set the intention to connect with the energies of the vortex in such a way that you feel as if you are seated there.
- Feel and receive the energies that will bring you to the most optimal state possible at this moment.

IMAGE 9.8. This is a picture of the location of a vortex of the morphogenetic grid of the primordial central dragons. The bottle marks the center.

- Ask the primordial central dragons to help you connect as optimally as possible with the whole primordial dragon group to integrate their energies and powers and to support this process.
- Sit in this energy for a while, and allow the process to unfold.
- Feel what has changed for you.
- Take a deep breath, and bring your awareness back to where you are seated. When you are ready, open your eyes.

——⁓⁓——

Integration

We have created connections with all seven primordial dragons individually. It is important to integrate these energies since integration helps to identify relationships and to recognize that the seven primordial dragons represent one functional system. Every integration will deepen our connection with the primordial powers and contribute to an increasing mastery of the energies connected with the elements.

Be aware that the path of mastery of the primordial powers is more difficult than all the other dragon groups. Working with the primordial dragons is a path of patience. Also, realize that the primordial dragons are not inclined to help in requests for personal gain (ego purposes). You may think you can deceive them, but that is an illusion. Therefore, always come from a place of love and with an intention that reflects that you work for the greater good of all.

Prepare again with the introductory meditation, and then continue with the following.

INTEGRATION MEDITATION

- Imagine a sphere with an equator. This sphere holds the energies of all the primordial dragons. The equator holds the energies of the primordial dragons connected with the elements.
- Imagine you are sitting in the west on the equator, the point of the primordial earth dragons. Feel yourself in that place. Feel the energies that come from your connection with that place.
- Ask the primordial earth dragons to help you connect as deeply as possible with the qualities of all solid manifestations. Feel that you are able to work with these manifestations as you never have been before.
- While you remain connected with the energies of the primordial earth dragons, imagine that you now move to the south point of the equator, the location of the primordial water dragons. Feel the energies that come from your connection with this place, and realize that these dragons connect you with the power of all fluid manifestations, especially with water, so that you can use it for the greater good of all.
- Ask the primordial water dragons to help you to connect as deeply as possible so that you can feel the power of

water and its ability to receive, hold, and create from the information received. Feel the power of destruction that water possesses. Also, feel how water always follows the path of least resistance.

- While you remain connected with the energies of the primordial earth and water dragons, move your awareness to the north. The north is the location of the primordial air dragons. Feel yourself in that place. Feel the energies that come from your connection with this place.

- Ask the primordial air dragons to help you connect as deeply as possible with all gaseous manifestations. Feel the movements of air and the movement of life force. Feel the power of the life force within the physical system of Gaia. Feel the power of thoughts, and use the energies of the primordial air dragons to help you to have only those thoughts that support the whole.

- While you remain connected with the energies of the primordial earth, water, and air dragons, focus your attention on the east, the location of the primordial fire dragons. Feel yourself in that place. Feel the energies that come from your connection with that place.

- Ask the primordial fire dragons to help you connect as deeply as possible, and feel the power of consciousness and the energies flowing through all systems in this physical reality, through this whole manifestation. Set the intention to use these energies only for the greater good of all.

- While you remain connected with the four groups of primordial dragons of earth, water, air, and fire, focus your attention on the south pole of the sphere, the location of the primordial black dragons. Feel yourself in that place. Feel the energies connected with that place.

- Ask the primordial black dragons to help you connect as deeply as possible. Feel the energies in the primordial dragon grid system that help you to connect with the energies of all the primordial dragons and the connected energies of the elements that are already in use and available.

- While staying connected to the five groups of primordial dragons, focus your attention on the north pole of the sphere, the location of the primordial white dragons. Feel yourself in that place. Feel the energies connected with that place.
- Ask the primordial white dragons to help you connect as deeply as possible. Feel the full potential of the primordial dragons and also feel your ability to connect with those energies and information in the morphogenetic field that can be brought into the grids to support the development of the potential of the Gaia system and humanity as a whole.
- While staying connected with the six groups of primordial dragons, now bring your attention to the center of the sphere. The center is the location of the primordial central dragons. Feel yourself at that center. Feel the energies connected to this location.
- Ask the primordial central dragons to help you connect as fully as possible. Feel your ability to bring the powers of the primordial dragons together in a dynamic whole and to function as the central dragon to support the evolution of the Gaia system.
- Feel the connection of all seven primordial dragons. Feel the power of these connections. Be aware that you can always connect with these powers to function optimally in this physical reality and to master the powers of the elements.
- Sit in the energies for as long as it feels comfortable.
- Take a deep breath, and bring your awareness back to where you are seated. When you feel ready, open your eyes.

We have now completed the connection with the primordial dragons. Again, be aware that this connection is just the first step. The next step is a deeper exploration of the energies of the elements and how the primordial dragons can help us accomplish that.

These dragons can also guide us to master these energies to a level that is optimal for each of us. We all are unique, and what we need will vary from person to person. I am strongly aware how little I know of the true powers of the elements, which often made it difficult to provide a good description. The connections with the primordial dragons and the powers of the elements are in their initial stages, and we all have a long way to journey.

Primordial Dragons and Chakras

Of all the dragon groups, the primordial dragons have a correspondence with the chakras that is the easiest to understand. It is a direct and linear relationship, as you can see in table 9.1.

DRAGON Specieꞟ	CHAKRA
Primordial Earth Dragon	Chakra 1 (root)
Primordial Water Dragon	Chakra 2 (sacral)
Primordial Fire Dragon	Chakra 3 (solar plexus)
Primordial Air Dragon	Chakra 4 (heart)
Primordial Black Dragon	Chakra 5 (throat)
Primordial White Dragon	Chakra 6 (third eye)
Primordial Central Dragon	Chakra 7 (crown)

TABLE 9.1. This is a list of correspondences between the primordial dragons and the human chakras.

Even though this relationship will make sense to most people, to fully comprehend all aspects of the primordial dragons is quite a journey. Therefore, it also is a journey to fully understand how these energies and the powers with which these dragons connect affect our chakra function and whole energy system. Mentioning the correspondences is an invitation for you to explore these powers, the way you work with them, and how that affects your chakras and other energy systems.

CHAPTER 10

Master Dragons

STUDYING THE THREE DRAGON GROUPS — the duality, oneness, and primordial dragons — posed challenges; however, there were clear definitions, and their grids were easy to locate. Also, I knew that there were dragons who had a more integrative role, and over time, I named them the master, or super, dragons.

I also was aware that there were cosmic dragons connected to the star system of Cassiopeia. However, their number, role, and names remained mysterious. My understanding of my dragon guide, Drasil-air, suffered the same fate throughout my confusion. Sometimes I believed that he was a master dragon, a super dragon, or even a cosmic dragon. When I reflect, it is obvious that it was premature for me to understand the master and cosmic dragons. I had not yet acquired the ability to feel and understand their different energies. My connection with Cassiopeia was especially superficial; however, I trusted that it would all become clearer over time.

When I was in the Netherlands a couple of years ago, I found a Cassiopeia portal in an old church in the town of Schipluiden (image 10.1), which stimulated more research during my visit. Relying on my intuition, I decided to focus mainly on churches. Soon it became clear that portals to Cassiopeia were very common in the Netherlands. Of the thirty-nine places I randomly visited, twenty-six had Cassiopeia portals. I have not found such a high ratio anywhere else.

We are all cosmic beings who originated from somewhere in the universe. This cosmic origin is also true for other beings and consciousness, such as dragons, unicorns, whales, and dolphins. In a cosmic sense, we all are brothers and sisters. The fact that beings choose different vehicles to incarnate on this planet does not change this. When we learn this perspective, we will see others' essences rather than their expressed forms.

The beings we call dragons are from a star system that is also the origin of many human souls. The fact that some beings use crystalline beings while we use physical bodies does not change that we are related. Because of our similar origin, some people may be more related than others, which may explain differences of attraction. There is no doubt that there are many souls in the Netherlands who are related to dragons or at least feel strongly attracted to them.

Connecting with Cassiopeia deepened my relationship with the dragons in a general sense. The connection brought many new insights and helped me to better understand the different species. It led to a more detailed grouping of the species. It also added five more species: the cosmic dragons, who will be reviewed in the next chapter. Remember that the master dragons are part of physical reality because of their connection with crystalline beings.

The seven master dragons can be arranged within a sphere in the same way as the seven primordial dragons (image 10.2). As we saw earlier, when you connect the six outer points, you create an octahedron. The octahedron connects to the element of air. It is the dual of a cube. A cube stands for the element of earth and represents manifestation. It means that without the element of air, all your creation will be dead. Those two interact strongly, as do water and fire, which are responsible for creation.

While the primordial dragons and the master dragons have one

IMAGE 10.1. This is a church in Schipluiden, the Netherlands, where I found a portal to Cassiopeia.

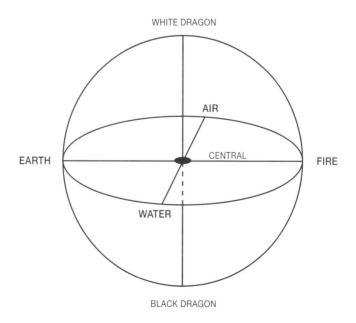

IMAGE 10.2. This is an image of the sphere of the seven master dragons.

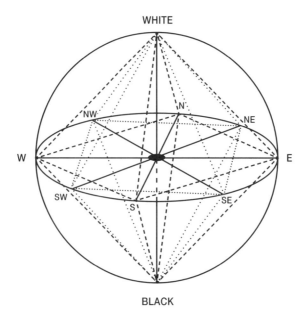

IMAGE 10.3. This is an image of the sphere of the duality dragons with two octahedrons.

octahedron, the duality dragons have two: a feminine and a masculine octahedron (image 10.3). The oneness dragons have three octahedrons: feminine, masculine, and child (or neutral).

Mastery

What does a master dragon master? In earlier chapters, we examined three groups of dragons — the primordial, duality, and oneness. These three groups have a total of six aspects of each of the four elemental powers. The master dragons group consists of the masters of all six aspects of the elemental powers. A summary of these six aspects may be helpful to refresh your memory. Realize that even though you may not remember, your system still knows.

We started with the duality, or three-dimensional, dragons. These dragons connect with two of the six aspects of the elemental powers. Let us use water as an example. The feminine aspect of water is emotion, which creates, and the masculine aspect is the maintenance of the proper conditions to allow the process of creation to unfold.

The group of the oneness, or four-dimensional, dragons has three aspects of each of the elemental powers: active, passive, and neutral (masculine, feminine, and child). For the elemental power of water, this means the aspect that receives (feminine) the energy of the fire lovingly (child) creates (masculine) in alignment with what it received from the fire.

The third group, which holds the sixth aspect, is the group of the primordial dragons. They are the dragons that help to connect to the power of the elements. For water, this means that we learn and understand what physical water does and how it shapes the world in which we live.

Because it is important for the understanding of the master dragons, I will repeat a statement made in the previous chapter. "The duality and oneness dragons help you to understand yourselves and how you function in this world. The primordial dragons help you to understand the manifested world in which you live and the powers that govern this manifested world."

Because you have connected with each of the six aspects of each elemental power through the dragons of the previous three groups does not mean that you have mastered these four elemental powers, let alone that you can integrate them into a functional understanding of these powers. We need the master dragons to bring the parts into a whole, realizing that the whole is far more than the sum of its parts. However, you cannot master the essence of the elemental power and integrate the six aspects if you have not sufficiently connected with these aspects.

You may wonder what "being sufficiently connected" means. To be honest: I do not know. I trust that since Drasil-air agreed to allow me to work with the master dragons and share information about them means that enough people have made enough connection with the previous three groups of dragons to do so. However, Drasil-air is also clear that working with the master dragons and deepening your understanding of the elemental powers is a life-long process for those who choose this path. When you make a connection with the master dragons, you cannot expect that this will lead to a full understanding of the elemental powers. However, you should realize that the level we need to master the elemental powers to be able to express who we are will be different for each person. Therefore, how much we have mastered these powers in comparison with others is useless, ego-bound, and a waste of energy.

The level of integration of the six aspects of each of the elemental powers is determined by the weakest of the six. For example, if your weakest point is the feminine aspect of fire of the oneness dragons, then that aspect will determine the level of integration of the six aspects of the elemental power, which will determine at what levels of consciousness you generally will function in your daily life. This does not mean you will be unable to attain higher levels of consciousness for moments, for example, while in meditation, giving healing, or channeling. However, these levels do not represent your daily functioning. The level of the consciousness at which you function overall in your daily life determines your vibrational state, which in turn determines your experience of reality.

The master dragons can help you understand aspects of your essence. The master dragon with whom you feel the strongest resonance gives you some idea about your purpose and optimal qualities. This state is different from feeling a connection with one of the dragons with whom we worked in the previous chapters. The master dragon with whom you resonate the most may be your strongest energy, and it also may be an invitation to draw in more of its energies to find balance.

At the moment of writing this book, there is only one dragon in each of the master dragon species different from the situation in the previous three groups. The group of duality dragons, for example, has a large number of dragons in each species. There are less oneness dragons but still many. The numbers of the primordial dragons are rather low, as we have seen in the previous chapter, but their numbers are higher than that of the master dragons. There are seven master dragons, implying that there are only seven in existence. However, my feeling is that this may change when more people are ready to work with them.

While it is easy to describe the role of the four master dragons of the elemental powers, it is even easier to describe the role of the three master dragons of the central axis. The master black dragon helps us to connect with all the dragon energies we work with now or have worked with in the past in this physical reality. These are the energies located in the morphogenetic grids of all the dragon species. It is important to remember that the dragons not only help us to connect with the energy and information of our reality in the fourth world but also of the other three realities (worlds) that exist in the Gaia system.

The master white dragon helps us to connect with the dragon morphogenetic field. It connects us with the total field, and the previous three white dragons connect us with the fields of the group they belong to, which is only a part of the total dragon morphogenetic field. We cannot even imagine the potential of this total field. Few people will work actively with this master dragon.

Finally, there is the master central dragon. We can rightfully call this dragon the super master dragon. This dragon can help you to master all dragon energies in the physical reality of the total Gaia system. There will be even fewer people who will be able to connect with the benefits offered by this master dragon.

The gifts offered by the master dragons are impressive, and we may think that we are not ready to connect with them. The fact that we received permission to connect means that we are ready. We each will receive the support to integrate what we are capable of in each moment and what is for our highest good. Opportunities preside, but it is up to each of us to use these opportunities to the best of our abilities.

From the perspective of where we are currently (the transition from the fourth to the fifth world), the master dragons will initially help with the integration of the six aspects of the elemental powers. However, once we have a sufficiently high level of mastery, we will increasingly use the elemental powers to create a world that has an increasing amount of Aether energy as a basis to move more fully into the fifth world, which is dominated by the element.

One day, Drasil-air reminded Jeanne and me that the fifth world exists now. It is fully present as a potential within the morphogenetic field of Gaia. We are unable to connect with it in this phase of our collective consciousness. However, as an individual, you can begin to see and connect with this fifth world. In its full expression, it can be called paradise or eden. It is not the paradise or eden of the past but a new eden, a new paradise.

The master dragons help us to create, manifest, and experience this new eden. We need the creative powers of the master fire, water, and air dragons to make it possible and the power of the master earth dragons to manifest this new eden. The master dragons of the central axis will provide the information and the support to allow all the energies to work together optimally.

The Master Fire Dragon

The master fire dragon is the guardian of all that the elemental power of fire represents within the Gaia system. It helps us to master the elemental power of fire as completely as is possible in this system. The master fire dragon helps us to integrate the qualities of all six fire dragons of the previous three groups into a mastery of that elemental power. The keywords are "energy" and "consciousness," which are directed through conscious intent.

Let us summarize the six aspects we have worked with so far: The two aspects that belong to the fire duality dragons are conscious intent and the way you see yourself as well as to what degree that is in alignment with your conscious self (higher self). The fire oneness dragons hold three aspects. The feminine aspect is the ability to receive from your essence (soul, higher consciousness); the child aspect ensures that you connect from a place of unconditional love, preventing a return to duality; and the masculine aspect sets the intention into motion, passing it on to water for creation.

When we refer to the sixth aspect of fire, which relates to the primordial fire dragons, we are discussing all the energies and the consciousness connected to the Gaia system. Of course, the energies of the Sun, planets, star systems, and other celestial bodies play a role and affect the energies of the Gaia system. I am referring to the energies as they flow through the Gaia system and all the systems within this system.

This energy, as everything else in the Gaia system, is influenced by human beings — their thoughts, feelings, and actions, which are aspects of human intentions. Therefore, they all contribute to the way the element of fire functions. In this way, we affect not only Gaia but also every aspect of our system. Fire stimulates new beginnings by destroying the old. All energies continuously renew themselves, and all possess characteristics of what we know as physical fire.

You can only work with the master fire dragon when you have at least made a connection with all six aspects of the elemental power of fire within physical reality. With such a connection, the process of integration can help you to master the use of the elemental power of fire within the Gaia system. You will start with integration at the level of the fourth world, the world in which we still live. While you grow and expand, you will include aspects of the other three worlds as far as they help you on your journey and help to create the new world. Understand that this is a life-long process.

The master fire dragon is the master dragon of conscious intent. The master fire dragon will not help you to master each of the six aspects of the elemental power of fire. That is the responsibility of the six dragons who are the guardians of these six aspects. The master dragon helps you to integrate these energies as part of you, into an increasingly larger understanding of the elemental power as it functions in this physical reality.

Integrating the six aspects of the elemental power of fire with the help of the master fire dragon will lead to mastery of consciousness and energies within this world at a level we can hardly imagine at this moment. It is important to begin this process in order to contribute to the creation of a new world. Our intentions (direction of consciousness and energy) are instrumental for this creation.

The level of integration and mastery we can reach depends in part on our willingness and courage to look honestly at our weaknesses. We need to ask ourselves, which of the six aspects of the elemental power of fire is weakest. It is not easy to determine this when we do not have a good connection with each of the six aspects, and it will be different for each person. For example, when we consider the two aspects of the duality fire dragons, do most people possess a strong self-image? There is no judgment when I say that most people need to work with all six aspects because none of them are strong. At the same time, we need to honor what we have achieved and ensure that this accomplishment is integrated optimally through work with the master fire dragon.

To connect with the energies of the master fire dragon, first connect with the picture of the location of a vortex of the morphogenetic grid of the master fire dragon (image 10.4). Start with the general introductory meditation, which I have included here, and then continue with the following meditation.

———〰〰———

GENERAL INTRODUCTORY MEDITATION

- Take a few deep inhalations and exhalations, and feel yourself relaxing.
- Bring your awareness as fully as possible to the present.
- Bring your awareness to your physical heart. Your heart is also the location of your spiritual (divine) essence.
- Imagine this essence as a sphere of white light. Allow this white light to shine through your entire physical body. Feel the unconditional love inherently connected with this light, and direct this love to yourself.
- Allow the love for yourself to permeate your whole physical system so that your frequency will increase. Feel this unconditional love for yourself, exactly as you are now, without the need to change anything.
- Allow the love to expand out of you and to fill the whole space in which you are seated. If you are with other people, animals, plants, or crystals, as well as the invisible subtle beings in the room, connect with them and together create a coherent field of unconditional love.
- Feel gratitude for all others present, knowing that they are supporting you on this journey.
- From your divine essence, connect with the divine essence of Mother Earth. Feel love for Mother Earth, and feel her love for you. Ask her to support you with her crystalline life force to enable you to optimally work with this energy, knowing that it will make your work with the dragons easier.

MASTER FIRE DRAGON MEDITATION

- Look at the picture of a vortex of the master fire dragon grid (image 10.4). Connect with the energies, and imagine that you are sitting in the center of that vortex.

IMAGE 10.4. This is a picture of the location of a vortex of the morphogenetic grid of the master fire dragon. The bottle marks the center.

- Feel the energies of the vortex, and take in the energies that will bring you to the most optimal state possible at this moment.
- Ask the master fire dragon to help you to connect with the elemental power of fire in an integrated way. Ask this dragon to help you connect with the six aspects of the element of fire to allow you to work with the elemental power and the power of the element of fire most optimally.
- Ask the master fire dragon to burn away all that no longer serves and supports you so that you can create new ways, connections, and intentions that contribute to the development of the new world.
- Finally, ask the master fire dragon to help you work with energies within you and in the Gaia system in such a way that you contribute to the greatest good of all while moving into the new world.

- Sit in this energy for a while, and allow the process to un-fold.
- Feel what has changed for you.
- Take a deep breath, and bring your awareness back to where you are seated. When you are ready, open your eyes.

—/\\/—

The Master Water Dragon

The master water dragon helps with the integration of all six aspects of the elemental power of water. The elemental power of water helps to deal with emotions and helps us to allow energies to flow. It helps to receive the impulses of energy and information that comes from fire (conscious intent) and ensures proper creation based on stability, flow, and wisdom, along with the ability to allow the unfolding.

I mentioned the different aspects of the elemental power of water earlier, but let us repeat them as part of the preparation for the medi-tation with the master water dragon. We started with the duality dragons. These dragons connect with two of the six aspects of the elemental powers. The feminine aspect of water receives intent (ener-gies) to induce the emotional state that creates, and the masculine aspect maintains the proper conditions to allow the creative process to unfold.

The group of the oneness dragons has three aspects of each of the elemental powers: the active, passive, and neutral (masculine, feminine, and child aspects respectively). For the elemental power of water, this means the aspect that receives the energy of fire (femi-nine) that lovingly (child) creates (masculine) in alignment with what it received from fire.

The third group, which holds the sixth aspect, is the group of the primordial dragons. They are the dragons that help us to connect to the power of the elements. For water, that means that we learn and understand what water does for us and how it shapes and affects the world in which we live.

In the same way the primordial fire dragon deals with all energy processes in the physical and energy bodies, so do the primordial water dragons deal with all water systems in our bodies: the water in all cells, the blood, the lymph system, the kidneys, the bladder, and the urinary tract. Also, these dragons help us to work with and understand our planet's bodies of water. The water dragons of the duality and oneness groups help us to learn to understand how to apply the power and energies of the elemental power of water in our lives.

Water is primarily a receiver and holder of energies and information. Water gathers all that is needed to create life and creates through collaboration with other elements. However, the creation aspect takes place with the elemental power of water within the element of water.

Once we begin to master the elemental power of water, we recognize there is no separation between the six aspects of the elemental power. They flow in alignment with what is needed in each moment of our lives depending on which aspect is needed to fulfill our purpose at that moment.

When we discussed the master fire dragon, we mentioned that most people have a limited development of the six aspects of the elemental power of fire. It is similar for the six aspects of the elemental power of water. For many people, the elemental power of water can pose more challenges because it deals with emotions. It is safe to say that humans, both at an individual and a collective level, have difficulties in dealing with emotions.

In many cultures, traditions, and families, it is necessary to suppress certain emotions, which implies that the movement of energy is limited or distorted, restricting the creative power. This situation will prevent people from using creative power at the oneness level because they are stuck in emotions that create polarity. Consequently, people will create only to a limited degree, and their creations will be mainly dualistic. Through working with the three groups of dragons, we will stimulate the development of the six aspects of the elemental power of water. Through continuous integration with the help of the master water dragon, we will master our emotions, allowing the most optimal manifestation of what we intend to create. Therefore, working with all water dragons is important for creation.

To connect with the master water dragon, connect first with the picture of a vortex of the morphogenetic grid of the master water dragon (image 10.5). Start with the introductory meditation, and then continue with the following.

IMAGE 10.5. This is a picture of the location of a vortex of the morphogenetic grid of the master water dragon. The bottle marks the center.

MAJTER WATER DRAGON MEDITATION

- Focus your awareness on the picture of a vortex of the grid of the master water dragon (image 10.5). Set the intention to connect with the energies of this vortex so that you feel you are sitting there.
- Feel and take in the energies that bring you to the most optimal state possible.
- Ask the master water dragon to help you connect as optimally as possible with the elemental power of water and the power of the element of water to understand its ability to receive energies, information, and its creative powers. Ask the master water dragon to support the process of integrating the six aspects of the element of water and its creative powers to the most optimal level for you.
- Tell the master water dragon that you understand the full

development of your creative powers is a journey, and ask the master water dragon to support this journey.

- Sit in this energy for a while, and allow the process to unfold.
- Feel what has changed for you.
- Take a deep breath, and bring your awareness back to where you are seated. When you are ready, open your eyes.

—⋙—

The Master Air Dragon

Let us review the six aspects of air. When we considered the two aspects connected to the duality dragons, we identified that the thoughts we hold about manifestation determine how much life and life force are available. We also discussed the aspect of conscious change: the awareness of what needs to change to be able to create at a higher level of vibration in the next cycle.

The oneness dragons are guardians of three aspects of the elemental power of air. They are the abilities to connect and receive life force (feminine) through pure thoughts of love (child), and they pass that on (masculine) in a direction that creates the optimal life force for the greatest good of all.

It may be more complex to understand the sixth aspect of which the primordial air dragon is the guardian. We have learned that our thoughts increase or decrease the amount of life force, emphasizing the importance of balancing how we think. However, our thinking is affected by our emotions in the same way our emotions affect our thinking. In other words, our minds influence our quality of life. This also affects the flow of air on the planet, which is connected to the movement of water, which we experience as rain. In this way, you can see that our minds have an impact on creation as much as wind and rain have an impact on creation and life on Earth. The master air dragon is a powerful ally to bring our thoughts to the most optimal state.

Mastering the elemental power of air gives us the ability to work with life force and love in a way that is beyond our comprehension. We need to work with all six aspects of the elemental power of air to master the connected powers. We can work with each of the aspects

IMAGE 10.6. This is a picture of the location of a vortex of the morphogenetic grid of the master air dragon. The bottle marks the center.

separately (which the dragons highly recommend), but we need the master air dragon to help us integrate and to obtain a deeper understanding of all that this elemental power can give us.

To connect with the master air dragon, first connect with the energies of a vortex of the morphogenetic grid of the master air dragon (image 10.6). Start with the introductory meditation, and then continue with the following.

—⟁⟁—

MAƧTƐR AIR DRAGON MƐDITATION

- Focus your awareness on the picture of a vortex of the morphogenetic grid of the master air dragon (image 10.6). Set the intention to connect with the energies of this vortex so that you feel you are sitting there. Feel and take in the energies that will bring you to the most optimal state possible at this moment.

- Ask the master air dragons to help you to connect as optimally as possible with the elemental powers of air and the powers of the element air, which means to help you connect with all six aspects of the elemental power of air.
- Ask the master air dragon to help you create pure loving thoughts to direct life force to where it is needed.
- Sit in this energy for a while, and allow the process to unfold.
- Feel what has changed for you.
- Take a deep breath, and bring your awareness back. When you are ready, open your eyes.

———

The Master Earth Dragon

The master earth dragon helps you to connect with all manifestation and the process of manifestation. Without manifestation, we would not be able to see and experience what we create. The power of the master earth dragon gives us a feeling of being able to deal with all aspects of this world, which comes with a tremendous responsibility. Therefore, it is beneficial that there are six aspects of this elemental power that needs to be mastered sufficiently to bring us to an optimal state of manifesting and working with manifestation.

To remind you of the six aspects, let us summarize them. The duality earth dragons are the guardians of two powers. These are manifestation and understanding the degree your manifestation fits within the natural cycles and systems of Gaia. This may be referred to as bringing awareness to what you are doing in this world and the consequences of it.

The oneness dragons hold three aspects of the element of earth. The feminine aspect receives all that is needed to allow the process of manifestation (masculine) to take place in love (child). This process creates manifestations that will help to increase the vibration of the manifested world to assist the process of ascension.

As mentioned in the previous chapter, a part of the mastery of the master earth dragon is the ability to master the power inherent in all material forms. Most people will think about crystals and stones, and while this is correct, it applies to every manifested form. The master earth dragon also helps us to work optimally with the vibration of the earth (8.1 Hz). When you are learning to work with the power of the electromagnetic energies of the earth, you work with both the master earth and the master fire dragons.

What is the weakest and most challenging aspect of the elemental power of earth for most people? The need to have. In the world of materialism and consumerism, many people feel that they do not have enough or that they may lose what they have. Manifestation connects them with the need to have things. This need ties in with emotions (fears) and beliefs (thoughts), which keep people in the lower aspects of the dualistic three-dimensional world. The earth dragons help us to see that manifestations are supposed to help the Gaia system as a whole thereby creating abundance for every being.

Working with the six dragons connected with the six aspects of the elemental power of earth will help us to see the world differently and to understand that most of what we think we need, we do not really need at all. Also, a shift in the way we see the world will help us to understand that the earth provides abundance if we are all willing to share resources. Continuous integration of the six aspects contributes to this shift and even accelerates it. We need the master earth dragon for this process.

To connect with the master earth dragon, we connect with the picture of a vortex of the morphogenetic grid of this dragon (image 10.7). Start with the introductory meditation, and then continue with the following.

‧‧‧〜〜〜‧‧‧

MAϟTER EARTH DRAGON MEDITATION

- Focus your awareness on the picture of a vortex of the grid of the master earth dragon (image 10.7). Set the intention to connect with the energies so that you feel you are sitting there. Feel the energies of this vortex, and draw in those energies that will bring you to the most optimal state possible at this moment.
- Ask the master earth dragons to help you to connect as optimally as possible with these energies and to help you to integrate the six aspects of the element of earth.

IMAGE 10.7. This is a picture of the location of a vortex of the morphogenetic grid of the master earth dragon. The bottle marks the center.

- Ask this dragon to help you to understand, explore, develop, and use the process of manifestation and the manifestation itself for the greater good of all, as well as to bring the manifestation to the highest vibration possible.
- Sit in this energy for a while, and allow the process to unfold.
- Feel what has changed for you.
- Take a deep breath, and bring your awareness back to where you are sitting. When you are ready, open your eyes.

The Master Black Dragon

The master black dragon is one of the trinity master dragons (grid, field, and central). It is also named the Aether (fifth element) dragon. The trinity invites us to look beyond the individual elemental powers and integrate them into something that is more than the sum of

244 ♦ DRAGONS: GUARDIANS OF CREATIVE POWERS

its parts. Within the trinity, the master black dragon is the feminine aspect that deals with the part that is manifested or already created (energy that was already received and worked with). That which is in the grids is already far beyond what most people can connect and work with even though the amount of information in the grids is limited compared to what is held in the field. In this phase of our spiritual evolution, the master black dragon is important because it can connect us with the information and energies that are the easiest to access.

Realize that the master black dragon helps us to connect with the information held in the grids of all dragon species. It also is the dragon that helps us to integrate the energies of the grids of which the three previously discussed black dragons are the guardians.

This master black dragon is important because it helps us to connect with all the grids and their respective dragons we need because we are continually in a creative process (even when this process produces destructive results). If you would like to connect with any of the dragons and the information already available, ask the master black dragon to help you. This dragon will guide you to the optimal connection, even when you may not be able to feel or sense it.

To connect with the master black dragon, make a connection first with the energies through the pictures of a vortex of the morphogenetic grid of the master black dragon (image 10.8). Start with the introductory meditation, and then continue with the following.

—⟋⟋⟍⟍—

MASTER BLACK DRAGON MEDITATION

- Focus your awareness on the picture of a vortex of the grid of the master black dragon (image 10.8). Set the intention to connect with the energies so that it feels as if you are seated there. Feel and take in those energies that will bring you to the most optimal state possible.

- Ask the master black dragon to help you to connect as optimally as possible with the three black dragons of the duality, oneness, and primordial dragon groups, as well as the grids of all dragons so that you can learn to optimally use all the information that is available to you on your path of mastering the elemental powers.

IMAGE 10.8. This is a picture of the location of a vortex of the morphogenetic grid of the master black dragon. The bottle marks the center.

- Sit in this energy for a while, and allow the process to unfold.
- Feel what has changed for you.
- Take a deep breath, and bring your awareness back to where you are seated. When you are ready, open your eyes.

—⚡—

The Master White Dragon

The master white dragon helps us to connect with and to tap into the morphogenetic field of all the dragons. This dragon can connect us with the full potential of all elemental powers and energies to help us to function optimally within this reality and to become a master of this reality. The master white dragon also helps us to connect to the three white dragons of the three dragon groups mentioned in the previous chapters.

While it is possible to tap more fully into what all the dragons offer, it is best to first master that which the master black dragon offers.

IMAGE 10.9. This is a picture of the location of a vortex of the morphogenetic grid of the master white dragon. The bottle marks the center.

Then we can invite the master white dragon to help us to bring more energy and information about the elemental powers from the field into the grids, depending on what is possible for us in each moment.

To connect with the master white dragon, connect first with the energies of a vortex of the morphogenetic grid of the master white dragon (image 10.9). Start with the introductory meditation, and then continue with the following.

—⟋ⱳⱳ—

MAJTER WHITE DRAGON MEDITATION

- Focus your awareness on the picture of a vortex of the mor-phogenetic grid of the master white dragon (image 10.9). Set the intention to connect with the energies of this vor-tex so that you feel you are sitting there. Feel and take in the energies that will bring you to the most optimal state possible at this moment.

- Ask the master white dragon to help you to connect as optimally as possible with the morphogenetic fields of all dragons. This will help you to receive the information that supports you personally in your ability to function and create optimally within the Gaia system. It will also help you connect with the information that supports the ascension of the Gaia system so that you can bring as much energy and information into the grids as is optimal for you and our world at this moment.
- Sit in this energy for a while, and allow the process to unfold.
- Feel what has changed for you.
- Take a deep breath, and bring your awareness back to where you are seated. When you are ready, open your eyes.

The Master Central Dragon

The master central dragon truly is the master dragon who integrates all the dragon energies into a complete masterpiece. Working with this dragon is powerful and can be overwhelming. Therefore, it is wise to have a clear intention when connecting with this dragon so that you are not overloaded. When you connect, always hold the intent of choosing that which is optimal for you and the greatest good of all.

The master central dragon is also the bridge to the cosmic dragons from Cassiopeia. Dragons are universal. Although their birthplace or origin is Cassiopeia, dragons have been invited to many planets and star systems to support the beings who live in these systems with their creative processes, attuning to the unique consciousness constructs of the planet or system in which these beings live.

You might be starting to understand that you cannot separate the elemental powers. Although they each have a unique function, they are also interdependent, emphasizing our need of the central dragons and especially the master central dragon. This dragon helps us to see this interconnectedness, and it helps us to move from the separation that we experience in the world of duality to the oneness that is needed for true integration, optimal functioning, and the development of the new fifth world.

The master central dragon is the true guide to master the elemental powers in the Gaia system. This mastery refers to the creative aspects of the four worlds that are part of Gaia. Only when we can do that sufficiently will we be able to connect to the fifth element and start the creation of this fifth world.

Drasil-air, Drasha-air, and Draphi-air will guide us. This next step is the development of the next level of mastery: the understanding of the elemental powers at a universal level in such a way as to cocreate the fifth world. Then new dragons will be created to support this process. The master central dragon, as the guardian of the doorway to the fifth world, blocks our passage if the level of mastery of the elemental powers of the four worlds is insufficient. We must accomplish this process from our current world, the fourth world, which is dominated by the element of earth.

It is only possible to rise above the physical (into the metaphysical) when you master the physical sufficiently. These master dragons, especially the central master dragon, are essential in this process.

To connect with the master central dragon, connect with the energies of the picture of a vortex of the morphogenetic grid of the master central dragon (image 10.10). Start with the introductory meditation, and then continue with the following.

———〜〰〜———

MASTER CENTRAL DRAGON MEDITATION

- Focus your awareness on the image of a vortex of the grid of the master central dragon (image 10.10). Set the intention to connect with the energies of this vortex so that it feels you are sitting there. Feel and take in the energies that bring you to the most optimal state possible at this moment.

- Ask the master central dragon to help you to connect as optimally as possible with the energies of all dragons who connect with the physical reality of the four worlds. Also, ask the master central dragon to help you to integrate those aspects of these powers so that you can most optimally support the Gaia system to move increasingly into the fifth world.

IMAGE 10.10. This is a picture of the location of a vortex of the morphogenetic grid of the master central dragon. The bottle marks the center.

- Sit in this energy for a while, and allow the process to unfold.
- Feel what has changed for you.
- Take a deep breath, and bring your awareness back. When you are ready, open your eyes.

Integration Meditation

The following meditation is important. You have connected with all the dragons who help you to function optimally in this physical reality. The dragons are wonderful allies who are also very practical. How do we function? And based on our functioning, how do we create? When we take an honest look at the world and at ourselves, we know that much needs to change and improve. The dragons are waiting for an invitation to help us in this process.

This integration meditation brings us to a powerful point in our journey with the dragons. From a certain perspective, we finished the journey of our first contacts. We still can choose to connect with the beings from Cassiopeia, whom I call the cosmic dragons, the guardians and guides of the dragons connected with the Gaia system, but that is only for those who are interested. We do not need to do this to understand what the dragons offer us on our journey in this physical world. Remember image 6.1 (see chapter 6). We must deal only with the dragons within the broken lines unless we feel guided to do otherwise.

—╱╲╲╱—

SPHERE INTEGRATION MEDITATION

- Imagine a sphere with an equator. This sphere holds the energies of all seven master dragons. The equator holds the energies of the four master dragons of the elemental powers.
- On this equator, imagine that you go to the east, the point of the master fire dragon. Feel yourself at this place. Feel the energies that come from your connection with this place. Ask the master fire dragon to help you to optimally integrate the six aspects of the element of fire to be able to connect with qualities, energies, and characteristics of the consciousness and intention needed to function optimally in the Gaia system.
- Feel the ability to work with the elemental power of fire and conscious intent as you were never able to do before. Feel the ability to work with all the energy systems of Gaia. Also feel that you can burn away everything that no longer serves you in order to expand even further.
- While you stay connected with the energies of the master fire dragon, imagine that you now move to the south point of the equator, the location of the master water dragon. Feel the energies that come from your connection with this place.
- Ask the master water dragon to help you to connect as deeply as possible. Ask the master water dragon to help you to integrate the six aspects of the elemental power of water.

- Feel the ability to receive all the energies that you need to create, the ability to be a master of creation, and the ability to master emotions in such a way that they optimally support the creative process for the greatest good of all.
- While you stay connected with the energies of both the master fire and water dragons, now bring your awareness to the north. The north is the location of the master air dragon. Feel yourself at this place. Feel the energies that come from your connection with this place.
- Ask the master air dragon to help you to integrate the six aspects of the elemental power of air. Ask the master air dragon to help you master the element of air within the Gaia system as optimally as possible.
- Feel the ability to master your thoughts in such a way that you connect only with loving thoughts that support creation for the greatest good of all. Feel your thoughts optimally supporting the flow of life force throughout all creation.
- While you stay connected with the energies of the master fire, water, and air dragons, bring your attention to the west, the location of the master earth dragon. Feel yourself at this place. Feel the energies that come from your connection with this place.
- Ask the master earth dragon to help you to integrate the six aspects of the elemental power of earth so that you can master this elemental power as optimally as possible and that you only manifest what is for the greater good of all, contributing to the increase of vibration of the physical reality that leads to ascension.
- While you stay connected with the four master dragons of fire, water, air, and earth, bring your attention to the south pole of the sphere, the location of the master black dragon. Feel yourself at this place. Feel the energies connected with this place.
- Ask the master black dragon to help you to connect as deeply as possible with the energies of all the dragons held in the grids — but only to the degree that is optimal for you.

- While you stay connected to the five master dragons, now bring your attention to the north pole. The north pole is the location of the master white dragon. Feel yourself at this place. Feel the energies connected with this place.
- Ask the master white dragon to help you connect as deeply as possible. Feel the full potential of all the dragons and also feel your ability to connect with this full potential of the elemental powers located in the morphogenetic field to the degree that is aligned with your journey and your soul's purpose, leading to your optimal support of Gaia's ascension.
- While you stay connected with the other six master dragons, bring your attention to the center of the sphere. The center is the location of the master central dragon. Feel yourself at this center. Feel the energies connected to this location.
- Ask the master central dragon to help you connect as fully as possible. Feel your ability to bring the powers of all the dragons together and to function as the central dragon, being a master of all elemental powers of the physical reality of Gaia.
- Feel your connection with all seven master dragons while feeling the power of these connections. Become aware that you are these connections.
- Be aware that you always can connect with all these powers to the highest degree possible to allow you to function optimally in this physical reality. Be aware that using these elemental powers as optimally as you can will contribute to the creation of the new world.
- Take a deep breath, and bring your awareness back to where you are seated. When you are ready, open your eyes.

—〰—

We have now finished the journey of making connections with the dragon species who are connected with physical reality. We defined these dragons as a combination of the essence of crystalline beings and beings from Cassiopeia.

As far as we currently understand, the dragons we have described are all the dragon species in existence. We are aware that there are other descriptions; however, those are based on imagined forms and not on energies and grids. Realize that many variations of dragons may appear as if they are different species. For instance, I have learned that a dragon can change colors based on the way it functions and on how it presents itself to you.

Feel proud that you have finished a journey that gives you the basis and the opportunity to grow into becoming a master of creation in physical reality.

Master Dragons and Chakras

We have reviewed the correspondence between the energies of which the dragons are the guardians and the human chakras. The correspondence between the master dragons and the chakras is different. We need to remember that the chakras function at four different frequency levels. The master dragons invite us to progress toward the highest frequency levels. The correspondences are summarized in table 10.1.

MAJTER DRAGON	CHAKRA(J)
Master Earth Dragon	Chakras 1, 2, and 3
Master Air Dragon	Chakras 4 and 5
Master Water Dragon	Chakra 6
Master Fire Dragon	Chakras 7, 8, and 9
Master Black Dragon	Chakra 10
Master White Dragon	Chakra 11
Master Central Dragon	Chakra 12

TABLE 10.1. Presented is a list of the correspondences between the master dragons and the human chakras.

It is important to remind yourself that these correspondences do not imply that these energies are identical. They correspond and thus resonate with each other. There remains much to explore about the effects that dragons have on us. Their correspondences with chakras are just one of the areas in which we still have much to learn.

The Dragon Journey

Working with dragons is a journey. If you have reached this point, you have already traveled an impressive path. Guided by the heart, you are able to achieve levels that you could not even have imagined. There remains much to explore before achieving mastery, assuming your heart will guide you there.

I wish to share an experience I had during a meditation in which I connected with Drasil-air. He invited me to sit in the east of the circle of the duality dragons. He asked me to observe the flow of energies. I began to feel the flow of energies throughout the circle. I felt the movement in all directions and the iterations between the eight steps. I also could feel the connection with the black and white dragons.

I became aware that although I first connected with the grids and field of the duality dragons, once I connected with the field, my level of consciousness determined whether I stayed at the level of duality dragons or started to connect with the oneness dragons or the primordial dragons. Everyone who connects with the field of one of the groups has the opportunity to go to any of the other groups, depending on the vibrational state of that moment.

Feeling through the different energies, I became aware that I felt the connection with the fire master dragon. Yes, you can choose to connect with a specific group, depending on what you want to create or experience. However, all dragons connect with the field, and once you are in the field, the level of your consciousness can guide you to an optimal level, moving you in the direction of true mastery.

CHAPTER 11

Cosmic Dragons

DISCOVERING THE DIFFERENT DRAGON SPECIES and learning to understand their role and function is a long and extremely satisfying journey if you are dedicated. When I started, I had no idea where this journey would lead me. Every step was a surprise and led to excitement, discoveries, and a deeper understanding of the elemental powers and the powers of the elements. When I was able to describe the role and functions of the master dragons, it seemed that I had completed my journey, at least concerning connecting with the dragon species. However, I learned that I was wrong. It turned out that there was still one more group. I named this group the cosmic dragons.

I mentioned in the previous chapter that there was a period when I was confused about the names and functions of the dragons I called master, super, or cosmic dragons. Once I had a better understanding, the only confusion remaining was about the cosmic dragons. Initially, I thought that the cosmic dragons were dragons who came from Cassiopeia and did not have a connection with Earth through the crystalline beings. As you may remember, Cassiopeia is the star system that provided information that, when combined with the crystalline beings, leads to the dragons as we have studied them. Therefore, I thought that cosmic dragons were Cassiopeia beings, which turned out to be partially true.

Many cosmic dragons are indeed beings from Cassiopeia who have no connection with Gaia. However, there also is a group of beings from Cassiopeia that has a relationship with the earth dragons and a role that is essential for the optimal functioning of the dragons on Earth. While they have a strong connection with Cassiopeia, they also are part of the Gaia system. Therefore, they are different from the beings from Cassiopeia who are not related to Gaia and from the dragons who live in and function within the Gaia system. These cosmic dragons are included in the overview of the dragon species (see image 6.1 in chapter 6). They are shown in the right lower corner between the broken lines of the groups of earth dragons and the broken lines with dots.

In previous chapters, we saw how the octahedron could help us to understand the dragon energies. For me, that was an exciting discovery, and I played extensively with this and other Platonic solids. I kept feeling I was missing something. One day, I looked at the spheres of the three dragon groups — the primordial, the duality, and the oneness dragons. In particular, I was intrigued by the role of the central dragons. I realized that when I connect the central dragon of each of the three groups, they form a triangle. I have a fascination with triangles and tetrahedrons.

Staring at the three groups and the triangle created an unexpected excitement. I could see that if I added the grids and the field as two additional points (as we did with the other dragon groups), I could create a double tetrahedron (image 11.1). The double tetrahedron has five points. Suddenly, I realized that I had discovered the five cosmic dragons.

My first question was whether my ideas had any validity. Was it my imagination, or do these cosmic dragons exist? My approach always is to go out into the field and look for morphogenetic grids of the possible species. I started with what I called the cosmic dragon of the primordial group. It was interesting to see that the grid I found was different from any dragon species I have studied. Each vortex of the grid had

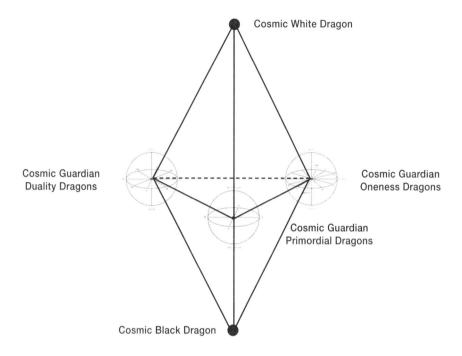

IMAGE 11.1. Here is a diagram of the five cosmic dragons and their connections presented in the double tetrahedron.

seven lines (image 11.2). No other dragon species has such a grid. When I studied the other four species, I found that they all had similar grids that do not differ much in size of the grids, the lines, and the vortexes.

Given who these cosmic dragons are, it was unsurprising to find that the grids differ from other dragon species. These dragons do not have a connection with the crystalline beings and are less earthy. I called them cosmic dragons because I felt that they were more connected with Cassiopeia than they were with the earth. They were not a blend of earth and Cassiopeia. Even though they were part of the earth morphogenetic system, their energy seemed more cosmic than earthly.

I also was fascinated by the number of dragon species. I thought that the four groups were complete, and there was a total number of forty dragon species. The number 40 is a higher order of the number 4. And the number four is the number of earth. The number 40 suggests that the dragons can help us to go to a state that brings Gaia to a higher vibration. With the addition of the five cosmic dragons, we

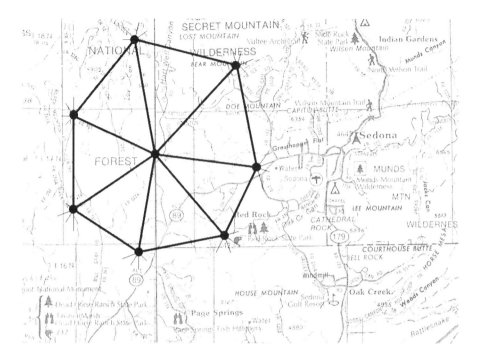

IMAGE 11.2. Here is a map of the morphogenetic grid of the cosmic guardian of the primordial dragons.

have forty-five species. Numerologically, this is the number 9 (4 + 5 = 9), which is the number of completion. The cosmic dragons bring the number of dragon species to a level that indicates completion.

Similar to the master dragons, there is only one for each of the five cosmic dragons. I prefer to call the cosmic dragons overseers. As we will see, this is their function.

In my attempts to understand the role of the cosmic dragons, I wondered what the difference is between them and the master dragons. For example, what is the difference between the master black dragon and the cosmic black dragon? We have already defined the role of the master black dragon. It helps us to master the information of all elemental powers and powers of elements in the grids. It is like a teacher helping us connect with that information. The cosmic black dragon is responsible for what is in the grids and makes sure that the information and energy there is in alignment with the laws and cycles of the earth and the cosmos.

Primarily, the cosmic dragons ensure that all the information in the grids and the field is aligned with the morphogenetic field of Gaia and the universal laws that determine the function of the elemental powers throughout creation. Next, they offer us the opportunity to clear and transform all ideas about dragons in general and the elemental powers in particular to align all information with the higher cosmic truths and values. To create this alignment, we need to accept responsibility for all our beliefs and creations.

The Double Tetrahedron

Image 11.1 shows how the five cosmic dragons create the double tetrahedron. The cosmic dragons of the three groups of elemental powers — the primordial, the duality, and the oneness dragons — create the triangle, which forms the basis of the two tetrahedrons. The cosmic black dragon forms the point below, and the cosmic white dragon forms the point above.

When I connected with the cosmic white dragon, I could feel that I stepped into the highest frequencies of the cosmic dragon field. Looking at the double tetrahedron, I felt that the energy of the cosmic black dragon held the lowest vibration of the five. The energy of the three cosmic dragons who are the overseers of the three dragon groups forms the next level.

There is an increase in vibration in these three overseers as well, moving from the overseer of the primordial to the duality to the oneness dragons. Realize that the differences in frequencies do not constitute a difference in importance. All groups are equally important, possessing differing functions and frequency ranges.

Finally, the cosmic white dragon forms the highest energy vibrations. We can contribute to the process of creating a dragon system that functions optimally by bringing more of the frequencies of the field into the grid. Because the master dragons connect to the three groups of dragons, the cosmic dragons (who are the guardians of the three groups) also are the guardians of the master dragons of the elemental powers. The cosmic dragons ensure that the total dragon potential available is pure and aligned with cosmic laws.

We decide the degree to which we open ourselves and use this potential. That is our journey — to develop our abilities and raise our vibrations to support the process of ascension of the Gaia system into the fifth world. The dragons are not the only beings and frequencies who support this journey. We can include unicorns and quartz crystals whose energies also have the double tetrahedron as a basis. There is a certain resonance among these systems. However, that is a topic beyond the scope of this book.

Because there are only five species, it seems that it would be easy to oversee and work with this group. However, it is difficult to allow our energies to resonate with these cosmic dragons. To increasingly match our energies with those of the dragons of the different groups is the purpose of our journey with them. If you begin to resonate with the cosmic field dragon, you truly are on the path of becoming a master of creation even beyond the physical world of Gaia. Because the five species compose one energy system with frequencies that increase and spiral upward, working with the cosmic dragons leads to mastery over all elemental powers and helps you to work with the fifth element of Aether, which leads to a higher resonance with the universal energies. Because the tetrahedron is the Platonic solid for the Aether element, it becomes clear that mastering all elemental powers through the dragons ultimately will lead to mastering the fifth element of Aether, represented by the tetrahedron.

In many traditions, people believe that we have lived in four worlds and are now entering the fifth world, as was mentioned in chapter 5. I want to expand on this understanding: The Kabbalah — an esoteric method, discipline, and school of thought that originated in Judaism — describes the four worlds as being connected to the elemental powers. The first world, Atzilut, is connected to the element of fire. The second world, Briah, is connected to the element of water. The third world, Yetzirah, is connected to the element of air. (There is a debate, however, whether Briah connects with air and Yetzirah with water. However, for many reasons, I prefer the former order.) The fourth world, Assiah, is connected to the element of earth.

We live in the fourth world, the world of manifestation, of physical form, which resulted in our current materialism. We are beginning to enter the fifth world. The fifth world is the world that integrates the previous worlds into something new, which will be the world of Aether, the world of the fifth element.

13 LEVELS OF HUMAN CONSCIOUSNESS

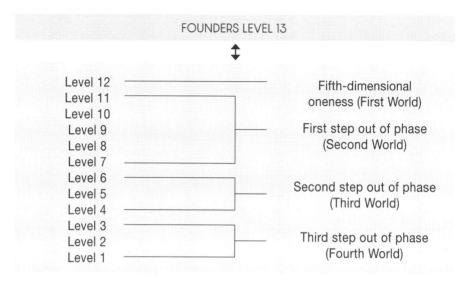

IMAGE 11.3. Shown is a hierarchy of the thirteen levels of human consciousness and how they relate to the four worlds.

This information is in alignment with the information the Founders (the consciousness of the first souls who came to Earth) provided me during my ongoing research. According to the Founders, there are thirteen levels of consciousness spread over four realities (image 11.3). I see the four realities as similar to the four worlds. We are in the lowest reality, the reality in which we are stuck in materialism and survival, the physical world. We are now integrating the thirteen levels of consciousness (the four realities, or worlds) into something new. Based on what you learned about dragons so far, it may be clear that they are helping us on this journey.

In the Kabbalah, each world has a Tree of Life. However, we can also see the four worlds within a single Tree of Life. Scholars have different opinions about how to do this. A Tree of Life consists of ten sephiroth, or divine emanations. The connections between these ten sephiroth are the twenty-two letters of the Hebrew alphabet and the corresponding cards of the major arcana of the tarot, indicating the Fool's journey.

In the same way, the forty-five dragons show us the steps of the journey of mastering our reality through the elemental powers and moving into a new world, into a new way of creating and being. Working with dragons is a process that can ultimately lead to enlightenment!

While a certain element is dominant in each of the worlds, all four elements are needed to create in these worlds. The different frequencies and consciousness systems of the different worlds help us to develop the ability to work with the four elemental powers.

Working with the five cosmic dragons does not complete the journey of mastering the elemental powers. As mentioned in the previous chapter, we need to work with all forty dragon species — which are both earth (crystalline beings) and cosmic (beings and aspects from Cassiopeia). However, working with the five cosmic dragons completes the process of connecting with all the existing dragon species in the Gaia system and the energies of the elemental powers for which they stand.

The journey can never be complete without a sufficient connection with all the powers and thus with all forty-five species. Such a journey may seem to be an impossible task. However, as has been mentioned several times, you do not have to become a master of each of the forty-five powers and their respective dragons. We are all unique, and we have come to Earth to express that uniqueness. Only rarely will that call for mastery over all forty-five energies. We need to connect with enough of each of these powers and their dragon guardians to allow us to express who we are and what we came to do to contribute to the shift into the new world. This process requires us to discover our unique form of mastery, whatever that means for you in this lifetime. In other words, it is not about mastering everything but about those aspects that are relevant to our journeys.

With this realization, there is no need to compare ourselves with others. The purpose is to cocreate a field in which we support each other in arriving at a connection that is optimal for all people in each moment of their lives.

I am aware of five species of cosmic dragons who have a grid system on Earth, indicating that, although they are cosmic, they are connected to the earth. However, there are three dragons that I know as guides and guardians that have no grid at all, which has always puzzled me. Originally, I thought that these three dragons were master dragons. Later, I realized that they did not have grids. Together, they seem to act like a central dragon. I believe that we can call them the three central dragons (the trinity) of the cosmic dragon system. While they do not have grids, they are the connection between the morphogenetic dragon field and the universal dragon consciousness that has its basis and origin in Cassiopeia.

These three dragons determine the field requirements needed to support the optimal ascension of the Gaia system. They can increase and change the field as required. I mentioned these three dragons earlier, referring to them as my guides, particularly Drasil-air. The other two (Drasha-air and Draphi-air) I met more recently while studying the cosmic dragons.

I see Drasha-air as the feminine aspect that holds the field while Drasil-air is the active masculine aspect. Draphi-air is the child aspect and the love who maintains the optimal harmony of the oneness and the trinity. Though I have worked with Drasil-air for many years, I have finally found his proper place and function within the dragon system.

Because it is so important, I am mentioning once again that even though we will finish our journey of connecting with the dragon species through connecting with the cosmic dragons, please do not see this as a completion of the journey with the dragons. You might decide, however, that this journey is rather complex and prefer to use other systems that can lead you into the fifth world. Because the double tetrahedron is a symbolic representation for entering into the fifth world, all systems that work with the double tetrahedron can help you do so. I previously mentioned unicorns and quartz crystals. Another possibility is to work with photons, which also have the shape of a double tetrahedron. However, these systems do not help you to learn to work with the creative energies, the elemental powers, as a basis.

You can compare that with the minor arcana of the tarot, which also has the four elemental powers. It is too far from our topic in this book to go into detail, but the tarot is also designed to help you to learn to work with the worlds and the elemental powers. It is a different system but may lead to the same result. From my perspective, the path with the dragons is simpler than the tarot. Also, we work with beings, who may make the journey more lively and interesting. Of course, you may have a different opinion.

Depending on how deeply you can connect with the dragons of the previous groups, it may be helpful to prepare yourself before making a deeper connection with the cosmic dragons. The fastest way to do that is through the three master dragons of the central axis. They hold and thus create the possibility of mastering the information of all forty dragon species. When you feel sufficiently prepared, you can start your connection with the five cosmic dragons.

Connect with the Cosmic Black Dragon

Let us go back to the image of the double tetrahedron (image 11.1). The cosmic black dragon is at the lowest point of the double tetrahedron. This dragon is the guardian of the lowest frequency system, the guide of all the grid dragons. It may be preferable to define this dragon as the guardian of all information held in the grids. Its task is to check whether the information in all the grids is in alignment with the dragon's universal principles and laws. If needed, they make changes through the guardians of the grids: the black dragons.

When you continue to work with dragons and begin to master certain principles of working with the elemental powers, you will increasingly work with this cosmic dragon, assuming that you have reached the level whereby you can work with it. The reason I formulate it this way is that you can only work with this dragon when you have connected sufficiently with the master black dragon. While the master black dragon helps you to master working with dragon energies within the Gaia system, the cosmic black dragon can help you to understand the creative principles on a grander scale.

It helps you to connect to the full aspect of the information in the grids of the Gaia system, and beyond that, it helps you to connect with the system that relates to the dragon grid information in our solar system, our galaxy, and beyond. It helps us to formulate an idea of how the Gaia system fits into a bigger picture. It also helps us to understand that what we do on Gaia affects the whole of the solar system, the Milky Way, and the universe.

Before doing the meditation, look at the picture of the location (grid) of a cosmic black dragon (image 11.4) to prepare yourself. Always start with the introductory meditation to connect with your essence and love before going into the specific connection with the cosmic black dragon. Again, I will provide the introductory meditation at the beginning of the first meditation.

—⟋⟍⟍—

GENERAL INTRODUCTORY MEDITATION

- Take a few deep inhalations and exhalations, and feel yourself relaxing.
- Bring your awareness as fully as possible to the present.
- Bring your awareness to your physical heart. Your heart is also the location of your spiritual (divine) essence.
- Imagine this essence as a sphere of white light. Allow this white light to shine through your entire physical body. Feel the unconditional love inherently connected with this light, and direct this love to yourself.
- Allow the love for yourself to permeate your whole physical system so that your frequency will increase. Feel this unconditional love for yourself, exactly as you are now, without the need to change anything.
- Allow the love to expand out of you and to fill the whole space in which you are seated. If you are with other people, animals, plants, or crystals, as well as the invisible subtle beings in the room, connect with them and together create a coherent field of unconditional love.
- Feel gratitude for all others present, knowing that they are supporting you on this journey.
- From your divine essence, connect with the divine essence of Mother Earth. Feel love for Mother Earth, and feel her love for you. Ask her to support you with her crystalline life force to enable you to optimally work with this energy, knowing that it will make your work with the dragons easier.

COSMIC BLACK DRAGON MEDITATION

- Focus your awareness on the picture of a vortex of the grid of the cosmic black dragon (image 11.4). Set the intention to connect with the energies to such a degree that you feel you are sitting on the vortex. Feel its energies, and draw in

IMAGE 11.4. This is a picture of the location of a vortex of the morphogenetic grid of the cosmic black dragon. The bottle marks the center of the vortex.

the energies that bring you to the most optimal state possible at this moment.

- Ask the cosmic black dragon to help you to connect as optimally as possible with all the information in all grids. Ask this dragon to help you connect with the energies of the grids in such a way that you will be able to use the energies always for the greatest good of all within the Gaia system and all the systems of which Gaia is a part. This process will support the creation of the fifth world, which will be in harmony with all universal systems.
- Sit in this energy for a while, and allow the process to unfold.
- Feel what has changed for you.
- Take a deep breath, and bring your awareness back to where you are seated. When you are ready, open your eyes.

To the best of your ability, bring into your awareness your experiences. Feel how these experiences relate to your belief system and consider which beliefs you would like to change.

Connect with the Cosmic Guardian of Primordial Dragons

I consider the energies of the cosmic black dragon as the lowest energy of the five cosmic dragons. This idea seems to be strange when we realize that the primordial, duality, and oneness dragons obtain their information primarily from the grids. However, the active use of the information in the grids is of a higher vibrational level than the energy of holding information in the grids.

As you may remember, the master dragons focus on the full elemental powers. The cosmic dragons are concerned with the proper functioning of the dragons in alignment with the universal dragon principles, which are held and guarded in the Cassiopeia system. That is the reason there is a cosmic dragon overseer of the primordial dragons and the two other groups. Each group works in a specific way with the elemental powers and their functions.

Based on their frequencies, the primordial dragons work with the lowest frequencies of the elemental powers, and the oneness dragons work with the highest. Again, realize that what we see as elemental powers is only a very small portion of what these elemental creative powers can do. Nonetheless, they need to be in harmony with all other systems, and the cosmic dragons have the task to ensure that this happens.

The cosmic dragon who is the overseer of the primordial dragons has the task of checking that the energy systems connected with these dragons are in harmony with the cosmic principles to ensure the essence of the power of the elements remains pure and uncorrupted. Purity is especially important because these are the powers that humans influence and try to control. If you control the powers of the elements, you control what happens on Earth, the dangers of which are clear. Remember the destruction of Atlantis.

We have the freedom to use powers for construction or destruction. However, if misusing them leads to a corruption of these powers, the effects could have an impact beyond the Gaia system. That is

IMAGE 11.5. This is a picture of the location of a vortex of the morphogenetic grid of the cosmic guardian of the primordial dragons. The bottle marks the center of the vortex.

why there are cosmic dragons whose function it is to prevent such a disaster.

Connect again through a picture (image 11.5) of the vortex of the grid of the cosmic guardian of the primordial dragon as preparation for the meditation. Begin with the introductory meditation, and then continue with the following.

—⟋⟍⟍—

COSMIC GUARDIAN OF THE PRIMORDIAL DRAGON MEDITATION

- Focus your awareness on the picture of a vortex of the grid of the cosmic overseer of the primordial dragons (image 11.5). Set the intention to connect with the energies to such a degree that you feel you are sitting on that vortex. Open yourself to the energies, and take in those that bring you to the most optimal state possible at this moment.
- Ask the cosmic guardian of the primordial dragons to help you to connect as optimally as possible with the primordial

dragons and the information they hold. Ask this dragon to help you to be in harmony with all that these dragons offer so that you can work optimally with the powers of the elements of our world to lay a foundation for the creation of a new world that supports the cosmic system.

- Sit in this energy for a while, and allow the process to unfold.
- Feel what has changed for you.
- Take a deep breath, and bring your awareness back to where you are seated. When you are ready, open your eyes.

To the best of your ability, bring into your awareness your experiences. Feel how these experiences fit into your belief system, and consider which beliefs you would like to change.

Connect with the Cosmic Guardian of Duality Dragons

Based on what we shared about the cosmic guardian of the primordial dragons, it is now easy to feel what the role is of the cosmic guardian of the duality dragons. As I mentioned, the frequency of the energies of the primordial dragons is lower than those of the duality dragons, which in turn are lower in frequency than those of the oneness dragons. In some ways, the job of the cosmic guardian of this group may be the most challenging.

Most of the problems that occur during creation in our world are with the aspects of the elemental powers — of which the duality dragons are the guardians. It is the most powerful reflection of the mess we, as a species, have created. We also have the strongest effect on the use of these powers in our world and, as a consequence, on all systems with which Gaia has a connection. Because we live in a freewill world, we can use the powers the way we feel or think we should use them. The dragons, even the cosmic dragons, cannot change our right to free will. The cosmic dragons can prevent the corruption of these powers but not their corrupted use and application.

We have the responsibility to use these powers for the greatest good of all. The dragons can help us when our connection with them is strong enough. The master dragons and the cosmic dragons

IMAGE 11.6. This is a picture of the location of a vortex of the morphogenetic grid of the cosmic guardian of the duality dragons. The bottle marks the center of the vortex.

can help the most. Also, the cosmic overseer of the duality dragons ensures that corrupted use of the elemental powers does not lead to them being changed and keeps them aligned with cosmic principles.

Connect through the picture (image 11.6) of the vortex of the grid of the cosmic guardian of the duality dragons as preparation for the meditation. Prepare further by doing the general introductory meditation, and then continue with the following.

—⁓🐍⁓—

COSMIC GUARDIAN OF THE DUALITY DRAGONS MEDITATION

- Focus your awareness on the picture of a vortex of the grid of the cosmic guardian of the duality dragons (image 11.6). Set the intention to connect with the energies to the degree you feel that you are sitting on the vortex. Feel and take in the energies that will bring you to the most optimal state possible at this moment.

- Ask the cosmic guardian of the duality dragons to help you to connect as optimally as possible with the duality dragons and the information they hold. Ask this dragon to help you to be in harmony with all that these dragons offer so that you can contribute to the improvement of the quality of the energies in this world to assist the creation of the fifth world in harmony with the universal system we are part of.
- Sit in this energy for a while, and allow the process to unfold.
- Feel what has changed for you.
- Take a deep breath, and bring your awareness back to where you are seated. When you are ready, open your eyes.

To the best of your ability, bring into your awareness your experiences. Feel how they fit into your belief systems, and consider which beliefs you would like to change.

Connect with the Cosmic Guardian of Oneness Dragons

The group of the oneness dragons holds the highest energies of the elemental powers in our world and reality. We have also called them the dragons of the fourth-dimensional reality in contrast to the duality dragons who belong to the creative processes of the third-dimensional world. The oneness dragons help to develop the full potential of our ability to create in the physical world. The cosmic dragon who is the guardian of this group ensures that the energies of the elemental powers at the fourth-dimensional level remain in pure form, which is the form aligned with the powers on all other levels and dimensions throughout the universe.

The cosmic dragons help us to connect with the purity of the unique energies of each of the three groups, allowing us to interact in such a way as to expand our abilities to contribute to the creation of a new world. Without a sufficient connection with the oneness dragons, it will be difficult to connect with new information from the morphogenetic field.

IMAGE 11.7. This is a picture of the location of a vortex of the morphogenetic grid of the cosmic guardian of the oneness dragons. The bottle marks the center of the vortex.

Prepare by looking at the picture (image 11.7) of a vortex of the grid of the cosmic guardian of the oneness dragons as preparation for meditation. Prepare further with the general introductory meditation, and then continue with the following.

———✕✕✕———

COSMIC GUARDIAN OF THE ONENESS DRAGON MEDITATION

- Bring your awareness to the picture of a vortex of the grid of the cosmic guardian of the oneness dragons (image 11.7). Set the intent to connect with the energies to feel as though you are sitting there. Feel its energies, and draw in what brings you to the most optimal state possible at this moment.

- Ask the cosmic guardian of the oneness dragons to help you to connect as optimally as possible with the oneness dragons and the information they hold. Ask this dragon to help you to be in harmony with all that these dragons offer so that you can raise the vibration of our world and contribute to the creation of a new world in harmony with the universal systems of which Gaia is a part.

- Sit in this energy for a while and allow the process to unfold.
- Feel what has changed for you.
- Take a deep breath, and bring your awareness back to where you are seated. When you are ready, open your eyes.

—⟋⟍⟍—

To the best of your ability, bring into your awareness your experiences. Feel how they fit into your belief structures, and consider which beliefs you would like to change.

Connect with the Cosmic White Dragon

We now have reached the top of the double tetrahedron, the location of the cosmic dragon who holds the highest frequencies. This cosmic white dragon is the guardian of the morphogenetic field of all dragons of the Gaia system. It makes sure that everything in that field is in alignment with the consciousness of the universal dragons, the beings from Cassiopeia.

The morphogenetic field of all the dragons connected with Gaia is in this phase of our development and state of consciousness far beyond our ability to grasp. The field includes the possibility of being able to work with the elemental powers in the four worlds and their connected levels of consciousness. To create the new fifth world, we need to be able to increasingly connect with the morphogenetic field and to take out of that field what we need to be able to contribute optimally to its creation. All the other white dragons can and will help us.

Training to work with the existing dragon species and the information available in the grids will help us to be increasingly capable of tapping into the morphogenetic field. Connecting with this cosmic white dragon helps us to tap into the field even more quickly and purely.

Prepare by looking at the picture (image 11.8) of a vortex of the grid of the cosmic guardian of the morphogenetic field of dragons (the cosmic white dragon) as preparation for the meditation. Prepare

IMAGE 11.8. This is a picture of the location of a vortex of the morphogenetic grid of the cosmic white dragon. The bottle marks the center of the vortex.

further by doing the introductory meditation, and then continue with the following.

⸺〰⸺

COꟻMIC WHITE DRAGON MEDITATION

- Focus your awareness on the picture of a vortex of the grid of the cosmic white dragon (image 11.8). Set the intention to connect with the energies so that you feel you are sitting on the vortex. Feel and take in the energies that will bring you to the most optimal state possible at this moment.
- Ask the cosmic white dragon to help you to connect as optimally as possible with the morphogenetic field and the information it holds. Ask this dragon to help you to be in harmony with all the energies in the field. Ask it to help you to optimally express yourself in this world in order to

contribute to the creation of a new world in harmony with the universal system of which we are a part.

• Sit in this energy for a while, and allow the process to unfold.

• Feel what has changed for you.

• Take a deep breath, and bring your awareness back to where you are seated. When you are ready, open your eyes.

To the best of your ability, bring into your awareness your experiences. Feel how these experiences fit into your belief structures, and consider what you would like to change.

Drasil-air, Drasha-air, Draphi-air and the Total Integration

In image 11.1, we presented five cosmic dragons. It was also previously mentioned that there is an additional trinity of dragons, shown in image 11.9 as the central black dot, that does not have a grid system. This dragon complex (trinity) expresses itself as three dragons. One is the masculine aspect (Drasil-air), another is the feminine aspect (Drasha-air), and the third is the child aspect (Draphi-air). They are ambassadors from Cassiopeia overseeing both the earth and cosmic dragons. They function as a bridge between the Gaia and the Cassiopeia systems; however, their main connection is with the Cassiopeia system. They represent the dragon morphogenetic field personified in these three dragons. Even the five cosmic dragons are an inherent part of their system.

I have always found the power of these three dragons overwhelming. Connecting with them connects you with all the dragons who are part of the Gaia system and with the Cassiopeia consciousness. These three dragons can help us to go beyond anything we can imagine. Seen from a cosmic perspective, they are the final step for those who explore the dragon energy at the highest spiritual level. You can connect with them through the following meditation. However deeply you connect, they can guide you to any of the dragon species that are most optimal for you at each moment in your life.

It may seem that you need to strive for a connection with these

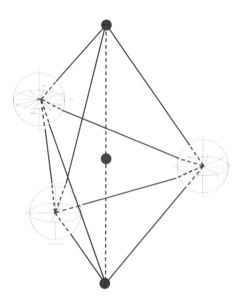

IMAGE 11.9. The central black dot represents the trinity of the Cassiopeia guardians of the earth dragons, named Drasil-air, Drasha-air, and Draphi-air.

three dragons. However, the contrary is true. Focusing on trying to make a connection will pull you off your path. The most important aspect of working with dragons is to connect with those who can help you to express your essence along every step of your journey. We need to learn to be open for these optimal connections that will help us to be authentic each step of the way. If this leads to a connection with these three dragons, wonderful. However, we will arrive at this connection only at the moment we are ready.

Always focus on inviting the dragons who can support you optimally. This book supports your connection with all the dragon species so that your system knows them and so that you can more easily work with them when it is most helpful for you.

Most people will never know which types of dragons they are working with. There is no need to know. Simply invite the dragons who can optimally help you, and be grateful for all they give. If you also know the dragon you connect with, great, but this is not essential and also unlikely until you have worked with them sufficiently to recognize their differences.

Because there is no grid, there also is no picture to help you connect. The only way to connect is to set a clear intent. Then observe and feel what happens. Of course, it is important to prepare as best as possible for the meditation that helps you to connect.

—⟋⟋⟍—

DRAGON OVERSEER MEDITATION

- Set the intent that you choose to connect to the three aspects of the Cassiopeia dragon complex that is the overseer of all dragons connected with the Gaia system. Call these three aspects of the overseer: Drasil-air, Drasha-air, and Draphi-air. Trust that there is at least some connection as soon as you mention their names. Feel and take in the energies that will bring you to the most optimal state possible.

- Now ask Drasil-air, Drasha-air, and Draphi-air to help you to connect as optimally as possible with their energies. Ask these three dragons to guide you in your work with dragons in such a way that you always work with the dragons who in each moment will optimally support you on your journey and in your contribution to the development of the Gaia system.

- Ask these three dragons to help you to bring all your connections with dragons to the most optimal levels. Also, ask them to help with the integration of the energies of the dragons in your system in such a way that you can work optimally with the dragon energies as part of your contribution to the ascension of Gaia and the creation of the fifth world.

- Sit in this energy for a while, and allow the process to unfold.

- Feel what has changed for you.

- Take a deep breath, and bring your awareness back to where you are seated. When you are ready, open your eyes.

—⟋⟋⟍—

To the best of your ability, bring into your awareness your experiences. Feel how these experiences fit into your belief systems and consider which beliefs you would like to change.

With this last meditation, we have completed the connection with all known dragon species. More importantly, we have made a connection and began to develop the ability to work with all aspects of the elemental powers that allow us to learn how to use these powers to create optimally. This journey is about the development of our abilities. The dragons are the best allies we can imagine for this journey. Honor and invite them from your heart to help you contribute in a wonderful way to the evolution of the human species and the evolution of the Gaia system as a whole.

The Trinity Guardians

I want to close this chapter with another experience I had with Drasil-air. While it seems that my connection is mainly with Drasil-air, he always is the entrance into the field of all three dragon guides. I had been used to thinking that it was only Drasil-air with whom I connected, and now I know that he is my connection point and that I connect with all three at the same time.

During one of the meditations, Drasil-air told me he wanted to show me something. When he says something like that, it means that he invites me to allow him to guide me to surrender to the process. He invited me to connect with the master central dragon.

The energy was almost overwhelming, to feel the power and potential of creation within the Gaia system. I could feel more than ever how limited we are in our ability to create. Suddenly, I felt a shift, and Drasil-air asked me, to the best of my ability, to connect with Cassiopeia. I felt myself moving somewhere, and I realized that I was on a connection within a portal about halfway between the energy of the master central dragon and Cassiopeia. It felt like I was a bridge.

Then Drasil-air said: "This is my role and that of Drasha-air and Draphi-air." He told me that there are many of these axes, or portals, emanating from Cassiopeia to different planets and star systems, each with a trinity guardian. The function of the trinity guardians is to ensure the purity of the creative powers in alignment with the system with which they connect. For this trinity, that system is Gaia.

The experience had a deep impact on me. Yes, the energies were powerful; however, what was even more important and touching for me was their trust in me to allow me to have this unique and amazing experience.

CHAPTER 12

More Beings Connected with Elemental Powers

FROM A CERTAIN PERSPECTIVE, THE TITLE OF THIS CHAPTER IS RATHER STRANGE. All beings always have four elemental powers integrated within their systems. However, that is not its meaning. In this chapter, we will examine beings we tend to connect with elemental powers because we believe that they have a special relationship to them, similar to those of dragons. The beings who people most frequently connect with the elemental powers are angels, devas, fairies, and elementals.

The question might arise whether this is true, and if so, how their role and function relates to that of the dragons. Is there any conflict? In this chapter, we will review these beings, their relationship to the elemental powers, and how they relate to dragons.

Archangels and Angels

There are many books about angels, describing them and their roles. As with dragons and many other beings, the tendency is to attribute human characteristics to them, something humans like to do. Giving them human characteristics makes them more familiar, less frightening, and easier to incorporate into our preferred view of the world.

The problem, however, is that it does not allow us to appreciate the uniqueness of these beings, because we have chosen to categorize them as if they are extensions of us. This perspective may be comfortable to a certain degree, but, again, it keeps us away from truly connecting with who they are. Angels especially are viewed as part of our spiritual reality, and consequently, there are various interpretations across religions, esoteric traditions, and more recently, the New Age movement.

I am not suggesting that anything shared about angels is incorrect. As this book comes from my point of view, everyone who writes about invisible beings does so from a personal perspective. I honor all viewpoints even when I may not resonate with them.

The distinction between different types of angels is complicated. I have never resonated with the often elaborate descriptions of angelic groups; therefore, I will not present them in this chapter. We can understand the function and characteristics of archangels to a certain degree by the meaning of their name. The word "archangel" comes from two Greek words: *angelos* and *Archein*. The word *angelos* means "messenger" or "envoy." Angels are the messengers of the Divine. They are spiritual beings who work with the manifestation of the divine plan in all its aspects. They are not material and therefore are invisible to most humans. They are energy beings who have never left the unity consciousness. The word *Archein* means "to be first," "to stand at the top," "to rule." Archangels are the first angels, the ones at the top of the angelic hierarchy.

People who have studied the angelic hierarchy identify seven to twelve groups organized in a specific order. There are, however, different opinions. Archangels cannot be known fully by what different authors provide. You need to experience archangels to understand them more fully. The same is true for dragons, unicorns, devas, and other invisible beings.

People also describe archangels as chief angels or angels of high rank. They are considered holy spiritual beings. They contribute to the building of universes and govern the powers and universal laws. As such, they serve creation, each in a unique way. They are beings of a tremendous responsibility with knowledge and power far beyond our comprehension. Each archangel has legions of other angels, and sometimes even archangels, to carry out its important and extensive work.

Each archangel represents a universal power. We only connect to the archangels who govern cosmic forces that are at play on Earth. That means we mostly connect with that aspect of the archangels who work in our reality. We understand only that aspect of their full power that we experience with our awareness.

It is important to realize that whenever we talk about archangels, we are talking only about a part or aspect of who they truly are. Often, we think we are talking about an archangel when we are talking only about an angel who is part of that archangel's legion. In other words, when people talk about Archangel Michael, they talk about their idea of Archangel Michael without understanding the fullness of who he is, or they talk about one of the angels from Michael's legion who has an Archangel Michael signature. The different interpretations about levels of archangels are not really important. Everybody connects with the energy of Archangel Michael to the degree he is capable and to that aspect of Archangel Michael's enormous energy field that is relevant for the person at that moment.

There is much confusion around archangels. In the literature, there is hardly any agreement about their number, names, and the different groups. In general, there are twelve orders of archangels, or there is one order of archangels with twelve groups. Some of these groups are thrones, authorities, dominions, principalities, overlords, seraphim, and cherubim with other named and unnamed groups. Few have attuned to them because their vibrations are too high for most human beings. Therefore, there are no clear descriptions of these groups of archangels.

Besides archangels, there are angels. Angels are part of the legion of the archangels. Some people call angels the elementals of the archangels.

An interesting aspect is the subject of guardian archangels. According to many, there is a guardian angel and not a guardian archangel. The belief is that when a human being descends into the world of separation, an angel accompanies him as a guardian angel. This angel will always care for the human being. Many people describe experiences in which they believe they were saved by their guardian angels.

The Hierarchy

The beginning of the Bible names three archangels: Michael, Raphael, and Gabriel. Many other names are mentioned later and by different sources and religions. As mentioned, there are strong opinions about the angelic hierarchies. Based on my experiences, my opinion may differ from the general points of view. I share it here because it demonstrates the parallel with the dragon system.

Initially, there was the One, the All, the Infinite Consciousness. The All is for us unknowable.[1] When the All reflected on Itself, it became Two. That moment of reflection was the creation of duality — opposites, polarities. I call the reflection a super-archangel, or Super Michael. The name Michael means "who is like God." The explanation of this may be different in various traditions. However, in the light of what I just mentioned, the name suggests the possibility that Michael was a reflection of the All who, in our language, is often called God.

Out of the two came the three from a need to balance and bring harmony again. We, with our very limited perceptions, call these three powers the sacred trinity. We know this sacred trinity in many forms and terms, depending how we look at them. As we mentioned earlier, these powers can be called the mother elements. Going back to the archangels, we know this trinity as the Archangels Michael, Gabriel, and Raphael. There is a relationship between these three archangels and the three mother elements. Traditionally, Archangel Michael connects to the elemental power of fire. There is some controversy concerning which elemental power connects with Raphael and Gabriel.

I connect Archangel Raphael with the elemental power of water and Gabriel with air. However, many authors see Gabriel connected with water and Raphael with air. If we look at the meaning of their names, it may explain why I prefer the first association. The name Raphael means "God heals." "El" means light. Raphael is "healing with light." Therefore some people call him the "divine physician" and connect Raphael with creativity.[2] I associate healing and creativity with the elemental power of water, not air. The name Gabriel means "God is my strength." He is called the herald of light.[3] A herald is a communicator. Communication belongs to the field of the elemental power of air.

We can see these three archangels as the highest vibrations of the angelic realm, and their energies, powers, and qualities are far beyond

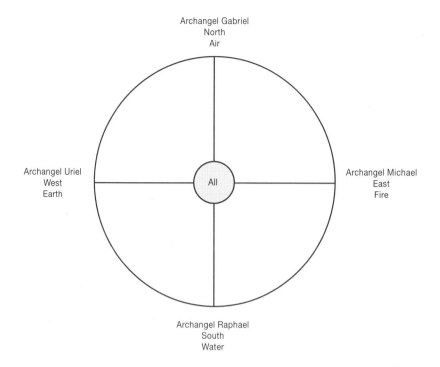

IMAGE 12.1. Shown are the four major archangels and their corresponding elements.

our comprehension. However, we can see that these three archangels connect with the mother elements at the highest levels, and that is far beyond the abilities of even the dragons. To begin to understand the relationship angels have with dragons, we need to proceed to the next step.

We mentioned the next step earlier. From the three mother elements came the fourth element, earth. The elemental power of earth also has an archangel guardian. This guardian is called Uriel. The name Uriel means "God is my light."[4] Archangel Uriel is in our reality as well as all the physical systems with higher vibrations responsible for manifestation. Archangel Uriel as the guardian of the fourth elemental power completes the four elemental powers that we need in our reality to create matter. The three elemental powers do not create matter. We need the fourth elemental power for that. The Egyptians possessed this knowledge.[5] Image 12.1 presents the four archangels as I prefer to position them on the wheel.

Michael, Raphael, Gabriel, and Uriel are the four major archangels. All angels, no matter their name or function, are part of the legions of these four archangels. This statement implies that every archangel or angel belongs, in one way or another, to these four energy beings and their consciousness construct. There are innumerable archangels and angels. Every time a new consciousness construct or entity is created or comes into being, there is an angel allocated to it. This angel will be an offshoot of one of the four major archangels (see image 12.2).

So far, we have described some steps of the creation of the angelic system. It is important to state that all angels who have a relationship with the manifested physical universe or multiverse have a connection with all four elemental powers. And similar to the dragons, they have a predominant elemental power. It cannot be otherwise, as image 12.2 shows. The image also shows that besides the four elemental powers, there always will be the twelve powers, as every elemental power has its trinity.

The twelve angels create a system similar to the one we have seen with the oneness dragons. We called this system of twelve the angel wheel. We first created this wheel at a spiritual retreat center and later also in our yard (image 12.3). This wheel consists of the four major archangels and the archangels who connect with them to form the trinity. The major archangels are the neutral essence of the elemental powers. The two archangels who connect with them are the feminine and masculine aspects of that elemental power. Creation, seen and experienced from our reality, always orients clockwise. The archangel at the right side of the main archangel, looking at it from the center, is always the active power, the masculine aspect, and the archangel at the left always holds the feminine aspect, the receiving aspect.

These systems keep each other in balance through feedback. We need to realize that everything is part of the whole and that each aspect of the whole influences all other aspects. Image 12.4 shows the twelve archangels of the circle. The solid lines connect the four major archangels and the neutral aspect or essence. The broken lines connect the four archangels that represent the feminine aspect of each of the four elements, and the broken lines with dots represent the masculine aspects.

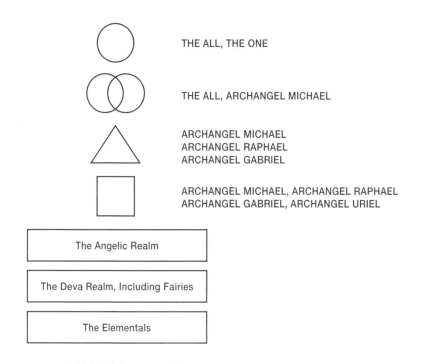

IMAGE 12.2. Depicted is an overview of the angelic system.

IMAGE 12.3. The angel wheel we constructed in our yard.

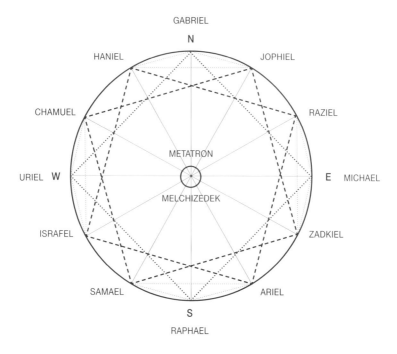

IMAGE 12.4. This is a diagram of the twelve archangels of the wheel and their names. The solid lines connect the four major archangels, who form the neutral aspects. The broken lines connect the four archangels that form the feminine aspect. The broken lines with dots represent the masculine aspects.

These twelve archangels are the major archangels with whom to work. The similarity with the oneness dragons is striking. It is even more striking when we add the two archangels of the center (image 12.4), Metatron and Melchizedek. Metatron is the archangel of above. We can compare this archangel with the white dragons or the master white dragon. This archangel is responsible for humanity's spiritual path, which has to be aligned with the morphogenetic field of the human species and is the consciousness construct of the full potential of humanity.

We can compare Archangel Melchizedek to the black dragons or the master black dragon. This archangel is responsible for guiding us, people, along our spiritual journey here on Earth. Melchizedek guides us to work with the consciousness aspects already available in the grids and helps us to expand that through an increasing connection with

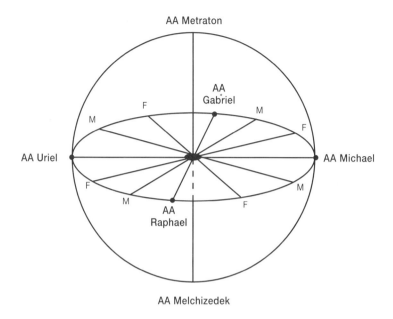

IMAGE 12.5. This is a cross-section of the archangel sphere and its properties.

Archangel Metatron. The addition of these two archangels also means that the angel wheel is the equator of a sphere that has Metatron at the top, the north pole, and Melchizedek at the south pole (image 12.5).

The fact that the archangel sphere has so many similarities with the oneness dragons again brings up the question of the difference in their functions. Or are they the same kind of beings? However, before answering these questions, we need to descend two more levels of the hierarchy.

Devas

Image 12.2 shows you that I see the deva world as part of the angelic world. Devas are also called Earthangels,[6] or the shining ones. Because they are part of the subtle realms, there is a lot of confusion and many opinions about what they are. Some people call devas nature spirits. From my perspective, there is not a difference. Nathaniel Altman in *The Deva Handbook* also does not show a difference between devas and nature spirits.[7] He also does not show a difference between angels and devas.

I have found very few authors who view the realms of angels, devas, and elementals the same way I do. Someone who views them similarly is William Bloom.[8] He goes so far as to use the words "angel" and "deva" interchangeably and sees elementals as devas too. Because they are all part of the hierarchy, his statement is correct. However, like many others, he uses the word "elementals" for the little devic beings who are also called the fairies. From my perspective, elementals have a different function. Based on their functions, I separate devas and elementals into different groups, as I will explain later in this chapter.

The world of the devas is large and holds an enormous variety. There are millions of devas. However, based on the Hermetic principle of "as above, so below," they are organized into four major groups, like the angels, based on the elemental powers. The parallel with angels goes even a step further. Also, devas have twelve main groups that we can describe in ways similar to the twelve archangels of the angel wheel. Each group based on the elemental powers has the trinity of feminine, masculine, and neutral (or child).

To understand devas, we need to look at their morphogenetic system. Interestingly, angels do not have a morphogenetic system connected to the Gaia system, which means they are not part of Gaia. The angels who have a morphogenetic system are the ones I call devas, or earth angels. There is much more research needed to understand the world of the devas. The deva system is so vast that it deserves its own book.

Initially, I thought that the deva morphogenetic field had twelve subfields. However, there are thirty-six subfields (image 12.6). Once again, each of the twelve subfields has a neutral (air [A]), feminine (water [W]), and masculine (fire [F]) aspect. These thirty-six subfields are the basis for the expression of the many deva species. Each deva species has its own morphogenic grid. It is difficult to imagine how many grids there are.

When I wrote *Gifts of Mother Earth*, I was aware of twelve systems.[9] The grid I had presented and designated a level 4, I would now call a deva grid dominated by the elemental power of water and connected to the neutral (air) aspect. This statement does not help us to understand what type of deva it is because there are many devas of all sizes and functions in this category. Unfortunately, at the moment

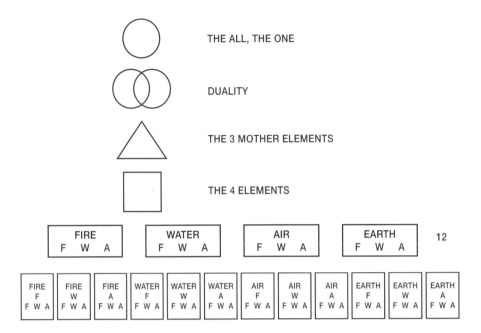

IMAGE 12.6. Here is an overview of the deva morphogenetic field and the thirty-six major groups of devas.

I researched that grid, I did not have a clear understanding of these grids, so I do not know which deva it was, only the type.

The research that will help to understand the groups, their function, and the structure of the hierarchy is an extensive and important study. If we want to expand into the fifth world, we need to collaborate with devas. It is helpful to have insight into their hierarchy to know which deva to connect with to create an optimal collaboration in each situation.

While this book is not about devas, I would like to share a bit more to help you understand the complexity of this realm. Each of the thirty-six morphogenetic subfields has an innumerable number of species. In each group, there are huge and powerful devas and tiny ones as well as every size in between. The size seems to have a certain correlation with the object or being they connect with. A deva of a continent, for example, Australia, is much larger than a deva connected to a mountain range, which is larger than the one connected with a mountain peak. Also, the fact that the deva of Australia belongs

IMAGE 12.7. The banana yucca has a deva who belongs to the water/water/air group.

to one of the thirty-six morphogenetic groups does not mean that all landscape aspects and biomes (ecological units) of Australia belong to the same group. The contrary is true. Altogether, the different units and levels create an optimal balance for that continent.

Another example is trees. There is a deva for all the trees. There is a deva for all types of trees, such as a deva for all pine trees or all oaks. Then there is a deva for each species. For example, there is a deva for all Ponderosa pines. Each Ponderosa pine has its own deva. These examples show the hierarchical structure in addition to the thirty-six main groups of devas.

Knowing the thirty-six groups as indicated in image 12.6, we can look at the deva of a certain plant or animal species and determine which of the thirty-six groups it belongs to. It is the start of getting a better understanding of the function of each of these groups. Following are a few examples.

Image 12.7 shows a plant named the banana yucca (*Yucca baccata*). Its deva belongs to the element of water. The trinity aspect of water for

IMAGE 12.8. The soaptree yucca has a deva who belongs to the water/water/air group.

this deva is also water, and the trinity aspect of that water aspect is air. I define the deva by saying that the deva of the *Yucca baccata* belongs to the water/water/air group. If we look at the deva of another yucca, the soaptree yucca (*Yucca elata*, see image 12.8), we see that this deva, although it is a different species, also belongs to the water/water/air group. When we look at the deva of an Arizona cypress (image 12.9), its deva belongs to the water/air/air group. By studying devas this way, we will begin to understand more of the deva world.

IMAGE 12.9. The Arizona cypress has a deva who belongs to the water/air/air group.

An aspect of devas I find fascinating is that they are caretakers of all creation. All creation is not restricted to only landscapes, mountains, biomes (lakes and rivers), minerals, plants, and animals. It also includes all that we create in our technological society. Every object is a coherent field and thus has a deva. That includes your house, car, computer, cell phone, and even the chair on which you sit. This awareness invites us to look at all objects differently. I needed, of course, to check which group the deva of my cell phone belongs to. It was the group of earth/air/air. The deva of my computer (PC) belongs to the same group.

While the study of the world of the devas may be huge and even overwhelming, we can start with the plants, animals, crystals, and objects around us. Learning to connect with the devas who are connected to all that exists, whether a living being or an object, will enhance our lives because they all are part of our lives. Only when we connect more fully with all around us with the help of devas will we create a new world.

I would like to finish this part of the information on devas by looking at the devas connected to human beings. These devas all belong to the fire/fire/air group, the full meaning of which continues to challenge me. So far, I have mentioned only devas connected to the visible world. However, we need to realize that the invisible worlds and beings also have devas.

While it is already difficult to understand the devas of the visible world, it is even more difficult to understand the devas of the invisible world. The importance of this realization is that there is a deva who oversees and cares for all dragons, one for each dragon species and one for each dragon. I have to admit that this realization was quite overwhelming for me. At the same time, it made me realize how wonderfully creation works — how all is interconnected and how all supports all.

Fairies

An often confusing subject related to devas is the subject of fairies. According to almost all books, fairies connect with the elements. Here, we are talking about elements and not elemental powers. However, a fairy (or little deva) connected to the element of water also has the dominant elemental power of water. In this sense, the devas we call fairies have a stronger connection with one of the elemental powers than the other devas. For this reason, people call them elementals, which I believe is incorrect.

Although opinions differ considerably, Nathaniel Altman describes the more common opinion well.[10] To him, and I concur, the fairies are not a separate group but are the devas, or nature spirits, connected with the four primary elements of creation.

Many call the devas, or nature spirits, of the earth dwarfs or gnomes, but Altman does not use this term. He defines them as the devas connected to the rocks, stones, earth, and mountains. He used the term "undines" for the water spirits. In Altman's definition, they are all devas connected to water, differing in size depending on the body of water. In folklore, people depict them as small, mostly female beings.

"Undine" is a term that appears in the alchemical writings of Paracelsus, a Renaissance alchemist and physician. It derives from the

Latin word *unda*, meaning "wave," and it first appears in Paracelsus's book *Liber de Nymphis, sylphis, pygmaeis et salamandris et de caeteris spiritibus*, published posthumously in 1658. Paracelsus believed that each of the four classical elements — earth, water, air, and fire — is inhabited by different categories of elemental spirits, liminal creatures who share our world: gnomes, undines, sylphs, and salamanders, respectively. He describes these elementals as the "invisible, spiritual counterparts of visible Nature ... many resembling human beings in shape, and inhabiting worlds of their own, unknown to man because his undeveloped senses were incapable of functioning beyond the limitations of the grosser elements."[11] This citation also explains why the terms "dwarfs," "undines," "sylphs" (devas connected with the element of air), and "salamanders" (devas connected with the element of fire) are commonly used.

While sometimes these terms are used in connection with fairies, they are based on limited perceptions of devas and restrict the separation of the devas to the four elements. As we have seen, there are not four but thirty-six groups. For this reason, I prefer not to use any of these four names or "fairies." I prefer to call them devas.

Elementals

The term "elementals" is also a confusing name. By now, you may understand that "elemental" applies to a number of beings. You can call all beings connected to elemental powers elementals, for example, dragons, devas, nature spirits, and angels. However, I use the term "elementals" for a group of beings who are different from any of the previously mentioned groups. All the beings from these previous groups are connected with all four elemental powers but have one of these four as their dominant power.

Besides being a confusing name, the basic definition of elementals is that they are mythological beings first appearing in the alchemical works of Paracelsus in the sixteenth century. Traditionally, there are four types, which returns us to the description just given to the fairies.

Does this mean that all these terms are descriptions of the same phenomenon, given by people in various ways with different terms? It appears so. It seems that the names devas, nature spirits, fairies (not faeries, which is a name that refers to the sidhe), and elementals all refer to the same group of beings who are not visible to us and have similar functions: to connect with and support all manifested forms.

Why do I use the term "elementals" separately instead of placing it under the heading of devas? The reason is that they are, from my perspective, different from the devas. The elementals, as I define them, are beings who are very tiny and connect to only one of the four elemental powers. I mentioned them in my book *Gifts of Mother Earth*, where I described their grids. I had found a vortex that was shared by the grids of all four elementals even though the grids themselves were different.[12]

Because the elementals connect to a single element, I consider them different from the devas. Also, their role is different. They are the worker bees of the subtle realms who support all that exist in manifested form. To become active, they need to be directed by a consciousness of higher order, be it the devas and angels or even us. By following the directed consciousness, they ensure that their energies support the processes of creation, healing, and restoration. I do not know how this process unfolds. It requires a "seeing" that is beyond my current abilities.

Dragons, Angels, Devas, and Elementals and Their Roles

The purpose of this chapter is to provide a clearer understanding of the functioning of dragons within the physical and subtle worlds and their relationship with other beings connected with elemental powers. Here are some simple definitions that indicate the role of the different groups and the beauty of their cooperation, relationship, and interconnectedness.

Angels support and guide any independent consciousness construct. Whenever an independent consciousness appears, there will be an angel to guide it. That is why every human being has a guardian angel, and so does a planet. However, when a soul has many physical expressions, there will be an angel connected with the soul but not the individual physical expressions. An example of this is plants. There are many daisies, and each has a deva. However, there is one soul for many daisies, and that group of daisies that belongs to one soul has only one angel.

Angels try to pass on messages that guide a consciousness in creating and functioning in alignment with its purpose. Human beings have forgotten that there is an angel who helps and guides them to function as optimally as possible. Devas, however, are connected with expressions or manifestations created by a consciousness. To use the same example, the soul of daisies that has many individual expressions as its manifestation has a deva for each of its manifestations. Therefore, far more devas exist in and are connected with the Gaia system than there are angels.

The devas help the manifestation to function as optimally as possible. In our situation, our angels guide and help our souls and our consciousnesses, and our devas guide our physical systems' functioning so that we can become optimal creators. Unfortunately, we have forgotten how to receive their messages and therefore do not act on them. When people have some awareness of their angels and devas, they often talk about their two guardian angels, not realizing that one of them is a deva with a function different from the angel.

Whenever we create, we need to know how to use the elemental powers optimally, which is the job of the dragons. While the angel helps us to connect with us to ensure that we create in alignment with our higher consciousnesses, the dragons help with the process of the creation itself. The process of creation induces the four types of elementals to enable the actual manifestation in alignment with the consciousness stream. Angels, dragons, and elementals will not change the outcome, because that would mean they were interfering with our free will.

Although this book focuses on the dragons to help us to optimize the process of creation, there always will be angels, devas, and elementals involved. Understanding the way everything functions together makes it clear that reconnecting with the subtle beings who work with us is of prime importance to be able to optimize our functioning in this world and the creation of a new world.

CHAPTER 13

Dragons and the Fifth World: Humans Develop a New Consciousness

MANY SPIRITUAL AND ESOTERIC TRADITIONS INFORM US that the purpose of our journey is to connect with our spiritual essence. I define it as expressing our spiritual essence through our physical system. Our challenge is not so much our spirituality. Our challenge is the system through which spirituality — our essence, our soul — tries to express itself. To rephrase this statement, we can say that our physical systems have minds of their own that are so strong they often overrule the subtle signals that come from our essence through our hearts.

For most people, these subtle signals never reach their active minds. Their minds are too busy dealing with an ever-increasing amount of triggers our environment offers. Most people are unable to be still long enough to hear the signals and messages from their hearts, which we often call intuition. While most people are unable to hear their hearts, they also are unable to hear the signals their bodies send them.

We are so occupied surviving in this demanding world that we have lost our ability to connect with the world at large, especially with the subtle aspects. This disconnection is a reflection of the separation from our physical systems, which causes us to be unaware of what happens within our bodies unless it is something uncomfortable or painful.

Because of the overall lack of awareness, most people are no longer conscious cocreators and are unaware of the elemental powers involved. In this book, you have learned, or at least have been presented the opportunity to learn, how to become a conscious cocreator. We learned that there are different aspects of the elemental powers. Understanding these powers helps us to increase our ability to create in alignment with who we are and to do so from an increasingly high vibration. Through this process, we can learn to become masters of the powers of the elements and masters of the elemental powers. This process is exciting!

However, the process is not for personal gain. It is to help us become the true guardians of the Gaia system and to help this system to ascend. The ascension of the Gaia system and our expanding consciousnesses lead us into the fifth world.

Earlier, we mentioned the existence of four worlds. Indigenous people, especially the Hopi[1] and Maya[2] predicted that we would move into the fifth world. Interestingly, the Kabbalah[3] also mentions the fifth world. That world is characterized by what they call the Adam Kadmon. Within the traditional information of the Kabbalah, the world of Adam Kadmon (the supreme man, or universal man, also referred to as the spiritual world) is above the other four worlds, and this was so before the emanation into the four worlds.

From the perspective of the lowest vibration of the fourth world — the world of Assiah, the world of action, the world dominated by the element of earth, the world characterized by "I have" — we need to increase our vibration in regard to Adam Kadmon. However, this is a new Adam Kadmon, who is the new human with a complete mastery of the spiritual and the physical aspects while living within the Gaia system. I believe that we are heading in the direction of the fifth world, the world of the new Adam Kadmon.

We need all the help we can get to be successful. Based on all you have experienced through the connection with the different dragons, it may be clear that the dragons are powerful allies on this journey.

For many people, the collaboration with dragons is essential to know how to master the forces that we need to create this new world. I wrote an article on the fifth world,[4] as I describe in the following.

For a moment, let us return to the four worlds. There are barriers between the four worlds induced by a shift in consciousness that causes the worlds to go out of phase. As most people cannot perceive these worlds, they do not connect with them, and it is as if these worlds do not exist. However, they do exist and are part of the collective consciousness of humanity.

Our DNA, which functions as antennae, attunes to that aspect of the morphogenetic field (certain consciousness grids) that connects with our consciousness in the fourth world. Therefore, all we experience and the way we function is a consequence of the attunement to the fourth world. It is imperative for you to understand this statement. It means that we can only use what the dragons offer us to the degree that it is in alignment with the consciousness construct of the fourth world. In other words, we use only a small part of what the dragons offer us. We attune partially, and most people are not even able to fully use that available part.

The Four Worlds
and the Connected Elemental Powers

Different levels of human consciousness connect with the four realities, or worlds, that connect with the four elemental powers. The first world has the elemental power of fire as the dominant element. In all of creation, you will always find all three mother elements — fire, water, and air — and in the manifested world, the element of earth is added. We associate the elemental power of fire with consciousness. So the dominance of fire indicates that there was a focus on consciousness in that world and that this consciousness was of a high level. This level of consciousness corresponds to the twelfth and thirteenth levels of consciousness in image 13.1. It was the world of the first experiences of the souls we call the Founders.

When consciousness descended in frequency, there was a loss of knowledge and understanding. The lowering of the frequency of consciousness induced a shift out of phase into the second world. According to the Hopi stories, the move into the second world was

13 LEVELS OF HUMAN CONSCIOUSNESS

FOUNDERS LEVEL 13

↕

Level 12	Fifth-dimensional
Level 11	oneness (First World)
Level 10	
Level 9	First step out of phase
Level 8	(Second World)
Level 7	
Level 6	
Level 5	Second step out of phase
Level 4	(Third World)
Level 3	
Level 2	Third step out of phase
Level 1	(Fourth World)

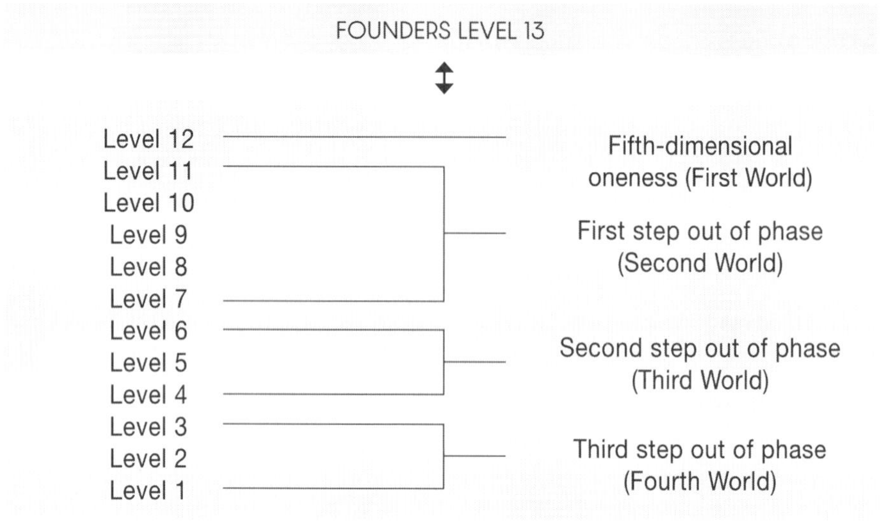

IMAGE 13.1. Here is a hierarchy of the thirteen levels of human consciousness and their relationship to the four worlds.

because of forgetting.[5] I agree. When the frequencies of consciousness decrease, we have less access to knowledge and information and begin to forget.

The second world's dominant elemental power was water. This world corresponds to the seventh through the eleventh levels of consciousness. This world was the world of almost unlimited creation. Many know this world as Lemuria, or Mu. Lemuria dominated this planet for millions of years. The story of the destruction of a world is an interpretation that comes from the perspective of those who survived the destruction and found themselves in the next world. However, there was no destruction in the sense of the world no longer existing. It was the inability to maintain such a high vibration that, seen from the perspective of the observer with the lower consciousness, that world with the higher consciousness no longer exists (is destroyed), because it is no longer perceived. This experience is true of all worlds. However, the shift in consciousness can be energetically very intense, amplifying the feeling of destruction, and even lead to actual physical destruction.

The second world, dominated by the element of water, existed the longest of all the four worlds. In fact, it still exists. Seen from the perspective of humanity, the destruction of the second world is a fact. Humanity shifted into the third world, the world with air as the dominant element. Before we look at that world, we need to go back to the statement that the second world still exists. It exists even though we cannot perceive it. However, we can make a connection with it again, and people are beginning to do so.

We make this connection through human beings (our family) who still live in this second world: the sidhe, an invisible human race who are our relatives. With the sidhe, I wrote a book called *Birth of a New Consciousness*.[6] The title of the book reflects what we are sharing in this chapter, but I did not know that then. We are living in a time that will give birth to a new consciousness. The sidhe live in a world (reality) that is not solid and fixed as is our world. Their world changes in a fluid way based on the way the energy moves within the consciousness construct (field) of the community. Such a fluid movement is very challenging, if not impossible, for us to understand.

The third world is dominated by the element of air. By the time human consciousness shifted into this world, its vibration was considerably lower. The consciousness of the third world includes the consciousness levels 4 through 6. Because the overall level of consciousness was so much lower, the third world grew into a world characterized by a mental approach. This world is also far more physical. We know this world as Atlantis. In this world, some people were still able to hold remnants of the Lemurian consciousness. Atlantis was a world of scientists and priests who increasingly dominated the masses in all areas of their lives. This world existed for a considerably shorter period than the second world. It existed around 170,000 years.

Presently, we live in the fourth world. The dominant elemental power of this world is the elemental power of earth. The consciousness of this, our, world connects to the levels 1 through 3. Our world is the densest. We see all forms as being solid and fixed. We started to believe that the world was physical, totally defined and unchangeable. It is the world of matter. Material forms began to rule our society, leading to a materialistic approach that continues to dominate us.

In our world, safety depends on having what we believe we need to have. This state of consciousness is the bottom of the barrel concerning consciousness, vibration, and awareness. The period in which this world exists is the shortest of the four worlds. So far, it has existed for around 35,000 years. We are at the end of this fourth world.

The biggest shift occurred when the second world shifted into the third world. The first two worlds connected to the two Platonic solids that form a dual: the dodecahedron in the first world and the icosahedron in the second world. However, shifting into the third world also meant shifting into the next dual: that of the octahedron (third world) and the cube (the fourth world). That shift, combined with a strong decrease in consciousness, created a barrier between the second and third worlds, which is the strongest barrier of all three.

Given that the sidhe live in the consciousness construct of the second world and we live in that of the fourth world indicates that there is a large degree of difference in consciousness between us. It will make collaborating with them to create the new world — the new consciousness — extremely challenging. However, challenging does not mean impossible. It all depends on our willingness to increase our vibration and open ourselves to our allies, like the dragons, the sidhe, and many others.

The Next Step

We are at the end of the fourth world and now moving into the fifth world. In the fifth world, consciousness and its vibrations begin to increase. It seems logical that we will use the experiences of the past to create this new world. Many people who read this may expect that we will proceed through the same worlds again but in reverse order. Of course, we can use experiences and information from these worlds. However, the purpose of the new world is not to repeat anything from the past. We will not go through the same four worlds in reverse order, because we would return to the Adam Kadmon at the beginning of the process. Instead, we will integrate the experiences of our ancestors from all worlds to create something entirely new.

The elemental power Aether will dominate the fifth world. The element of Aether integrates the four elements into something new. This new situation is more than the sum of the four elements. The

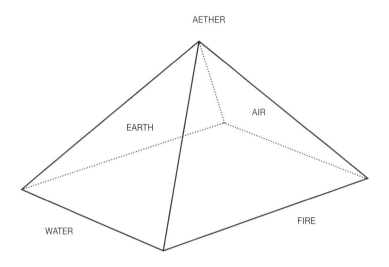

IMAGE 13.2. Shown is a pyramid that represents the relationship between the five elemental powers. The elemental powers of fire, water, air, and earth form the base of the pyramid; the elemental power of Aether is on the top.

best way to illustrate this is through a pyramid (image 13.2). The basis of the pyramid has four sides, each representing one of the four elemental powers, indicating the equality of these four elemental powers. We see this equality reflected in the circle in which all its points are equally important. The top of the pyramid represents the fifth element of Aether, indicating that it differs from the other four elemental powers and stands above them. However, without the base, there is no top. Each has unique functions and qualities, and they will all be required in the fifth world.

There has never been a world on Earth with a predominance of the elemental power of Aether. Every person presently living on Earth has chosen to contribute to the shift. Nobody knows how this next world will look. There is no previous example, no precedent. It is entirely up to us to create this world. There is an infinite number of possibilities. However, there is a framework within which the process of creating the fifth world will take place.

The Morphogenetic Field

The framework within which the new fifth world will unfold is the morphogenetic field of Gaia. We have mentioned this field many times because the dragon morphogenetic field is a subfield of the Gaia morphogenetic field. You will find general information about this field in *Gifts of Mother Earth.*[7] This field belongs to the consciousness of Gaia and holds the full potential of the Gaia system.

When the first souls who came to Earth seeded human consciousness, only a small part of the morphogenetic field was active. The energies and information of the actualized aspects of the field are present in morphogenetic grids that form networks of lines. During the different worlds, different aspects of the morphogenetic field were used and are consequently available in the grids. To this day, we only work with a part of the full potential of the field.

The grids represent the groundwork of all the gathered information obtained during the developments in each of the four worlds. We, starting at the beginning of the fifth world, will increasingly use the aspects of each world (the morphogenetic grids) and at the same time increasingly add aspects from the morphogenetic field. Ultimately, during the fifth world, the full potential of the field will be expressed and experienced. That is the work we as the human race will do. The human race includes humanity, the sidhe, and some smaller groups who live in the Inner Earth. Ultimately, we will all work together to achieve this goal. We have to, or we might destroy this world thereby never become able to create a balanced fifth world.

Realizing that the field holds the full potential does not mean that the form of the fifth world is defined. On the contrary, it is up to us together to give it the form that fits in each moment. While this form changes, it will do so within the framework of the morphogenetic field. In other words, the fifth world will be a dynamic world that shifts and changes with the unfoldment of consciousness within the framework of the morphogenetic field.

We are already functioning within the morphogenetic field, but we only use a small fraction of it. The same is true for the sidhe. Therefore, it is important to begin our collaboration. Image 13.3 shows this graphically. Members of humanity and the sidhe are aware of the importance of collaboration. Both groups need to expand by pulling information from the field into their consciousness to become increasingly connected to the total field. From our perspective, this

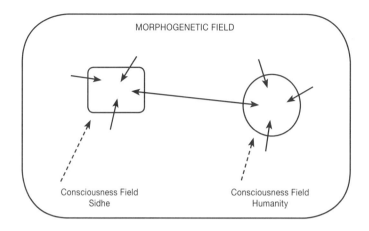

IMAGE 13.3. The morphogenetic fields of both humans and the sidhe form only a small part of the morphogenetic field of Gaia. Both groups need to draw more information from the field of Gaia to bridge their differences.

process has started, and we see the first signs of the development of the fifth world.

As we see in image 13.3, both the sidhe and we cover only a small part of the morphogenetic field. We will increasingly pull more information into our consciousnesses, recognizing that this is a long journey. We can speed up the journey by collaborating with other beings such as angels, devas, elementals, and of course, the dragons. There are many beings we can work with, but in this book, we mainly discussed the dragons. Mastering the elemental powers is a fast way to grow and to bring the world in which we live to higher vibrations.

Pulling the Cart

Many might wonder how the development of a fifth world can happen while the largest part of humanity is unaware or even disinterested in personal and spiritual development. However, in many messages I receive from different beings, it is pronounced that a shift in consciousness is inevitable. Therefore, it is also inevitable that we will move into the fifth world. This process is an inherent part of the morphogenetic field. It is up to us to decide how we will give form to this process. Will it be a smooth or a bumpy ride, a long or a short journey, or a fun or painful and difficult experience?

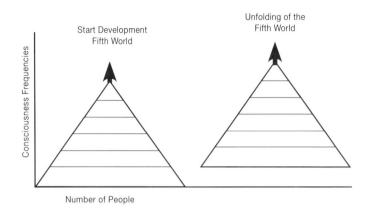

IMAGE 13.4. This image demonstrates the concept of human consciousness as shaped like a pyramid. The top will naturally pull those with lower vibrations into higher ones.

Some people have incarnated with the main purpose to be at the forefront of change, to be part of the movement from the fourth into the fifth world. Image 13.4 illustrates the principle of this process. Presently, most people function in the lower levels of the collective consciousness of the fourth (current) world. They form the base of the consciousness pyramid as presented in image 13.4. People who are contributing to the forefront of change form the top. They hold the highest levels of the current consciousness pyramid. The natural tendency of this top group is to evolve, which is their souls' purpose. They seek ways to increase their frequencies and to function from higher levels of consciousness. In doing so, they increase the overall frequencies of the human morphogenetic grid system. As a consequence, even those functioning at the lowest level will experience an increase in their level of consciousness.

As the people at the top of the pyramid continue to increase their vibrations and consciousnesses, this will influence the people throughout the pyramid, including the bottom, and will naturally raise their vibrations and consciousnesses, causing a shift in the whole pyramid. This development is the path of humanity. Humanity will inevitably increase in consciousness and consequently expand within the morphogenetic field. Ultimately, the top of the pyramid will reach a frequency that makes it possible to blend the paths of the sidhe and humanity into one. That will be the moment when we can truly say, "We now live in the new fifth world."

Support Systems: Crystals and Crystal Skulls

We know that dragons have a strong connection with crystalline energies. After all, they are a blend of crystalline beings and beings from Cassiopeia. Working with crystals in whatever form stimulates our ability to work with dragons. It also stimulates our connection with crystalline life force, which helps our physical system to raise its vibration. Therefore, working with crystals and crystal skulls creates a powerful support system on many levels, raising our vibrations and accelerating the process of ascending into the fifth world. We also stimulate and deepen our connection with the dragons.

We begin to remember that crystals and crystal skulls functioned as computers in the different worlds. Finding and working with these computers (which hold a tremendous amount of information) is a powerful way to bring more information into the morphogenetic grids or awaken information in the grids that have lain dormant. This process will enable us to connect with more information from the field as well. In other words, working with crystals and crystal skulls is exceedingly beneficial.

Each of the four worlds has at least one information system stored in quartz. Because the information from the other worlds is outside the reach of humans in this world in this phase of development, it is not useful to discuss them. We are aware of the locations of these quartz crystal information systems. We also know that all these systems are based on the number 12 with a central crystal or crystal skull. With our current level of consciousness, their information is inaccessible, but we are making a beginning with accessing the crystal skulls, the information system of the fourth world.

You might wonder how people from the past could have had such high consciousness levels while the general belief is that millions of years ago humans were primitive. You may think of primitive forms like Lucy (*Australopithecus afarensis*, an extinct hominid, who lived between 3.9 and 2.9 million years ago and is thought to be more closely related to the genus *Homo* than any known primate from the same time) and earlier *Homo* species, like *H. habilis* and *H. erectus*. We are referring to the form through which consciousness expresses itself in physical reality. Through the evolution of the form that is the basis for the creation of *H. sapiens*, we have our species through which our souls or our essences express into this world in current times. This human form was created to make it possible for souls to function in the fourth world. However, it also already has the qualities needed to function in the fifth world. In the first three worlds, the form was not as physical and solid as we know it now.

We cannot find any remnants of the different forms used in these previous worlds. We only can learn to understand the levels of consciousness through different lines, grids, and portals. Therefore, when we discuss humanoid consciousness and its evolution throughout the four worlds, we are not discussing the form through which the consciousness expresses itself. We are discussing solely the energetic messages and signals our less physical ancestors with higher consciousness left behind for us.

The mentioned three quartz systems that the people of the first three worlds created are all linked to the system of the twelve main chakras. When our vibrations and consciousnesses increase, we will be able to increasingly access these information systems. This information, in turn, will increase our consciousnesses and consequently the frequencies of our chakras, increasingly matching the vibrations and consciousness that will allow the creation of the fifth world.

Currently, we have access to only the crystalline information system of the fourth world. We know this system as the crystal skulls. Initially, these crystal skulls were all quartz crystal skulls. The survivors of the shift from the third to the fourth world developed this information system. They developed crystal skulls as a system to store information. They did that with beings from the Star Nations, beings from twelve different star systems. Like the informational systems of the previous three worlds, the crystalline information system of the fourth world is also based on the number 12.

The number 12 relates to the twelve chakras, which reflect the different ways of interacting with this information. As we have seen, the number 12 allows the expression of the full potential of a consciousness system in physical reality. We can define each world as a consciousness construct that has its possibilities and potentials and therefore will always have the number 12 as a basis.

I believe that the four main quartz crystalline information systems resonate with each other. These systems also reflect the different levels of vibration of our chakras. Working with crystal skulls, especially quartz, helps us to open ourselves to the information systems of the other worlds. Working with crystal skulls made of other materials helps us to prepare for our training to access information in the quartz systems. I have written two books on crystal skulls that present the foundation for working with these important information systems.[8]

Metaphysical Ecology

In the process of developing a new world, we need to work increasingly with the morphogenetic field. Currently, we still focus mainly on the information held in the morphogenetic grids. These grids, as we have seen, hold information about the visible and invisible worlds. If we want to bring these worlds into the new world, it is important to understand and work with the existing world.

The understanding and description of the visible and invisible worlds and their interactions is what I call metaphysical ecology. This term was introduced at the beginning of the book. I now will expand on this definition. Metaphysical ecology is the practical understanding and functioning in alignment with the morphogenetic field of Gaia. In other words, metaphysical ecology helps us to understand the Gaia system from a perspective that goes beyond the physical world as we perceive with our five physical senses. This whole book is an invitation to do so. Metaphysical ecology includes much more than just working with dragons. However, the dragons can help us with this process. They help us to function beyond the limitations of the fixed, physical world of the fourth dimension.

Parallel with the development of becoming aware of and working with metaphysical ecology, we recognize another process. This process is what I call the development, or evolution, of consciousness. This term is not completely correct because consciousness is infinite and is either expressed or is a potential. What evolves is awareness, that part of the infinite consciousness with which we actively work.

Our evolution of consciousness will remain confined to the boundaries of the morphogenetic field of the human species. This field is in turn part of the morphogenetic field of Gaia. The evolution of human consciousness is an integrated part of that of the Gaia system, and this understanding will be appreciated as increasing knowledge of metaphysical ecology.

The Gaia system is one dynamic system in which the physical and subtle worlds and their beings interact. Most people are unaware of these interactions, as they function solely at the solid, physical level. We call the understanding of these interactions in the observable physical world ecology. Hardly anybody is aware of the interaction between the physical and subtle systems, that which we call metaphysical ecology. This awareness will change in the near future.

When we have a certain understanding of metaphysical ecology, we will establish a foundation for the understanding of our role in the creation of a new world. We can do that when we collaborate with all beings, visible and invisible. Working with dragons helps us to become increasingly aware of the importance of beings from the invisible worlds. It also is training in partnering and building relationships with subtle, invisible beings.

It has been fascinating for me to see how much information and how many images of dragons exist. The interest in dragons strengthens their energy field. While I prefer a positive perspective about them, even a negative one strengthens their field. This book supports the awareness that dragons are wonderful allies and important beings with whom we are invited to work. This approach contributes to the increasing awakening of the concept of metaphysical ecology.

A Journey Ends, a Journey Begins

We have come to the end of our journey of connecting with the guardians of the powers of creation. The information that has been provided will help you to connect with everything you need to become a master in working with the elemental powers as tools for optimal creation. However, in the sense of making the connection and having an understanding of the powers involved, the journey has ended. At the same time, a journey begins.

Based on the connections you have made, you have reached the door that can give you access to the fifth world. You have to decide whether you would like to enter. To move forward, you have to set the intention that you choose to develop your potential and develop the skills to express that potential into this world in such a way that you cocreate this new world. You may think that you can do this alone. However, acting independently characterizes functioning in the fourth world.

In the fifth world, you have to collaborate and cocreate with the visible *and* invisible beings. We all have to do that in our unique ways. If we want to make things as easy as possible for ourselves, we accept the hand, paw, or wing that reaches out to support us. Dragons stretch out to you any part of themselves that you may wish to accept to offer a partnership such that you can work together and give form in the most optimal way to your contribution to the fifth world. Will you join me on this enlightened path of ascension?

Endnotes

INTRODUCTION

1. Jaap van Etten, *Gifts of Mother Earth: Earth Energies, Vortexes, Lines, and Grids* (Flagstaff, AZ: Light Technology Publishing, 2011), pp. xviii–xix.

2. See the following websites for more information on metaphysical ecology: http://metaphysicalecology.com and http://ucme.international.

3. Christopher Paolini, *Eragon: The Inheritance Cycle, Book 1* (New York: Alfred A. Knopf, 2003). *Eragon* was also produced as a movie by 20th Century Fox Home Entertainment with Director Stefen Fangmeier (2006).

4. Read about dragon bone discoveries on Wikipedia at http://en.wikipedia .org/wiki/Dragon.

5. van Etten, *Gifts of Mother Earth*, pp. 175–190.

6. van Etten, *Crystal Skulls: Expand Your Consciousness* (Flagstaff, AZ: Light Technology Publishing, 2013), pp. 20–21.

7. Ernest Ingersoll, *Dragons and Dragon Lore: A Worldwide Study of Dragons in History, Art, and Legend* (Chicago, IL: Aristeus Books, 2012), p. 131.

8. David Spangler, *Subtle Worlds: An Explorer's Field Notes* (Everett, WA: Lorian Press, 2010).

9. See Wikipedia "dark matter" at http://en.wikipedia.org/wiki/Dark_matter.

10. Univers-Review.ca. A Review of the Universe: The Observable Universe and Beyond: https://universe-review.ca/F02-cosmicbg08.htm.

11. National Geographic's *Your Brain: 100 Things You Never Knew, A User's Guide* (Washington, DC: National Geographic Society, 2012), p. 56.

12. Michael Shermer, *The Believing Brain: From Ghosts and Gods to Politics and Conspiracies* (New York City, NY: St. Martin's Griffin, 2012).

13. Lynne McTaggert, The Heart: The First Brain, https://lynnemctaggart .com/the-heart-the-first-brain/ (January 8, 2016).

CHAPTER 1

1. J. R. R. Tolkien, *The Hobbit* (Boston, MA: Houghton Mifflin Harcourt, 2012).

2. *How to Train Your Dragon*, directed by Dean DeBlois and Chris Sanders (DreamWorks Animation LLC, 2010).

3. Jaap van Etten, *Gifts of Mother Earth: Earth Energies, Vortexes, Lines, and Grids* (Flagstaff, AZ: Light Technology Publishing, 2011), p. 170–172.

4. Ernest Ingersoll, *Dragons and Dragon Lore: A Worldwide Study of Dragons in History, Art, and Legend* (Chicago, IL: Aristeus Books, 2012), p. 6.

5. Ingersoll, *Dragons and Dragon Lore*, p. 6.

6. Ingersoll, *Dragons and Dragon Lore*, p. 7.

7. Peter Dickinson, *The Flight of Dragons* (New York: Harper and Row Publishers, 1979), p. 103.

8. Judy Allen and Jeanne Griffiths, *The Book of the Dragon* (Secaucus, NJ: Chartwell Books Inc., 1979).

9. Judy Allen and Jeanne Griffiths, *The Book of the Dragon*, p. 17.

10. See "Tiamat" on Wikipedia at https://en.wikipedia.org/wiki/Tiamat.

11. Allen and Griffiths, *The Book of the Dragon*, p. 19.

12. R. A. Boulay, *Dragon Power: The Origin of the Fiery, Flying Serpent and Its Obsession with Gemstones* (Clearwater, FL: Galaxy Books, 1992), p. 10.

13. Annalee Newitz, "The Evolutionary History of Dragons Illustrated by a Scientist" (Gizmodo.com, August 20, 2012). Accessed July 22, 2017 at http://io9.gizmodo.com/5936427/the-evolutionary-history-of-dragons -illustrated-by-a-scientist.

14. Dugald A. Steer, *Dr. Ernest Drake's Dragonology: The Complete Book of Dragons* (Cambridge, MA: Candlewick Press, 2003).

15. See "Chinese dragon" on Wikipedia at https://en.wikipedia.org/wiki /Chinese_dragon.

16. See NationsOnline.org, "Guan Yin, Guan Yim, Kuan Yim, Kuan Yin," http:// www.nationsonline.org/oneworld/Chinese_Customs/Guan_Yin.htm.

17. See Jiulongbaguazhang.com, "The Dragons of China," http://www .jiulongbaguazhang.com/history/the-dragons-of-china/.

18. See Draconian.com, "Chinese Dragons," accessed on July 23, 2017 at http://www.draconian.com/dragons/chinese-dragon.php.

19. See Draconika.com, "Wyverns," accessed on August 10, 2017 at http://www.draconika.com/wyverns.php.
20. See "dragons" on Wikipedia at https://en.wikipedia.org/wiki/Dragon.
21. Susan J. Morris, *A Practical Guide to Dragon Magic* (Renton, WA: Wizards of the Coast LLC, 2010).
22. Dugald, *Dr. Ernest Drake's Dragonology*, chapter II.
23. Ingersoll, *Dragons and Dragon Lore*, p. 131.
24. van Etten, *Gifts of Mother Earth*, p. 4.
25. See HeartMath.org, "What Is Intuition?" (October 8, 2012) https://www.heartmath.org/articles-of-the-heart/the-math-of-heartmath/what-is-intuition/.
26. Bob Samples, *The Metaphoric Mind: a Celebration of Creative Consciousness* (Boston, MA: Addison-Wesley Pub. Co, 1976), p. 26.

CHAPTER 2

1. Jaap van Etten, *Gifts of Mother Earth: Earth Energies, Vortexes, Lines, and Grids* (Flagstaff, AZ: Light Technology Publishing, 2011), pp. 175–191.
2. Jaap van Etten, "Breaking through the Confines of Space and Time," *Sedona Journal of Emergence*, (Flagstaff, AZ: Light Technology Publishing, September 2016).

CHAPTER 3

1. Jaap van Etten, *Crystal Skulls: Interacting with a Phenomenon* (Flagstaff, AZ: Light Technology Publishing, 2007), pp. xv–xvii.
2. Jaap van Etten, *Crystal Skulls: Expand your Consciousness* (Flagstaff, AZ: Light Technology Publishing, 2013), pp. 59–78.
3. Jaap van Etten, *Gifts of Mother Earth: Earth Energies, Vortexes, Lines, and Grids* (Flagstaff, AZ: Light Technology Publishing, 2011), pp. 191–201.
4. van Etten, *Crystal Skulls: Expand your Consciousness*, pp. 141, 159.

CHAPTER 4

1. Cait Johnson, *Earth, Water, Fire & Air: Essential Ways of Connecting to Spirit* (Woodstock, VT: Skylight Paths Publishing, 2003) and Deborah Lipp, *The Way of Four: Create Elemental Balance in Your Life* (St. Paul, MN: Llewellyn Publications, 2004).
2. Aryeh Kaplan, *Sefer Yetzirah: The Book of Creation* (Boston, MA: Weiser Books, 1997).
3. Kaplan, *Sefer Yetzirah*, p. 146.
4. Gregg Braden, *The God Code: The Secret of Our Past, the Promise of Our Future* (Carlsbad, CA: Hay House Inc., 2004).
5. Braden, *The God Code*, p. 79.

6. Kaplan, *Sefer Yetzirah*, pp. 152–154.
7. Braden, *The God Code*, p. 100.
8. Braden, *The God Code*, p. 82.
9. Braden, *The God Code*, p. 101.
10. Braden, *The God Code*, p. 107.
11. Jaap van Etten, *Gifts of Mother Earth: Earth Energies, Vortexes, Lines, and Grids* (Flagstaff, AZ: Light Technology Publishing, 2011), pp. 89–154.
12. van Etten, *Gifts of Mother Earth*, pp. 11–123.
13. Richard Cassaro, *Written in Stone: Decoding the Secret Masonic Religion Hidden in Gothic Cathedrals and World Architecture* (New York City: Deeper Truth Books LLC, 2011).
14. van Etten, *Gifts of Mother Earth*, pp. 77–86.
15. James Bailey, Discover the Ida and Pingala Nadis: https://www.yogajournal.com/yoga-101/balancing-act-2.
16. See NaturalChakraHealing.com, "Healing the Chakras with the Elements," at http://naturalchakrahealing.com/elements.html, or see EnergyEnhancement.com, "The Qualities of the Five Lower Chakras," at http://www.energyenhancement.org/chakras/fantastic%20chakras/chap4.htm.
17. van Etten, *Gifts of Mother Earth*, p. 84.
18. Sun Bear and Wabun Wind, *The Medicine Wheel: Earth Astrology* (New York: Simon & Schuster, Touchstone, 1980).

CHAPTER 5

1. Dr. Masaru Emoto wrote several books about water. The following are worth the read:
    *   *The Hidden Messages of Water* (Hillsboro, OR: Beyond Words Publishing Inc., 2004).
    *   *The True Power of Water: Healing and Discovering Ourselves* (Hillsboro, OR: Beyond Words Publishing Inc., 2005).
    *   *The Secret Life of Water* (New York, NY: Atria Books, 2005).
2. Dr. Mu Shik Jhon, *The Water Puzzle and the Hexagonal Key: Scientific Evidence of Hexagonal Water and Its Positive Influence on Health* (St. Louis, MO: Uplifting Press Inc., 2004).
3. Love Nature, *The Memory of Water: H2O Remembers Everything*, published on February 3, 2011 at https://www.youtube.com/watch?v=ILSyt_Hhbjg&feature=youtu.be.
4. Callum Coats, *Living Energies: Viktor Schauberger's Brilliant Work with Natural Energy Explained* (Dublin: Gateway, Gill & Macmillan Ltd., 2001).
5. Alick Bartholomew, *The Spiritual Life of Water: Its Power and Purpose* (Rochester, VT: Park Street Press, 2010).
6. Jaap van Etten, *Gifts of Mother Earth: Earth Energies, Vortexes, Lines, and Grids* (Flagstaff, AZ: Light Technology Publishing, 2011), pp. 74–80.

7. The Flower of Life has become a popular symbol. Following are books that offer a good introduction of the subject:
   - Drunvalo Melchizedek, *The Ancient Secret of the Flower of Life, Volume 1* (Flagstaff, AZ: Light Technology Publishing, 1998).
   - Drunvalo Melchizedek, *The Ancient Secret of the Flower of Life, Volume 2* (Flagstaff, AZ: Light Technology Publishing, 2000).
8. Belle Dumé, "Is the universe a dodecahedron?" PhysicsWorld.com, posted on October 8, 2003 at http://physicsworld.com/cws/article/news/2003/oct/08/is-the-universe-a-dodecahedron.
9. Joseph "Joe" Panek, "Aether: The Fifth Element (Alchemy, Astrology, Symbolism)," aSeekersThoughts.com, posted on April 17, 2009 at http://www.aseekersthoughts.com/2009/04/aether.html.
10. See Wikipedia, "Aether (classical element)," https://en.wikipedia.org/wiki/Aether_(classical_element).
11. Anders Sandberg, "Some Random Thoughts About the Occult Correspondences of the Platonic Solids and Their Symmetries," Aleph.se, http://www.aleph.se/Nada/weirdness/polyhedr.txt.
12. Willem Witteveen, *The Great Pyramid of Giza: A Modern View on Ancient Knowledge* (Amsterdam, the Netherlands: Frontier Publishing, 2016).
13. Andrija Puharich, "A Way to Peace, Through ELF Waves," *Journal of Borderland Research*, vol. 39, no 2: https://borderlandsciences.org/journal/vol/39/no2/Puharich_ELF_Waves.html.
14. The citation attributed to Nikola Tesla, "If you only knew the magnificence of the 3, 6 and 9, then you would have a key to the universe," is available throughout the internet, for example, https://www.youtube.com/watch?v=GnEWOYKgI4o&t=5s.

CHAPTER 6

1. It is possible to obtain an essence of any of the dragon species by going to the Metaphysical Ecology Shop (http://metaphysicalecology.com/shop) and ordering a personal essence, specifying which you want.

CHAPTER 7

1. John Anthony West, *Serpent in the Sky: The High Wisdom of Ancient Egypt* (Wheaton, IL: Quest Books, Theosophical Publishing House, 1993), p. 34.
2. Three Initiates, *The Kybalion: A Study of the Hermetic Philosophy of Ancient Egypt and Greece* (San Bernadino, CA: Rough Draft Printing, 2012), pp. 16–17.
3. Three Initiates, *The Kybalion*, p. 18.
4. West, *Serpent in the Sky*, pp. 51–52.
5. Wikipedia, "Wu Xing," https://en.wikipedia.org/wiki/Wu_Xing.

CHAPTER 8

1. James Cameron, *Avatar*, 20th Century Fox Home Entertainment LLC, 209.
2. E. Battaner and E. Florido, *The Egg-Carton Universe* (February 1988). Cornell University Library: https://arxiv.org/abs/astro-ph/9802009v1.
3. Jaap van Etten, *Crystal Skulls: Interacting with a Phenomenon* (Flagstaff, AZ: Light Technology Publishing, 2007), pp. 123–141.
4. John Anthony West, *Serpent in the Sky: The High Wisdom of Ancient Egypt* (Wheaton, IL: Quest Books, Theosophical Publishing House, 1993), p. 53.

CHAPTER 9

1. M. Night Shyamalan, *The Last Airbender* (Hollywood, CA: Paramount Pictures, 2010). Based on the animated Nickelodeon series: *Avatar: The Last Airbender* (Hollywood, CA: Paramount Pictures, 2005–2008).
2. Three Initiates, *The Kybalion: A Study of the Hermetic Philosophy of Ancient Egypt and Greece* (San Bernadino, CA: Rough Draft Printing, 2012), pp. 16–17.
3. The Wachowski siblings, *The Matrix* (Burbanks, CA: Warner Bros Pictures, 1999).
4. Willem Witteveen, *The Great Pyramid of Giza: A Modern View on Ancient Knowledge* (Amsterdam, the Netherlands: Frontier Publishing, 2016), pp. 201–236.
5. Shaun K. Riebl, MS, RD, PhD student and Brenda M. Davy, PhD, RD, FACSM, associate professor, "The Hydration Equation: Update on Water Balance and Cognitive Performance." *ACSMs Health and Fitness Journal* (2013 November/December, 17(6): 21–28). doi: 10.1249/FIT.0b013e3182a9570f. https://www.ncbi.nlm.nih.gov/pmc/articles/PMC4207053/.

CHAPTER 12

1. Three Initiates, *The Kybalion: A Study of the Hermetic Philosophy of Ancient Egypt and Greece* (San Bernadino, CA: Rough Draft, 2012), pp. 27–31.
2. Richard Webster, *Communicating with the Archangel Raphael for Healing and Creativity* (Woodbury, MN: Llewellyn Publications, 2007).
3. Richard Webster, *Communicating with the Archangel Gabriel for Inspiration and Reconciliation* (Woodbury, MN: Llewellyn Publications, 2005).
4. Richard Webster, *Communicating with the Archangel Uriel for Transformation and Tranquility* (Woodbury, MN: Llewellyn Publications, 2006).
5. John Anthony West, *Serpent in the Sky: The High Wisdom of Ancient Egypt* (Wheaton, IL: Quest Books, Theosophical Publishing House, 1993), p. 37.

6. Petra Schneider and Gerhard K. Pieroth, *Archangels and Earthangels: An Inspiring Handbook on Spiritual Helpers in the Metaphysical and Earthly Spheres* (Twin Lakes, WI: Arcana Publishing, 2000).
7. Nathaniel Altman, *The Deva Handbook: How to Work with Nature's Subtle Energies* (Rochester, Vermont: Destiny Books, 1995), p. 7.
8. William Bloom, PhD, *Working with Angels, Fairies & Nature Spirits* (London, England: Judy Piatkus [Publishers] Limited, 1998).
9. Jaap van Etten, *Gifts of Mother Earth: Earth Energies, Vortexes, Lines, and Grids* (Flagstaff, AZ: Light Technology Publishing, 2011), pp. 186–188.
10. Altman, *The Deva Handbook*, pp. 8–10.
11. See "undine" on Wikipedia at https://en.wikipedia.org/wiki/Undine, accessed February 1, 2018.
12. van Etten, *Gifts of Mother Earth*, pp. 184–186.

CHAPTER 13

1. See "Native American Mythology" on Wikipedia at https://en.wikipedia.org/wiki/Fifth_World_(Native_American_mythology), accessed February 15, 2018.
2. Aluna Joy and the Ancient Ones from San Bartolo, "The Prophecy of the Fifth World," (AlunaJoy.com, March 2006) http://www.alunajoy.com/2006march.html.
3. See "four worlds" on Wikipedia at https://en.wikipedia.org/wiki/Four_Worlds, accessed February 15, 2018.
4. Jaap van Etten, "The Fifth World." *Sedona Journal of Emergence* (Flagstaff, AZ: Light Technology Publishing, February 2018), pp. 15–19.
5. BibliotecaPleyades.net, "The Four Worlds of the Hopi," https://www.bibliotecapleyades.net/esp_orionzone_6a.htm.
6. Jaap van Etten, *Birth of a New Consciousness: Dialogues with the Sidhe* (Flagstaff, AZ: Light Technology Publishing, 2015).
7. Jaap van Etten, *Gifts of Mother Earth: Earth Energies, Vortexes, Lines, and Grids* (Flagstaff, AZ: Light Technology Publishing, 2011), pp. 175–191.
8. Jaap van Etten, *Crystal Skulls: Interacting with a Phenomenon* (Flagstaff, AZ: Light Technology Publishing, 2007) and *Crystal Skulls: Expand your Consciousness* (Flagstaff, AZ: Light Technology Publishing, 2013).

About Jaap van Etten

JAAP VAN ETTEN, PHD was born and edu-
cated in the Netherlands. He received his
Phd in biology in Amsterdam, specializ-
ing in ecology. For the past twenty years,
his focus has been on metaphysical ecology. He studies and teaches about human
and Earth energies and the energies of
stones, crystals, and crystal skulls; he
also looks at how these energies interact.
He is the author of *Crystal Skulls: Interacting with a Phenomenon, Crystal Skulls:*

Expand Your Consciousness, Gifts of Mother Earth, and *Birth of a New
Consciousness.* Since 1998, he has lived in the United States with his
wife, Jeanne Michaels. They currently reside in Sedona, Arizona.

TO ORDER PRINT BOOKS
Visit LightTechnology.com, Call 928-526-1345 or 1-800-450-0985,
or Check Amazon.com or Your Favorite Bookstore

BOOKS THROUGH JAAP VAN ETTEN

Birth of a New Consciousness
Dialogues with the Sidhe

BIRTH OF A
NEW CONSCIOUSNESS

Dialogues with the Sidhe
Jaap van Etten, PhD

We usually base our perception of reality on what our five main senses receive, particularly our visual interpretation of the world, but the world we live in actually consists of many different worlds, most of which are invisible to us. All these worlds are part of Gaia and make up the reality we live in.

This book contains dialogues with the Sidhe, a race of human-like beings who are our direct relatives. Invisible to us, they occupy one of the subtle worlds of Gaia.

As the Sidhe and the author share their views on their respective worlds, explore the similarities and differences and gain a different perspective. Learn to recognize our respective gifts and self-induced limitations.

By collaborating with beings from the subtle realms, such as nature spirits and unicorns, we can create a new consciousness — and a new world. Embark on the journey available to every soul who comes to Earth, and raise your vibration and expand your view of reality.

$16.95 • Softcover • 6 x 9 • 192 PP.
ISBN 978-1-62233-033-1

CHAPTERS INCLUDE
• Meeting the Sidhe
• Getting to Know Each Other
• Our Origins and the Influence of the Stars
• The Separation
• Thoughts and Emotions
• Energy Systems and Healing
• Procreation and Hereditary Factors
• Teaching and Learning: the Education Systems
• Relationships with Plants and Animals
• Crystalline Energies

All Our Books Are Also Available as eBooks from Amazon, Apple iTunes, Google Play, Barnes & Noble, and Kobo.

ༀ Light Technology PUBLISHING Presents

TO ORDER PRINT BOOKS
Visit LightTechnology.com, Call 928-526-1345 or 1-800-450-0985,
or Check Amazon.com or Your Favorite Bookstore

BOOKS THROUGH JAAP VAN ETTEN

Crystal Skulls
Interacting with a
Phenomenon

Discover your energetic connection with crystal skulls. Learn how to utilize these energies for your personal growth and how these special energies affect your awareness and expand your consciousness.

Dr. van Etten's book reveals the skulls' ancient mysteries, their different characteristics and special energies, and the effects they have on humans and on Earth.

A few of the many theories surrounding these skulls are that they are shaped by higher or alien powers, they come from another world, or they are from an ancient Mayan civilization. Enhanced by 16 pages of color photos, this book invites you to delve deep into the mystical world of the crystal skulls.

$19.95 • Softcover • 6 x 9 • 240 PP.
ISBN 978-1-891824-64-7

TOPICS INCLUDE

- Characteristics of Crystal Skulls
- Some Famous Crystal Skulls and Their Caretakers
- Why a Skull Shape?

- Contemporary Crystal Skulls and How to Find Yours
- How to Categorize Crystal Skulls
- Piezoelectricity

- Original, Singing, Fully Activated, and Contemporary Crystal Skulls
- The Effects of Crystal Skulls on Human Beings

℣ Light Technology PUBLISHING Presents

BOOKS THROUGH DRUNVALO MELCHIZEDEK

THE ANCIENT SECRET OF THE FLOWER OF LIFE, VOLUME 1

Also available in Spanish as *Antiguo Secreto Flor de la Vida, Volumen 1*

Once, all life in the universe knew the Flower of Life as the creation pattern, the geometrical design leading us into and out of physical existence. Then from a very high state of consciousness, we fell into darkness, and the secret was hidden for thousands of years, encoded in the cells of all life.

$25.00 • 240 PP. • Softcover • ISBN 978-1-891824-17-3

THE ANCIENT SECRET OF THE FLOWER OF LIFE, VOLUME 2

Also available in Spanish as *Antiguo Secreto Flor de la Vida, Volumen 2*

Drunvalo shares the instructions for the Mer-Ka-Ba meditation, step-by-step techniques for the re-creation of the energy field of the evolved human, which is the key to ascension and the next dimensional world. If done from love, this ancient process of breathing prana opens up for us a world of tantalizing possibility in this dimension, from protective powers to the healing of oneself, others, and even the planet.

$25.00 • 272 PP. • Softcover • ISBN 978-1-891824-21-0

LIVING IN THE HEART

Also available in Spanish as *Viviendo en el Corazón*

Long ago we humans used a form of communication and sensing that did not involve the brain in any way; rather, it came from a sacred place within our hearts. What good would it do to find this place again in a world where the greatest religion is science and the logic of the mind? Don't I know this world where emotions and feelings are second-class citizens? Yes, I do. But my teachers have asked me to remind you who you really are. You are more than a human being, much more. Within your heart is a place, a sacred place, where the world can literally be remade through conscious cocreation. If you give me permission, I will show you what has been shown to me.

— Drunvalo Melchizedek

Includes
Heart
Meditation CD

$25.00 • 144 PP. • Softcover • ISBN 978-1-891824-43-2